D0106196

PERU

TOP SIGHTS, AUTHENTIC EXPERIENCES

THIS EDITION WRITTEN AND RESEARCHED BY

Phillip Tang, Greg Benchwick, Alex Egerton,
Carolyn McCarthy, Luke Waterson

Welcome to Peru

Peru is as complex as its most intricate and exquisite weavings. Festivals mark ancient rites, the urban vanguard beams innovation and nature brims with splendid diversity.

Peru's rich cultural heritage is never more real and visceral than when you are immersed street-side in the swirling madness of a festival. Deities of old are reincarnated as Christian saints, pilgrims climb mountains in the dead of night and icons are paraded through crowded plazas. History is potent here and still pulsing, and there is no better way to experience it.

Visitors make pilgrimage to the glorious Inca citadel of Machu Picchu, yet this feted site is just a flash in a 5000-year history of peoples. Explore the dusted remnants of Chan Chan, the largest pre-Columbian ruins in all the Americas. Fly over the puzzling geoglyphs etched into the arid earth at Nazca. And spend time in Lima's great museums, which reveal the sophistication and skill of these lost civilizations.

Few destinations have such madly diverse terrain. From the glaciated peaks of the Cordilleras to the sweltering untamed Amazon – the world's most biodiverse forest – Peru dazzles with opportunities to explore outdoors. Trekking routes abound, rafting is increasingly popular, as is mountain biking and surfing. Then grab your binoculars to see a staggering array of bird and animal life.

One question haunts all Peruvians: what to eat? Ceviche with slivers of fiery chili and corn, slow-simmered stews, velvety Amazonian chocolate – in the capital of Latin cooking, the choices dazzle.

Giant sand dunes, chiseled peaks and Pacific breaks a few heartbeats away from the capital's rush-hour traffic: take this big place in small bites and don't rush. And that's when you realize: in Peru the adventure usually lies in getting there.

Giant sand dunes, chiseled peaks and Pacific breaks

Cañón del Colca (p110)

NORTH PACIFIC OCEAN

✪ **QUITO**

ECUADOR

PERU

Caqu

Napo

Santiago

Tumbes ⊙

Tumbes

Talara ⊙

Piura ⦿

Jaén ⊙ **Bagua Grande** ⊙

Marañón

Moyobamba ⦿

Chiclayo ⊙

Cajamarca ⊙

Huallaga

Lagunas ⊙

Reserva Nacional Pacaya Samiria

Yurimaguas ⊙

Tarapoto ⊙

Ucayali

Juanjuí ⊙

Pacasmayo ⊙

TRUJILLO p221 ⊙

Reserva Nacional Calipuy

Parque Nacional Río Abiseo

Parque Nacional Cordillera Azul

Huallaga

Pucallpa ⊙

Chimbote ⊙

THE CORDILLERAS p235

Casma ⊙

Huaraz ⊙

Parque Nacional Huascarán

⦿ **Huánuco**

Parque Nacional Yanachaga Chemillen

Santuario Histórico Chacamarca

Río Tambo

Río Cañete

Tarma ⊙

Parq Nacio Otis

Chancay ⊙

LIMA p35 ✪

Huancayo ⦿

Reserva Nor Yauyos-Cochas

Huancavelica ⦿

Ayacuch ⊙

Pisco ⊙

ISLAS BALLESTAS p69

Andahuaylas ⊙

Ica ⊙

Reserva Nacional Paracas

NAZCA p79

SOUTH PACIFIC OCEAN

⌃
Ⓝ
0 ——————————— 400 km
0 ——————————— 200 miles

Llamas in the Cordilleras (p235)
CHARTON FRANCK/GETTY IMAGES ©

Plan Your Trip
Peru's Top 12

Machu Picchu

One of the most famous ruins on the planet

A fantastic Inca citadel lost to the world until its rediscovery in the early 20th century, Machu Picchu (p197) stands as a ruin among ruins. With its emerald terraces backed by steep peaks, and Andean ridges echoing on the horizon, the sight simply surpasses the imagination. This marvel of engineering has withstood six centuries of earthquakes, foreign invasion and howling weather (not to mention millions of foreign travelers). Discover it for yourself: wander through the stone temples and scale the dizzying heights.

1

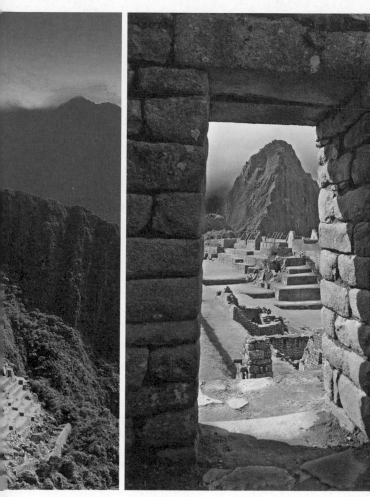

Nazca

Mysterious giant geoglyphs

Made by aliens? Laid out by prehistoric balloonists? Conceived as a giant astronomical chart? No two evaluations of Peru's giant geoglyphs and biomorphs – known as the Nazca Lines (p82) – are the same. The mysteries have attracted outsiders since the 1940s but no one has been able to fully crack the code. The lines remain unfathomed, enigmatic and loaded with historic intrigue.

Top: Condor biomorph; Bottom: Spider biomorph

2

RIGAMONDIS / GETTY IMAGES ©

Islas Ballestas

The Pacific Ocean's most astonishing fauna

A barren collection of guano-covered rocks, the Islas Ballestas (p69) support an extraordinary ecosystem of birds, sea mammals and fish. They also represent one of Peru's most successful conservation projects. Boat trips around the island's cliffs and arches allow close encounters with barking sea lions, huddled Humboldt penguins and tens of thousands of birds.

3

Lake Titicaca

Floating reed islands and traditional living

Less a lake than a highland ocean, Titicaca (p123) is home to fantastical sights – none more surreal than the floating islands crafted entirely of tightly woven *totora* reeds. Requiring near-constant renovation, the reeds are also used to build thatched homes and elegant boats. There are plenty of other islands to choose from, such as Isla Taquile, where rural Andean life from centuries long gone lives on, and the quinoa soup recipe has been perfected.

Reed boats

Cuzco

The ancient Inca capital

With ancient cobblestone streets, grandiose baroque churches and the remnants of masterful Inca temples, no city looms larger in Andean history than Cuzco (p143), which has been continuously inhabited since precolonial times. Cuzco also serves as the gateway to Machu Picchu. Mystic, commercial and chaotic, this unique city is still a stunner. Where else would you find ornately dressed women walking llamas on leashes, a museum for magical plants, and the wildest nightlife in the high Andes?

View over Plaza de Armas (p156)

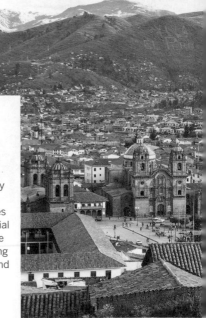

BJORN HOLLAND / GETTY IMAGES ©

Cañón del Colca

Scenic hiking, biking, rafting and zip-lining

First colonized by pre-Inca civilizations, the cultural history of the Cañón del Colca (p107) is as alluring as the endless trekking possibilities. Stretching 100km from end to end and plunging over 3400m at its deepest, the canyon has been embellished with terraced agricultural fields, pastoral villages, colonial churches, and ruins that date back to pre-Inca times.

6

JOHN COLETTI / GETTY IMAGES ©

Lima

World-class food and museums

Want to understand Peru's ancient civilizations? Begin your trip in Lima (p35). The city's museums hold millennia worth of treasures. Want to understand modern living in Peru? It's all about the diversity reflected in Lima's cuisine.The coastal capital is replete with options ranging from street carts to haute-cuisine eateries.

7

Trujillo

Colonial architecture and modern culture

Rising from the sand-strewn desert like a mirage of colonial color, old Trujillo (p221) boasts a dazzling display of preserved splendor. The city's historic center is chock-full of elegant churches, mansions and otherwise unspoiled colonial constructions, which are steeped today in a modern motif that lends the city a lovely, livable feel. Add the close proximity of impressive ruins such as Chan Chan, and the pyramids at Las Huacas del Sol y de la Luna, and Trujillo easily trumps its northern rivals in style and grace.

ANDREW WATSON / GETTY IMAGES ©

PAUL HARRIS / GETTY IMAGES ©

The Amazon Basin

The world's most biodiverse forest

The Amazon Basin (p253) is as close to visiting an alien planet as you can get on Earth. The abundance of plants and animal life can make it seem as if new creatures are created here. The forest's diversity is matched only by the uniqueness of its people, with tribes that have still never had any interaction with external civilization. Set aside ample time to visit the national parks, which grow more intriguing the deeper you get.

ELOJO TORPE / GETTY IMAGES ©

COPYRIGHT ALENGEL / GETTY IMAGES ©

ROSEMARY CALVERT / GETTY IMAGES ©

The Sacred Valley

Village markets and ancient ruins

Andean villages, crumbling Inca military outposts and agricultural terraces used since time immemorial are linked by the Río Urubamba as it curves through the Sacred Valley (p181). Located between Cuzco and Machu Picchu, this picturesque destination is an ideal base for exploring the area's famed markets and historic structures and remote agricultural villages.

Top: A woman weaving; Bottom left: Market, Pisac (p190); Bottom right: Sacred Valley

10

GLOWIMAGES / GETTY IMAGES ©

Arequipa

Cuisine and architecture in an ethereal cityscape

Crowned by dazzling baroque *mestizo* (mixed indigenous and Spanish) architecture hewn out of the local white *sillar* rock, Arequipa (p89) is primarily a Spanish colonial city that hasn't strayed far from its conception. Its beautiful natural setting amid volcanoes and high pampa is complemented by a 400-year-old monastery, a huge cathedral and innovative fusion cuisine.
La Catedral (p98)

11

MIKADUN / SHUTTERSTOCK ©

The Cordilleras

Ground zero for outdoor adventure in Peru

The Cordilleras (p235) are one of the pre-eminent hiking, trekking and backpacking spots in South America. Every which way you throw your gaze, perennially glaciated white peaks razor their way through expansive mantles of lime-green valleys. The Cordillera Blanca is one of the highest mountain ranges in the world and boasts the enigmatic 3000-year-old ruins of Chavín de Huántar.
Cordillera Huayhuash (p240)

12

Plan Your Trip
Need to Know

When to Go

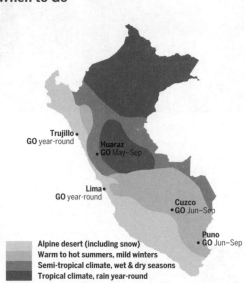

Trujillo•
GO year-round

Huaraz
• GO May–Sep

Lima•
GO year-round

Cuzco
•GO Jun–Sep

Puno
• GO Jun–Sep

Alpine desert (including snow)
Warm to hot summers, mild winters
Semi-tropical climate, wet & dry seasons
Tropical climate, rain year-round

High Season (Jun–Aug)

o Dry season in Andean highlands and eastern rainforest.

o Best time for festivals, highland sports and treks.

o Peak time due to North American and European holidays.

Shoulder (Sep–Nov & Mar–May)

o Spring and fall weather in the highlands.

o Ideal for less crowded visits.

o September to November good for rainforest trekking.

Low Season (Dec–Feb)

o Rainy season in the highlands and in the Amazon.

o The Inca Trail closes during February for cleanup.

o High season for the coast and beach activities.

Currency
Nuevo sol (S)

Languages
Spanish, Aymara and Quechua

Visas
Generally not required for stays of up to 183 days.

Money
ATMs widely available in larger cities and towns. Credit cards widely accepted. Traveler's checks not widely accepted.

Cell Phones
Local SIM cards (and top-up credits) are cheap and widely available, and can be used on unlocked tri-band GSM 1900 world phones.

Time
Eastern Standard Time (EST), five hours behind Greenwich Mean Time (GMT); same as New York City, without daylight savings time.

Daily Costs

Budget: Less than S300

○ Budget hotel room or dorm bed: S25–85

○ Set lunches or supermarket takeout: less than S15

○ Entry to historic sights: around S10

Midrange: S300–S550

○ Double room in midrange hotel: S140

○ Multicourse lunch at midrange restaurant: S40

○ Group tours: from S120

Top end: More than S550

○ Double room in top-end hotel: S300

○ Private city tour: from S180

○ Fine restaurant dinner: from S70

Useful Websites

Lonely Planet (lonelyplanet.com/peru) Destination information, hotel bookings, traveler forum and more.

Bus Portal Peru (www.busportal.pe) Tickets for buses throughout the country.

Exchange Rates (www.xe.com) Current exchange rates.

Expat Peru (www.expatperu.com) Useful for government offices and customs regulations.

Latin America Network Information Center (www.lanic.utexas.edu) Diverse, informative links including academic research.

Living in Peru (www.livinginperu.com) An English-language guide with articles and restaurant reviews.

Peru Reports (www.perureports.com) Alternative English-language news.

Peruvian Times (www.peruviantimes.com) The latest news, in English.

Opening Hours

Opening hours vary throughout the year. We've provided high-season opening hours; hours will generally decrease in the shoulder and low seasons.

Banks 9am–6pm Monday to Friday, some 9am–6pm Saturday

Government offices and businesses 9am–5pm Monday to Friday

Museums Often close on Monday

Restaurants 10am–10pm, many close 3pm–6pm

Shops 9am–6pm Monday to Friday, some open Saturday

Arriving in Peru

Many flights arrive in the wee hours, so be sure to have a hotel booked ahead.

Aeropuerto Internacional Jorge Chávez, Lima (p65)

Taxi Thirty minutes to one hour (rush hour) from the airport to Miraflores, Barranco or San Isidro, faster for downtown Lima; should cost S45 to S60.

Getting Around

Public transport in Peru is cheap, with options plentiful and frequent.

Light Rail Lima's Metropolitano offers efficient, fast service to downtown.

Train Expensive and geared toward tourists.

Car Useful for traveling at your own pace, though cities can be difficult to navigate and secure parking is a must.

Bus Cheapest option, with reclining seats on better long-distance buses.

Taxi A good option for sightseeing, shared taxis are common in the provinces.

For more on **getting around**, see p308

Plan Your Trip
Hot Spots For...

Peruvian Cuisine

Peru's food scene is going through a delicious renaissance, bringing modern appreciation to the classics from the coast to the Andes.

Ancient Ruins

Machu Picchu is just the start, with plenty of ruins, temples and secrets from the Incas and other cultures to discover.

Time-Traveling Cultures

The strong traditions of indigenous cultures are living and breathing all around you in Peru. Get even closer with homestays.

Wildlife Adventures

Natural wonders are outdoors and free in Peru. Catch sight of wildlife anywhere from soaring over canyons to swimming in jungle waters.

Lima (p40)
The capital caters to fancy fusion tastes with modern Asian and European influences and Andean classics.

Gastronomic Tours
Discover culinary treasures with Lima Tasty Tours (p54).

Iquitos (p262)
Great restaurants show off local Amazon flavors such as river fish ceviche and tasty *chupín de pollo* soup.

Real Amazonian Food
Food of the jungle at manic Belén Mercado (p265).

Cuzco (p146)
An unbelievable range of Andean crops from highland potatoes and quinoa to avocados and *ají picante* (hot chili).

Iconic Drink
Andean-style hot cocoa at Choco Museo (p162).

Sacred Valley (p181)
The Andean countryside is dotted with villages, high-altitude hamlets and isolated ruins.

Machu Picchu
This Incan citadel (p200) will live up to the hype.

Cuzco (p143)
The cosmic realm of the ancient Incans, fused with colonial and religious splendors of Spanish conquest.

Inti Raymi
Celebrate the solstice (p149) at Sacsaywamán.

Chan Chan (p224)
Wander the ruins of the largest pre-Columbian city in the Americas, north in Trujillo.

Bird's Eye View
Aerial shots at the museum reveal the city's sprawl.

Huaraz (p246)
The vast cordilleras have isolated communities with unique traditions.

Community Tourism
Book a homestay with Respons Sustainable Tourism (p249).

Arequipa (p89)
The colonial past meets *sillar* (white volcanic stone) in fascinating museums.

Monasterio de Santa Catalina
Traipse the grounds of a convent (p94) by candlelight.

Islas Uros (p126)
Floating reed islands reveal a people finding refuge by living on Lake Titicaca.

Unique Culture
Stay on Isla Taquile (p130) to experience its unique culture.

Islas Ballestas (p69)
An incredible ecosystem of birds, sea mammals and fish, nicknamed the 'poor man's Galápagos.'

Boat Tours (p74)
You can't get onto the island but you can get very close.

Cañón del Colca (p107)
Canyons here are as deep as the mountains are high, and full of untamed beauty stretching to the horizon.

Cruz del Cóndor (p113)
Witness condors gliding just above you.

Amazon Basin (p253)
Being vast and impenetrable has protected the diverse, sometimes bizarre, wildlife from the outside world.

Parque Nacional Manu (p256)
One of the best places in South America to see tropical critters.

Plan Your Trip
Local Life

FRANK GAGLIONE / GETTY IMAGES ©

Rug vendor, Cuzco (p143)

Activities

You could scale the highest tropical mountain peaks in the world, or stay in the capital, hang glide over the ocean and still have ample time for a coastal walk. Peru is big, with huge opportunities in the jungle, snow, desert and ocean to raft, zip and ride across. Or get your heart racing without breaking a sweat. You could spot a pink dolphin in the Amazon, watch the sun dissolve over lost ruins, see a condor ride canyon air currents, whip up your own pisco or step foot on an island made of reeds.

Shopping

Peru has a bonanza of arts and crafts. Popular souvenirs include alpaca-wool sweaters and scarves, woven textiles, ceramics, masks, gold and silver jewelry and the backpacker favorite: Inca Kola T-shirts.

Bargaining is the norm at street stalls and markets, where it's cash only. Upscale stores may add a surcharge for credit-card transactions.

Eating

There are dining and snacking options galore in Peru. The traveler hot spots are having a foodie boom; you can dine on Peruvian classics with modern twists. Traditional, complete meals can be tried in local restaurants with a *menú* (set menu). Eating with a family at a homestay can be a rewarding experience, not just for your palate but for the family, especially if you pay directly.

Staples such as beans and quinoa soup are easy options for vegetarians. Even in small towns, simple *chifas* (Chinese restaurants) are a common fallback. Peru caters to chili lovers with *ají* (chili) but it is easily avoided for the chili phobic.

Street snacks aren't meant to be complete meals like in other countries, but tasty whims, which include charcoal corn, *anticuchos* (cow's heart kebabs) or quail eggs.

Every region has its specialty, with standouts being seafood on the coast, tropical *chonta* (palm hearts) and river snails in the Amazon, and soups and *cuy* (guinea pig) in

Salkantay Trek (p165)

the highlands. In the land where potatoes originated, the humble spud is elevated to a starring role on a national level.

Drinking & Nightlife

Peruvians are passionate about their drinks: pisco is a source of pride and competition (it originated in Peru, not Chile, you'll be told); if you love the fluoro-coloured soft-drink brand Inca Kola, you have truly become a local; and lunch without a jug of *chicha* (corn beer or drink) isn't a Peruvian lunch. In the mountains, coca-leaf tea might get you through altitude sickness but is also a homely drink.

Beer is the favoured tipple of a night out, with Brahma, Cristal and Cusqueña topping the local brands; the microbrewery trend has hit the big cities too. Bars are abundant, though drinking for the sake of it is not nearly as popular as drinking and eating at *picanterías* (informal country restaurants) and other restaurants.

★ Best Markets

Mercado San Pedro (p169), Cuzco

Mercado Indio (p55), Lima

Mercado de Artesanía (p190), Pisac

Belén Mercado (p265)

Entertainment

Peru's larger towns and cities have plenty to keep your weekends full. The club scene begins well after midnight and keeps up the energy until dawn. Electronic beats, live bands and a range of Latin and jazz styles are all on offer, sometimes in restaurants.

Peruvian folk music and dance is performed on weekends at *peñas*. The *folklórica* style here is typical of the Andean highlands, while *criollo* is a coastal music pulsing with African-influenced beats. Dinner is often included.

Film screenings and theatre are sometimes offered with English translation, while art exhibits and dance need no translation.

Plan Your Trip
Month by Month

HUGHES HERVÁ © / HEMIS.FR / GETTY IMAGES ©

Semana Santa, Cuzco

January

January to March is the busiest (and most expensive) season on the coast. In the mountains and canyons, it's rainy season and best avoided by trekkers and mountaineers.

✥ Año Nuevo

Partygoers wear lucky yellow (including underwear) to ring in the New Year.

☆ Fiesta de la Marinera

Trujillo's national dance festival is held the last week in January.

February

The Inca Trail is closed all month. Many Peruvian festivals echo the Roman Catholic calendar and are celebrated with great pageantry, especially in highland villages.

✥ La Virgen de la Candelaria

Held on February 2, this highland fiesta, also known as Candlemas, is particularly colorful around Puno, where folkloric music and dance celebrations last for two weeks.

March

Beach resort prices go down and crowds disperse, though the coast remains sunny. Orchids bloom on the Inca Trail.

April

Crowds and high-season prices mark Semana Santa (Holy Week), a boon of national tourism in March or April. Hotel prices spike and availability is low. Reserve way ahead.

✥ Semana Santa

The week before Easter Sunday, Semana Santa is celebrated with spectacular religious processions almost daily.

May

The heaviest rains have passed, leaving the highlands lush and green. With the return of drier weather, trekking season starts to take off in Huaraz and around Cuzco.

Inti Raymi, Cuzco

☆ Noche en Blanco
Inspired by Europe's White Nights, the streets of Miraflores in Lima are closed to cars in early May, while arts, music and dance take over.

✱ Q'oyoriti
A fascinating indigenous pilgrimage to the holy mountain of Ausangate, outside of Cuzco, in May or June.

✱ Festival of the Crosses
This religious festival is held on May 3 in Lima, Apurímac, Ayacucho, Junín, Ica and Cuzco.

June
High season for international tourism runs June through August, with Machu Picchu requiring advance reservations for train tickets and entry. It's also the busiest time for festivals in and around Cuzco.

★ Best Events
Semana Santa, March/April
Q'oyoriti, May/June
Inti Raymi, June
Fiestas Patrias, July
Feast of Santa Rosa de Lima, August

✱ Corpus Christi
Processions of this Catholic celebration in Cuzco are especially dramatic. Held on the ninth Thursday after Easter.

✱ Inti Raymi
The Festival of the Sun (also the Feast of St John the Baptist and Peasant's Day) is the greatest of Inca festivals, celebrating the winter solstice on June 24.

✱ San Juan
The feast of San Juan is all debauchery in Iquitos, where dancing, feasting and cockfights go until the wee hours on the eve of the actual holiday of June 24.

✤ San Pedro y San Pablo

The feasts of Sts Peter and Paul provide more fiestas on June 29, especially around Lima and in the highlands.

July

The continuation of high-season tourism. In Lima the weather is marked by *garúa*, a thick sea mist that lingers over the city for the next few months.

✤ La Virgen del Carmen

Held on July 16, this holiday is mainly celebrated in the southern sierra – with Paucartambo and Pisac near Cuzco, and Pucará near Lake Titicaca being especially important centers.

✤ Fiestas Patrias

The National Independence Days are celebrated nationwide on July 28 and 29; festivities in the southern sierra begin with the Feast of St James on July 25.

August

The last month of high tourist visitation throughout Peru is also the most crowded at Machu Picchu. Book well ahead.

✤ Feast of Santa Rosa de Lima

Commemorating the country's first saint, major processions are held on August 30 in Lima, Arequipa and Junín to honor the patron saint of Lima and of the Americas.

September

Low season everywhere, September and October can still offer good weather to highland trekkers without the crowds.

✗ Mistura

For one week in September, this massive international food festival is held in Lima, drawing up to half a million visitors.

✤ El Festival Internacional de la Primavera

A don't-miss, the International Spring Festival features supreme displays of horsemanship, as well as dancing and cultural celebrations during the last week of September in Trujillo.

October

The best time to hit the Amazon runs from September to November when drier weather results in better wildlife-watching.

⚑ Great Amazon River Raft Race

The longest raft race in the world flows between Nauta and Iquitos in September or early October.

✤ La Virgen del Rosario

On October 4, this saint's celebration comes to Lima, Apurímac, Arequipa and Cuzco. Its biggest event is held in Ancash, with a symbolic confrontation between Moors and Christians.

November

A good month for festivals, with plenty of events to choose from. Waves return, calling all surfers to the coast.

✤ Todos Santos

November 1 is All Saints' Day, a religious precursor to the following day celebrated with Catholic masses.

✤ Día de los Muertos

All Souls' Day is celebrated on November 2 with gifts of food, drink and flowers taken to family graves.

✤ Puno Week

Starting November 5, this week-long festival involves several days of spectacular costumes and street dancing to celebrate the legendary emergence of the first Inca, Manco Cápac.

December

Beach season returns with warmer Pacific temperatures. Skip the Amazon, where heavy rains start falling from the end of the month through early April.

✤ Fiesta de la Purísima Concepción

The Feast of the Immaculate Conception is a national holiday celebrated with religious processions in honor of the Virgin Mary. It's held on December 8.

Plan Your Trip
Get Inspired

Read

Turn Right at Machu Picchu (2012) Mark Adams retraces explorer Hiram Bingham's early journeys to Machu Picchu.

Aunt Julia & the Scriptwriter (1977) Nobel laureate Mario Vargas Llosa's comic novel about a radio scriptwriter in love with his much older, divorced sister-in-law.

The Conquest of the Incas (1970) A gripping historical classic by John Hemming.

At Play in the Fields of the Lord (1965) Peter Matthiessen's true-to-life novel about conflicts in the Amazon.

The Last Days of the Incas (2007) Kim MacQuarrie's page-turner about the history-making clash between two civilizations.

Watch

El mudo (2013) A dark comedy about a government official who refuses to succumb to corruption.

Undertow (2009) A fictional tale about a married fisherman coming to terms with his dead boyfriend's ghost.

La muralla verde (The Green Wall; 1970) Armando Robles Godoy's classic feature film about an idealistic city couple who move to the Amazon.

La teta asustada (The Milk of Sorrow; 2009) Claudia Llosa's film about a girl suffering from a trauma-related affliction.

Listen

Arturo 'Zambo' Cavero (1993) The eponymous album of the crooner best known for his soulful Peruvian waltzes.

Chabuca Granda: Grandes Éxitos (2004) Breathy lyrics full of longing and nostalgia by the legendary singer and composer.

Eva! Leyenda Peruana (2004) Bluesy *landós* performed by premiere Afro-Peruvian songstress Eva Ayllón.

The Roots of Chicha (2007) Retro-psychedelic Amazon-meets-the-Andes-meets-Colombian-*cumbias* dance music.

Coba Coba (2009) Groovy fusion of Peruvian classics and chilled-out electronica.

The Sacred Valley (p181)

Plan Your Trip
Five-Day Itinerary

Southern Highland Jaunt

This brisk itinerary allows two days to see the capital's main sights, then heads south for a visit to the charming highland city of Arequipa, known for its rich history and spicy cuisine, and throws in the fabulous Cañón del Colca for good measure.

1 Lima (p35) Spend a couple of days in Lima, exploring colonial churches, the Museo Larco and some of the city's internationally acclaimed eateries. ✈ 1½ hrs to Arequipa

3 Cañón del Colca (p107) On the last day, get an early start (as in 4am early) for a day trip to see one of Peru's most famous natural sights. At Cruz del Condor, you'll stand a dizzying 1200m over the valley floor as condors cruise the currents before you. Totally unforgettable.

2 Arequipa (p89) Allocate the next two days to handsome Arequipa. Wander the Plaza de Armas, visit the massive Catedral and the Museo Santuarios Andinos. Explore the citadel-sized Monasterio de Santa Catalina before grabbing a table at one of Arequipa's renowned *picanterías* (local restaurants). 🚌 4 hrs by tour bus to Cañón del Colca

Plan Your Trip
10-Day Itinerary

A Tour of Inca Country

Ten days allows you ample time to soak up the wonders of the ancient Inca capital and the Sacred Valley. Starting with a couple of days in Lima ensures that you won't head to the highlands without a few exquisite meals in your belly.

1 Lima (p35) Two days in Lima is a great start to any adventure. Learn about Peru's history and cultures in the city's colonial churches and museums. Head to Miraflores to dine on delectable seafood.
✈ 1¼ hrs to Cuzco

4 Aguas Calientes (p216) Arrange to spend two to three nights at Aguas Calientes, the bustling transit point that serves as a base for exploring the sprawling Machu Picchu. The scenery is spectacular and there are some great day hikes in the area.

3 Ollantaytambo (p194) Ollantaytambo is a charismatic indigenous village that retains its inherently Inca form. Bed here for the night, then wake up early to see its Inca ruins. 🚌 2 hrs to Aguas Calientes

2 Cuzco (p143) Spend a couple of days in Cuzco. Wander the Plaza de Armas and visit La Catedral. Don't miss Sacsaywamán, a jaw-dropping fortress, or the Qorikancha, once the Incas' most important temple.
🚗 40 mins to Ollantaytambo

Plan Your Trip
Two-Week Itinerary

Highland/Jungle Combo

On this two-week trip through the Andes and then down into the Amazon, you'll see a little bit of everything that Peru has to offer: Inca ruins, pastoral highland settings, steamy lowland jungle, and more wildlife than you've ever dreamed of.

4 Aguas Calientes (p216) Base yourself at Aguas Calientes. Try to stick around for at least two days – Machu Picchu is huge. Head back to Cuzco, then 🚌 4½ hrs to Parque Nacional Manu

1 Lima (p35) Ease into the journey with a relaxed day in Lima. Sample the city's tasty food and explore your pick of museums. ✈ 2 hrs then 🚗 1 hr to Puno

5 Parque Nacional Manu (p256)
Try to factor in at least three nights
in this area of the Amazon Basin to
see a wonderland of jaguars, tapirs,
monkeys and birds.

5

3 Cuzco (p143) Explore the ancient
capital of the Inca empire, starting
with Qorikancha and Sacsaywamán.
Don't miss La Catedral. 🚌 3 hrs to
Aguas Calientes

4

3

2 Puno (p132) High above sea level,
visit La Catedral and stroll around the
Coca Museum. The next day, take a
day trip to one of Lake Titicaca's
islands. ✈ 1 hr to Cuzco

2

Plan Your Trip
Family Travel

HUGHES HERVÁO / GETTY IMAGES ©

Machu Picchu (p200)

Traveling with children to Peru can bring some distinct advantages; in this family-oriented society, little ones are treasured. For parents, it makes an easy conversation starter with locals and ultimately aids in breaking down cultural barriers. In turn, Peru can be a great place for kids, with plenty of opportunities to explore and interact.

Inspiration

Routine travel, such as train rides or jungle canoe trips, can amount to adventure for kids. In rural areas, community tourism is a great option. Many of the activities aimed at adults can be scaled down for children. Activities such as guided horseback rides and canyoning often have age limits (usually eight and up), but are invariably OK for teenagers. Some rivers may be suitable for children to float or raft; make sure outfitters have life vests and wet suits in appropriate sizes.

Other ideas include rafting near Cuzco, horseback riding in the Andean foothills, splashing about in the hot pools in Cañón del Colca's La Calera, canopy zip-lining in the Sacred Valley, cycling the coastal paths of Lima and spying wildlife in the Amazon.

Need to Know

Babysitting Babysitting services or children's activity clubs tend to be limited to upmarket hotels and resorts.

Dining While restaurants don't offer special kids' meals, most offer a variety of dishes suitable for children or may accommodate a special request. You can also always order meals *sin picante* (without spice). High chairs are available in some larger restaurants

Driving Car seats are not widely available with rental cars, so it is best if you can bring one with you.

Expecting and new mothers Expecting mothers enjoy a boon of special parking spaces and grocery-store lines. Breastfeeding in public is not

Sea lions, Islas Ballestas (p72)

uncommon, but most women discreetly cover themselves.

Flights Children under the age of 12 may receive discounts on airline travel, while infants under two pay only 10% of the fare, provided they sit on their parent's lap.

Hotels Most midrange and top-end hotels will have reduced rates for children under 12 years of age, provided the child shares a room with parents. Cots are not normally available, except at the most exclusive hotels. Cabins or apartments, more common in beach destinations, usually make a good choice, with options for self-catering.

Infant supplies Stock up on diapers (nappies) in Lima or other major cities before heading to rural areas. Bring your own infant medicines and a thermometer. Formula and baby food are easily found.

★ **Best Destinations for Kids**

Lima (p35)

Cuzco (p143)

Islas Ballestas (p69)

Machu Picchu (p197)

Public toilets In general, public toilets are poorly maintained. Always carry toilet paper. While a woman may take a young boy into the ladies' room, it would be socially unacceptable for a man to take a girl into the men's room.

Public transportation In Peru, kids are a common sight on public transportation. Often someone will give up a seat for a parent and child or offer to put your child on their lap. On buses, children aren't normally charged if they sit on their parent's lap.

Cerro San Cristóbal

Panorama of Paseo de la República, across from the Museo de Arte de Lima

N
0 — 2 km
0 — 1 mile

MUSEO LARCO

San Isidro
Swanky area with
sumptuous hotels,
frothy cocktails
and fusion haute
cuisine (p53)

Miraflores
Lima's modern hub, full
of restaurants, shops
and nightspots (p53)

*PACIFIC
OCEAN*

Barranco
Lima's nightlife hub,
full of thumping clubs
and bars (p53)

Paseo de los Héroes Navales

Palacio de Justicia

Estación
mparados

Lima Centro
The city's colonial
heart, filled with
bustling narrow streets
and ornate baroque
churches (p50)

**MUSEO DE
ARTE DE LIMA**

**ASTRID Y GASTÓN
CASA MOREYRA**

ámaZ

PACHACAMAC

(8km)

Corte Superior de Justicia de Lima

LIMA

Parque Universitario

Estación Central Grau

Lima at a Glance...

Fresh sophistication has come to a civilization that dates back millennia. Galleries debut edgy art, stately museums give new angles to sacrifice vessels, solemn religious processions recall the 18th century, and crowded nightclubs dispense tropical beats. No visitor can miss the capital's culinary genius, part of a gastronomic revolution more than 400 years in the making. This is Lima. Shrouded in history, gloriously messy and full of aesthetic delights. Don't even think of missing it.

Lima in Two Days

Start the day with a **walking tour** (p48) of the city's colonial heart and end the day with a most important pilgrimage: a pisco sour, either at **El Bolivarcito** (p63) or **Museo del Pisco** (p63). On the second day, go pre-Columbian and view breathtaking Moche pottery at **Museo Larco** (p38) and explore **Huaca Pucllana** (p53), a centuries-old adobe temple in the middle of Miraflores, which also boasts a sophisticated **restaurant** (p60).

Lima in Three Days

On the third day, make the day trip to **Pachacamac** (p44) to explore sandy ruins with several civilizations' worth of temples. Spend the afternoon haggling for crafts at the **Mercado Indio** (p55) in Miraflores.

GREG VAUGHN / GETTY IMAGES ©

Parque del Amor, Miraflores

Arriving in Lima

Aeropuerto Internacional Jorge Chávez Lies 12km west of downtown, or 20km northwest of Miraflores. Take the 45- to 60-minute trip in an official airport taxi, Taxi Green, for about S60.

Bus There is no central terminal; each company operates independent arrival points. Cruz del Sur has most luxury arrivals at La Victoria, from where it's a 15-minute taxi ride south to Miraflores.

Where to Stay

From diminutive family *pensións* to hotel towers armed with spas, Lima has every type of accommodations imaginable. It is also one of the most expensive destinations in the country (other than the tourist mecca of Cuzco).

The favored traveler neighborhood is Miraflores, offering a bounty of hostels, inns and upscale hotel chains, and vigilant neighborhood security. Nearby Barranco is certainly one of the most walkable areas, with lots of gardens and colonial architecture. More upscale – and generally more tranquil – is the financial hub of San Isidro.

For more on where to stay, see p67.

Fundación Museo Amano

Top Museums

Lima is a masterpiece of cultures, artefacts and architecture. A glut of art of the pre-Incan, colonial and contemporary kind is matched with eye-openers like erotic pots, Mario Testino snaps and Inquisition torture devices.

Great For...

☑ Don't Miss

Museo Larco's gold ceremonial suit, and the erotic ceramics of indigenous cultures.

Museo Larco

In an 18th-century viceroy's mansion, **Museo Larco** (☎01-461-1312; www.museo larco.org; Bolívar 1515, Pueblo Libre; adult/child under 15 S30/15; ⊙9am-10pm) offers one of the largest, best-presented displays of ceramics in Lima. Founded by pre-Columbian collector Rafael Larco Hoyle in 1926, the collection includes over 50,000 pots, with ceramic works from the Cupisnique, Chimú, Chancay, Nazca and Inca cultures. Highlights include the sublime Moche portrait vessels, presented in simple, dramatically lit cases, and a Wari weaving in one of the rear galleries that contains 398 threads to the linear inch – a record.

Chimú sculpture, Museo Larco

STEPHEN COLLECTOR / GETTY IMAGES ©

Need to Know

Most museums are closed Mondays.

Take a Break

Larco has a beautiful on-site garden cafe, Museo Mario Testino an arty one, and the one at MALI pushes pisco sours.

Top Tip

Explore Lima Centro's concentration of museums by day, then taxi back to Miraflores for cosmopolitan nightlife.

Museo de Arte de Lima

Known locally as **MALI** (01-204-0000; www.mali.pe; Paseo Colón 125; adult/child S12/4; 10am-8pm Tue, Thu & Fri, to 5pm Sat & Sun), Lima's principal fine-art museum is housed in a striking beaux arts building that was recently renovated. Subjects span from pre-Columbian to contemporary art, and there are also guided visits to special exhibits. On Sunday, entry is just S1. A satellite museum is under construction in Barranco.

Museo de la Inquisición

A graceful neoclassical structure facing the Plaza Bolívar houses the diminutive **Museo de la Inquisición** (Map p52; 01-311-7777, ext 5160; www.congreso.gob.pe/museo.htm; Jirón Junín 548; 9am-5pm) FREE where the Spanish Inquisition once plied its trade. In the 1800s the building was expanded and rebuilt into the Peruvian senate. Today, guests can tour the basement, where morbidly hilarious wax figures are stretched on racks and flogged – to the delight of visiting eight-year-olds. The old 1st-floor library retains a remarkable baroque wooden ceiling. After an obilgatory half-hour tour (in Spanish or English) guests can wander.

Fundación Museo Amano

The well-designed **Fundación Museo Amano** (Map p56; 01-441-2909; www.museoamano.org; Retiro 160; 3-5pm Mon-Fri, by appointment only) FREE features a fine private collection of ceramics, with a strong representation of wares from the Chimú and Nazca cultures. It also has a remarkable assortment of lace and other textiles produced by the coastal Chancay culture. Museum visits are allowed by a one-hour guided tour only, in Spanish or Japanese.

Museo Mario Testino

The wonderful and small **Museo Mario Testino** (MATE; Map p62; 01-251-7755; www.mate.pe; Av Pedro de Osma 409; adult/student S15/5; 11am-8pm Tue-Sun) is dedicated to the work of the world-renowned photographer Mario Testino, a native of Peru and a *barranquino* (Barranco local). The permanent exhibition includes iconic portraits of Princess Diana, Kate Moss and notable actors. There are also beautiful portraits of Andean highlanders in traditional garb.

Anticuchos (beef-heart skewers)

Eating in Lima

The gastronomic capital of the continent, Lima is where you will find some of the country's most sublime culinary creations: from simple cevicherías *(ceviche counters) and corner* anticucho *(beef-heart skewer) stands to outstanding molecular cuisine, nutty chicken stews (*ají de gallina*) from Arequipa and cocktails infused with Amazon berries.*

Great For...

ⓘ **Need to Know**

A *menú* (set-menu meal) is a delicious way to taste-test local flavours.

★ **Top Tip**

In Miraflores, casual places with cheap *menús* abound on the tiny streets east of Av José Larco just off the Parque Kennedy.

Where to Eat

Lima's prime position on the coast gives it access to a wide variety of staggeringly fresh seafood, while showcasing regional specialties. The city has such a vast assortment of cuisine, in fact, that it's possible to spend weeks here without tasting it all. Pack your appetite, you'll need it.

ámaZ   Amazonian $$

(Map p56; ☑01-221-9393; www.amaz.com.pe; Av La Paz 1079; mains S12-44; ⊙12:30-11:30pm Mon-Sat, to 4:30pm Sun; ☑) Chef Pedro Miguel's latest wonder is wholly dedicated to the abundance of the Amazon. Start with tart jungle-fruit cocktails and oversized *tostones* (plantain chips). Banana-leaf wraps, aka *juanes*, hold treasures like fragrant Peking duck with rice. There's excellent *encurtido* (pickled vegetables), and the generous vegetarian set menu for two (S270) is a delicious way to sample the diversity.

Isolina   Peruvian $$

(Map p62; ☑01-247-5075; Av San Martín 101; mains S22-48; ⊙10am-midnight) Go old school. This is home-style *criollo* (a blend of Spanish, Andean, Chinese and African influences) food at its best. Isolina doesn't shy away from tripe and kidneys, but also offers loving preparations of succulent ribs, *causa escabechada* (with marinated onions) and vibrant green salads on the handwritten menu. Family-sized portions come in old-fashioned tins, but you could also make a lighter meal of starters.

Central   Peruvian $$$

(Map p56; ☑01-242-8515; centralrestaurante. com.pe; Santa Isabel 376; mains S52-88; ⊙12:45-3:15pm & 7:45-11:15pm Mon-Fri) ☑ Part

Ceviche

restaurant, part laboratory, Central reinvents Andean cuisine and rescues age-old Peruvian edibles you'd find nowhere else. Dining here is an experience, evidenced by the tender native potatoes served in edible clay. Chef Virgilio Martinez wants you to taste the Andes. He paid his dues in Europe and Asia's top kitchens, but it's his work here that dazzles.

Astrid y Gastón
Casa Moreyra   Novo Andino $$$
(Map p56; ☑01-442-2775; www.astridygaston. com; Av Paz Soldan 290; mains S53-89; ⊘12:30-3:30pm & 6:30pm-midnight Mon-Sat) Spearheading *novoandina* (Peruvian

nouvelle cuisine) in Lima, Gastón Acurio's flagship French-influenced restaurant as run by Lima native Diego Muñoz remains a culinary tour de force. The seasonal menu features traditional Peruvian fare, but it's the exquisite fusion specialties that make this such a sublime fine-dining experience. The 28-course tasting menu showcases the depth and breadth of possibility here – just do it.

What to Eat

In Lima, food inspires as much reverence as religion. So, the agonizing question is always, what to eat? Start by sampling these local staples.

○ Lima's most tender *anticuchos* can be found at street carts and a posh Miraflores eatery, Panchita (p59).

○ Sublime renditions of ceviche, the country's most seductive dish, can be found in places both economical, such as El Rincón del Bigote (p60), and upscale, such as Pescados Capitales (p61); for something truly different, try it seared at Fiesta (p61).

○ The country's fusion cuisine, *criollo* cooking is without parallel at neighborhood eateries Isolina (p42) and **El Rincón que No Conoces** (☑01-471-2171; Av Bernardo Alcedo 363, Lince; mains S21-55; ⊘12:30-5pm Tue-Sun), in addition to the superchic Restaurant Huaca Pucllana (p53).

○ First-rate service, encyclopedic wine lists and sculptural dishes that blend the traditional and the nouveau find their apex at Astrid y Gastón Casa Moreyra (p43) and Central (p42).

○ Celebrating the humble potato, *causas* are cold potato dishes that are as beautiful as they are delectable, and are found in any traditional restaurant.

> ☑ **Don't Miss**
> The experience of tucking into ceviche with a view of the moody ocean.

FOODIO / SHUTTERSTOCK ©

> ✖ **Take a Break**
> For eating on the go, grab a tasty Peruvian *sanguche* – 'sandwich' by name, panino by flavour.

Pachacamac

Situated about 31km southeast of the city center, the archaeological complex of Pachacamac is a pre-Columbian citadel made up of adobe and stone palaces and temple pyramids.

Great For...

☑ Don't Miss

The Templo del Sol for vistas of the Pacific Ocean and the Andes foothills.

❶ Need to Know

☏01-430-0168; http://pachacamac.peru cultural.org.pe; admission S10; ⊘9am-4pm Tue-Sat, to 3pm Sun

★ **Top Tip**

In summer take water and a hat –
there is no shade once you hit the
trail.

History

If you've been to Machu Picchu, Pachacamac may not look like much, but this was an important Inca site and a major city when the Spanish arrived. It began as a ceremonial center for the Lima culture beginning at about AD 100, and was later expanded by the Waris before being taken over by the Ichsma. The Incas added numerous other structures upon their arrival to the area in 1450. The name Pachacamac, which can be variously translated as 'He Who Animated the World' or 'He Who Created Land and Time,' comes from the Wari god, whose wooden, two-faced image can be seen at the on-site museum.

The Site

Most of the buildings are now little more than piles of rubble that dot the desert landscape, but some of the main temples have been excavated and their ramps and stepped sides revealed. You can climb the switchback trail to the top of the **Templo del Sol** (Temple of the Sun), which on clear days offers excellent views of the coast. The most remarkable structure on-site, however, is the Palacio de las Mamacuna (House of the Chosen Women), commonly referred to as the **Acllahuasi**, which boasts a series of Inca-style trapezoidal doorways. Unfortunately, a major earthquake in 2007 left the structure highly unstable. As a result, visitors can only admire it from a distance. Without funding to repair the extensive damage, it has been listed as one of the planet's most endangered sites.

New Discoveries in Pachacamac

The widespread looting of Peru's archaeological treasures has left many ruins with more puzzling questions than answers. So the discovery in May 2012 of an untouched 80-person burial chamber in Pachacamac is considered nothing less than a coup. Archaeologists from the Free University of Brussels discovered an 18m (60ft) oval chamber in front of the Temple of Pachacamac, hidden under newer burials. The perimeter was laced with infants and newborns encircling over 70 skeletons in the center of the tomb. The mummies were wrapped in textiles and buried with valuables, offerings, and even dogs and guinea pigs. According to *National Geographic,* investigators think the tomb may contain pilgrims who were drawn to the site to seek cures for serious illnesses.

Visiting Pachacamac

Various agencies in Lima offer guided tours (half-day around S115 per person) that include transport and a guide.

✕ Take a Break

There is a visitors center and cafe at the site entrance, on the road to Lurín.

A simple map can be obtained from the ticket office, and a track leads from here into the complex. Those on foot should allow at least two hours to explore. Those with a vehicle can drive from site to site.

Alternatively, catch a minibus signed 'Pachacamac' from Av 28 de Julio or the sunken roadway at the corner of Andahuaylas and Grau in Lima Centro (S3, 45 minutes); minibuses leave every 15 minutes during daylight hours. From Miraflores, take a bus on Av Benavides headed east to the Panamericana and Puente Primavera, change here for the bus signed 'Pachacamac/Lurín' (S3, 30 minutes). For both services, tell the driver to let you off near the *ruinas* (ruins) or you'll end up at Pachacamac village, about 1km beyond the entrance. To get back to Lima, flag down any bus outside the gate, but expect to stand. You can also hire a taxi per hour (from S40) from Lima.

A restored section of Pachacamac

STUART GRAY / GETTY IMAGES ©

★ **Top Tip**
Mountain-bike tours can be an excellent option.

MANX_IN_THE_WORLD / GETTY IMAGES ©

Downtown Lima Walking Tour

In the historical center of Lima, every turn is a blast from the city's colonial past. This is the best of its architecture in churches, palaces, plazas and catacombs.

Start Plaza San Martín
Distance 3km
Duration 2 hours

Classic Photo
from the Plaza de Armas

4 Explore **Plaza de Armas** (p50), including the **Catedral de Lima** (p50) and the **Palacio Arzobispal** (p50), home to some of the city's best-preserved Moorish balconies.

Plaza de Armas (Plaza Mayor)

4

Camaná
Callao
Ica
Ucayali
Carabaya
Lampa
Miró Quesada

2 Walk the pedestrian street of **Jirón de la Unión**; once the heart of aristocratic city life, it's now lined with cinemas and bargain shoe stores.

Emancipación

Estacion Jiron de la Union

Jirón de la Unión

3

1 Begin in **Plaza San Martín** (p52) to imbibe the faded grandeur of **Gran Hotel Bolívar** (p53), the city's first fine hotel.

2

Nicolás de Piérola (Colmena)
Camaná

1

START

Plaza San Martín

3 Iglesia de la Merced (⊙10am-noon & 5-7pm), was originally built in 1541. It held the first Mass in Lima. Peek inside at the impressive mahogany altars.

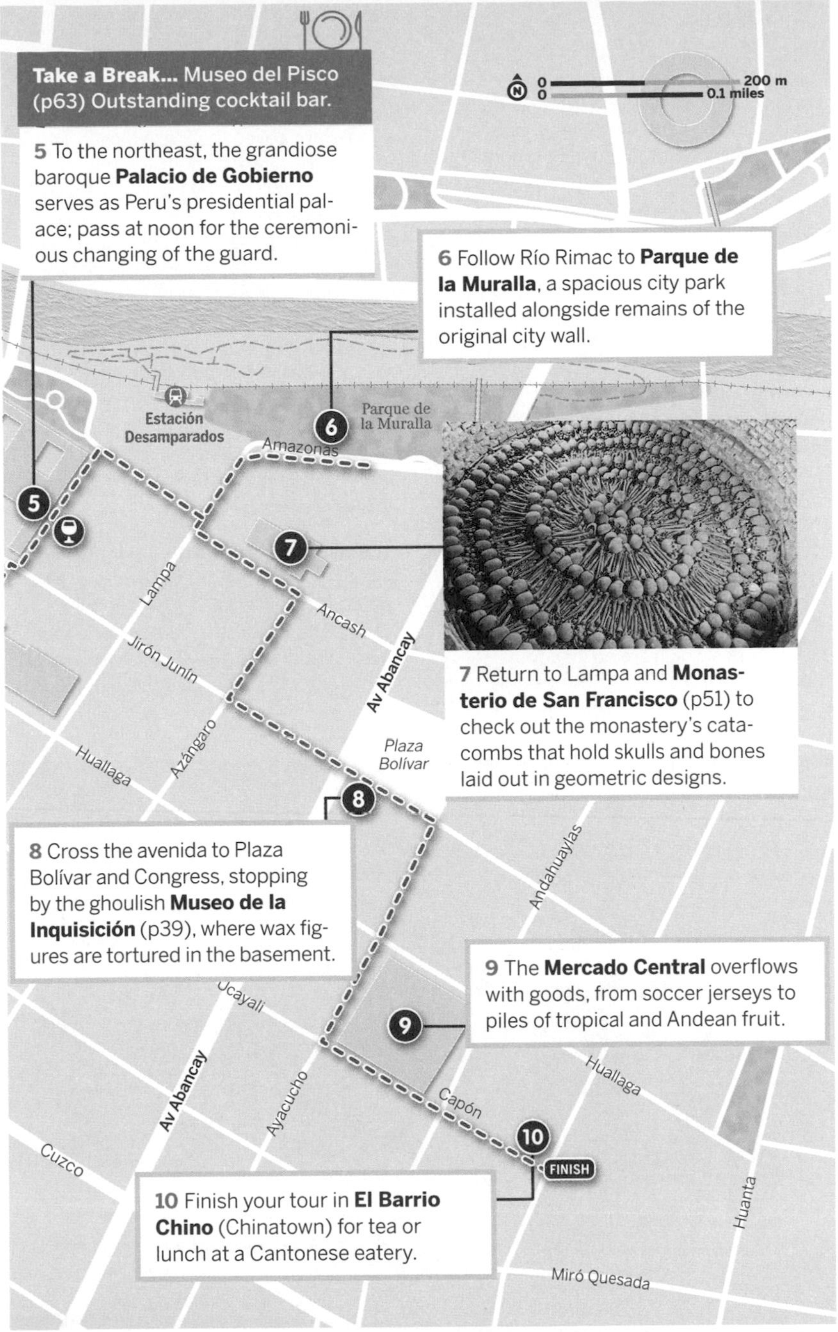

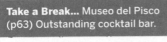

Take a Break... Museo del Pisco (p63) Outstanding cocktail bar.

5 To the northeast, the grandiose baroque **Palacio de Gobierno** serves as Peru's presidential palace; pass at noon for the ceremonious changing of the guard.

6 Follow Río Rimac to **Parque de la Muralla**, a spacious city park installed alongside remains of the original city wall.

7 Return to Lampa and **Monasterio de San Francisco** (p51) to check out the monastery's catacombs that hold skulls and bones laid out in geometric designs.

8 Cross the avenida to Plaza Bolívar and Congress, stopping by the ghoulish **Museo de la Inquisición** (p39), where wax figures are tortured in the basement.

9 The **Mercado Central** overflows with goods, from soccer jerseys to piles of tropical and Andean fruit.

10 Finish your tour in **El Barrio Chino** (Chinatown) for tea or lunch at a Cantonese eatery.

Estación Desamparados

Parque de la Muralla

Amazonas

Lampa

Ancash

Jirón Junín

Av Abancay

Azángaro

Huallaga

Plaza Bolívar

Andahuaylas

Ucayali

Av Abancay

Ayacucho

Capón

Huallaga

Cuzco

FINISH

Huanta

Miró Quesada

200 m
0.1 miles

⊙ SIGHTS

The city's historic heart, Lima Centro (Central Lima) is home to most of the city's surviving colonial architecture. Well-to-do San Isidro is Lima's banking center. It borders the seaside neighborhood of Miraflores, which serves as Lima's contemporary core, bustling with restaurants and nightlife. Immediately to the south lies Barranco, a hip bohemian center with hopping bars and nice areas to stroll.

⊙ Lima Centro

Bustling narrow streets are lined with ornate baroque churches in the city's historic and commercial center, located on the south bank of the Río Rímac. Few colonial mansions remain since many have been lost to expansion, earthquakes and the perennially moist weather. The best access to the Plaza de Armas is the pedestrian-only street **Jirón de la Unión** (Map p52).

Finding street names in this area can be maddening; to top it off, tiles label colonial street names which are no longer in use. Your best bet is to look for the green street signs and use well-known landmarks for orientation.

Plaza de Armas   Plaza

(Map p52) Lima's 140-sq-meter Plaza de Armas, also called the Plaza Mayor, was not only the heart of the 16th-century settlement established by Francisco Pizarro, it was a center of the Spaniards' continent-wide empire. Though not one original building remains, at the center of the plaza is an impressive bronze fountain erected in 1650.

Surrounding the plaza are a number of significant public buildings: to the east resides the **Palacio Arzobispal** (Archbishop's Palace; Map p52), built in 1924 in a colonial style and boasting some of the most exquisite Moorish-style balconies in the city. To the northeast is the block-long Palacio de Gobierno.

La Catedral de Lima   Church

(Map p52; ☏ 01-427-9647; museum S10; ⊙ 9am-5pm Mon-Fri, 10am-1pm Sat) Next to the Palacio Arzobispal, the cathedral resides on the plot of land that Pizarro designated for the city's first church in 1535. Though it

Plaza de Armas and La Catedral de Lima

retains a baroque facade, the building has been built and rebuilt numerous times: in 1551, in 1622 and after the earthquakes of 1687 and 1746. The last major restoration was in 1940.

A craze for all things neoclassical in the late 18th century left much of the interior (and the interiors of many Lima churches) stripped of its elaborate baroque decor. Even so, there is plenty to see. The various chapels along the nave display more than a dozen altars carved in every imaginable style, and the ornate wood **choir**, produced by Pedro de Noguera in the early 17th century, is a masterpiece of rococo sculpture. A **museum**, in the rear, features paintings, vestments and an intricate sacristy.

By the cathedral's main door is the mosaic-covered **chapel** with the remains of Pizarro. Their authenticity came into question in 1977, after workers cleaning out a crypt discovered several bodies and a sealed lead box containing a skull that bore the inscription, 'Here is the head of the gentleman Marquis Don Francisco Pizarro, who found and conquered the kingdom of Peru...' After a battery of tests in the 1980s, a US forensic scientist concluded that the body previously on display was of an unknown official and that the brutally stabbed and headless body from the crypt was Pizarro's. Head and body were reunited and transferred to the chapel, where you can also view the inscribed lead box.

Guide services in Spanish, English, French, Italian and Portuguese are available for an additional fee.

Iglesia de Santo Domingo   Church

(Map p52; ☏01-427-6793; cnr Camaná & Conde de Superunda; church free, convent S7; ◷9am-1pm & 5-7:30pm Mon-Sat) One of Lima's most storied religious sites, the Iglesia de Santo Domingo and its expansive **convent** are built on land granted to the Dominican Friar Vicente de Valverde, who accompanied Pizarro throughout the conquest and was instrumental in persuading him to execute the captured Inca Atahualpa. Originally completed in the 16th century, this im-

Street Names

The same street can have several names as it traverses Lima, such as Av Arequipa (aka Garcilaso de la Vega or Wilson). Some names reappear in different districts, so indicate the right neighborhood to taxi drivers. Streets also may change names – for practicality we have used the most common names.

pressive pink church has been rebuilt and remodeled at various points since.

It is most renowned as the final resting place for three important Peruvian saints: San Juan Macías, Santa Rosa de Lima and San Martín de Porres (the continent's first black saint). The convent – a sprawling courtyard-studded complex lined with baroque paintings and clad in vintage Spanish tiles – contains the saints' tombs. The church, however, has the most interesting relics: the skulls of San Martín and Santa Rosa, encased in glass, in a shrine to the right of the main altar.

Monasterio de San Francisco   Monastery

(Map p52; ☏01-426-7377; www.museocatacum bas.com; cnr Lampa & Ancash; adult/child under 15 S7/1; ◷9:30am-5:30pm) This bright-yellow Franciscan monastery and church is most famous for its bone-lined **catacombs** (containing an estimated 70,000 remains) and its remarkable **library** housing 25,000 antique texts, some of which predate the conquest. Admission includes a 30-minute guided tour in English or in Spanish. Tours leave as groups gather.

This baroque structure has many other treasures: the most spectacular is a geometric Moorish-style **cupola** over the main staircase, which was carved in 1625 (restored 1969) out of Nicaraguan cedar. In addition, the **refectory** contains 13 paintings of the biblical patriarch Jacob and his 12 sons, attributed to the studio of Spanish master Francisco de Zurbarán.

Plaza San Martín · Plaza

(Map p52) Built in the early 20th century, Plaza San Martín has come to life in recent years as the city has set about restoring its park and giving the surrounding beaux arts architecture a much-needed scrubbing. It is especially lovely in the evenings, when illuminated. The plaza is named for the liber-ator of Peru, **José de San Martín**, who sits astride a horse at the center of the plaza.

At the base of the statue, don't miss the bronze rendering of **Madre Patria**, the symbolic mother of Peru. Commissioned in Spain under instruction to give the good lady a crown of flames, nobody thought to iron out the double meaning of the word

Lima Centro

Sights

1 Iglesia de la Merced	B2
2 Iglesia de Santo Domingo	B1
3 Jirón de la Unión	B2
4 La Catedral de Lima	C2
5 Monasterio de San Francisco	D2
6 Museo de la Inquisición	D2
7 Palacio Arzobispal	C2
8 Plaza de Armas	C2
9 Plaza San Martín	B3

Activities, Courses & Tours

10 Lima Tours	A2

Eating

11 Domus	C3
12 El Cordano	C1
13 L'Eau Vive	C2
14 Tanta	B1
15 Wa Lok	D3

Drinking & Nightlife

El Bolivarcito	(see 18)
16 Museo del Pisco	C2

Entertainment

17 Teatro Segura	B2

Sleeping

18 Gran Hotel Bolívar	A3

'flame' in Spanish (llama), so the hapless craftsmen duly placed a delightful little llama on her head.

The once-stately **Gran Hotel Bolívar** (Map p52; ☑01-619-7171; www.granhotelbolivar. com.pe; Jirón de la Unión 958; s/d/tr S247/ 278/309; @), built in the 1920s, presides over the square from the northwest.

El Circuito Mágico
del Agua Fountain

(Parque de la Reserva, Av Petit Thouars, cuadra 5; admission S4; ☺3:30-10:30pm) This indulgent series of illuminated fountains is so over-the-top it can't help but induce stupefaction among even the most hardened cynic. A dozen different fountains – all splendiferously illuminated – are capped, at the end, by a laser light show at the 120m-long Fuente de la Fantasía (Fantasy Fountain). The whole display is set to a medley of tunes comprised of everything from Peruvian waltzes to ABBA. It has to be seen to be believed. Access to the area is free by day when fountains are off.

◉ San Isidro & Around

A combination of middle- and upper-class residential neighborhoods offer some important sights of note.

Huaca Huallamarca Ruin

(Map p56; ☑01-222-4124; Nicolás de Rivera 201, San Isidro; adult/child S10/5; ☺9am-5pm Tue-Sun) Nestled among condominium towers and sprawling high-end homes, the simple Huaca Huallamarca is a highly restored adobe pyramid, produced by the Lima culture, that dates to somewhere between AD 200 and 500. A small on-site **museum**, complete with mummy, details its excavation.

Museo Nacional de Antropología, Arqueología e Historía
del Perú Museum

(National Anthropology, Archaeology & History Museum; ☑01-463-5070; http://mnaahp.cultura. pe; Plaza Bolívar, cnr San Martín & Vivanco, Pueblo Libre; adult/child S10/1; ☺9am-5pm Tue-Sat, to 4pm Sun) Trace the history of

Peru from the pre-ceramic period to the early republic. Displays include the famous Raimondi Stela, a 2.1m Chavín rock carving from one of the first Andean cultures to have a widespread, recognizable artistic style. Late-colonial and early republic paintings include an 18th-century *Last Supper* in which Christ and his disciples feast on *cuy* (guinea pig). The building was home to revolutionary heroes San Martín (from 1821 to 1822) and Bolívar (from 1823 to 1826).

◉ Miraflores

The city's bustling, modern hub – full of restaurants, shops and nightspots – overlooks the Pacific from a set of ragged cliffs.

Huaca Pucllana Ruin

(Map p56; ☑01-617-7138; cnr Borgoño & Tarapacá; adult/student S12/5; ☺9am-4:30pm) Located near the Óvalo Gutiérrez, this *huaca* (tomb or grave) is a restored adobe ceremonial center from the Lima culture that dates back to AD 400. In 2010 an important discovery of four Wari mummies was made, untouched by looting. Though vigorous excavations continue, the site is accessible by regular guided tours in Spanish (for a tip). In addition to a tiny on-site **museum**, there's a celebrated restaurant that offers incredible views of the illuminated ruins at night.

◉ Barranco

A tiny resort back at the turn of the 20th century, Barranco is lined with grand old *casonas* (stately homes), many of which have been turned into eateries and hotels.

Museo Pedro de Osma Museum

(Map p62; ☑01-467-0141; www.museopedro deosma.org; Av Pedro de Osma 423; admission S20; ☺10am-6pm Tue-Sun) Housed in a lovely beaux arts mansion surrounded by gardens, this undervisited museum has an exquisite collection of colonial furniture, silverwork and art, some of which dates back to the 1500s. Among the many fine pieces, standouts include a 2m-wide canvas that depicts a Corpus Christi procession in turn-of-the-17th-century Cuzco.

Mistura Food Fair

One serious eating event, **Mistura** (www.mistura.pe; Parque de la Exposicion, Lima Centro) is Lima's prestigious week-long international food fair held every September. Get a ticket and sample an astonishing diversity of delicacies from the finest restaurants to the best street food.

Traditional food at Mistura
AFP / STRINGER / GETTY IMAGES ©

Puente de los Suspiros   Bridge
(Bridge of Sighs; Map p62) A block west of the main plaza, look for this recently renovated, narrow wooden bridge over an old stone stairway that leads to the beach. Especially popular with couples on first dates, the bridge has inspired many a Peruvian folk song.

Choco Museo   Museum
(Map p62; ☏01-477-3584; www.chocomuseo.com; Av Grau 264; 2hr workshop adult/child S75/55; ☉11am-10pm) A quickie cacao 101 museum better known for its daily chocolate-making workshops, with a few locations in the city. The specialty of this outlet is the bean-to-bar chocolate factory housed on-site. Fair-trade chocolate is also sold here.

> *sample an astonishing diversity of delicacies*

🪂 ACTIVITIES

Peru Fly   Paragliding
(Map p56; ☏01-959-524-940; www.perufly.com) A paragliding school that also offers tandem flights in Miraflores.

Andean Trail Peru   Paragliding
(andeantrailperu.com) Offers tandem flights over Miraflores and Pachacamac, along with basic paragliding courses.

🎯 TOURS

Bike Tours of Lima   Bicycle Tour
(Map p56; ☏01-445-3172; www.biketoursoflima.com; Bolívar 150, Miraflores; 3hr tour S105; ☉9am-7pm Mon-Sat) Highly recommended for organized day tours around Barranco, Miraflores and San Isidro, as well as Sunday excursions into downtown. Rentals available.

Lima Tasty Tours   Food
(☏01-958-313-939; www.limatastytours.com) Excellent gastronomic tours, with tailored options and insider access to lesser-known culinary treasures, available in English.

Lima Tours   Tour
(Map p52; ☏01-619-6900; www.limatours.com.pe; Nicolás de Piérola 589, 18th fl, Lima Centro) A travel agency that is not exclusively gay, but that organizes gay-friendly group trips around the country.

Lima Vision   Tour
(Map p56; ☏01-447-7710; www.limavision.com; Chiclayo 444, Miraflores) Lima Vision has various four-hour city tours (S70), as well as day trips to the ruins at Pachacamac.

🔒 SHOPPING

Small shops selling crafts dot the major tourist areas around Pasaje de los Escribanos in Lima Centro, and near the intersection of Diez Canseco and La Paz in Miraflores. Credit cards and traveler's checks can be used at some spots, but you'll need photo identification.

Quality pisco can be bought duty-free at the airport just prior to departure.

Dédalo — Handicrafts

(Map p62; ☏01-652-5400; http://dedaloarte.
blogspot.com; Sáenz Peña 295, Barranco;
◷10am-8pm Mon-Sat, 11am-7pm Sun) A vintage
casona houses this contemporary crafts
store with a lovely courtyard cafe.

Las Pallas — Handicrafts

(Map p62; ☏01-477-4629; www.laspallasperu.com;
Cajamarca 212, Barranco; ◷10am-7pm Mon-Sat)
For special gifts, check out this handicrafts
store featuring a selection of the highest-
quality products from all over Peru; it's even
on the radar of Sotheby's. Ring the bell if the
gate is closed during opening hours.

Mercado Indio — Market

(Map p56; Av Petit Thouars 5245, Miraflores)
The best place to find everything from
pre-Columbian-style clay pottery to
alpaca rugs to knockoffs of Cuzco School
canvases. Prices vary; shop around.

LarcoMar — Mall

(Map p56; Malecón de la Reserva 610) A well-to-
do outdoor mall wedged into the cliff top
beneath the Parque Salazar, full of high-end
clothing stores, trendy discotheques and

Paraglider above LarcoMar

a wide range of eateries. There's also a
bowling alley.

El Virrey — Books

(Map p56; ☏01-444-4141; www.elvirrey.com;
Bolognesi 510, Miraflores; ◷10am-7pm) Includes a room stocked with thousands of
rare vintage editions.

🍴 EATING
🍴 Lima Centro

Miraflores and San Isidro may have the
city's trendiest restaurants, but Lima's
downtown spots offer cheap deals and
history, from functional *comedores* (simple
dining rooms) packed with office workers
to atmospheric eateries that count Peruvian presidents among the clientele. *Menús*
(set meals) in the vicinity of S10 can be
found at many of the cheaper restaurants.

El Cordano — Cafeteria $

(Map p52; ☏01-427-0181; Ancash 202; mains
S10-32; ◷8am-9pm) A Lima institution since
1905, this old-world dining hall has served
practically every Peruvian president for

Miraflores & San Isidro

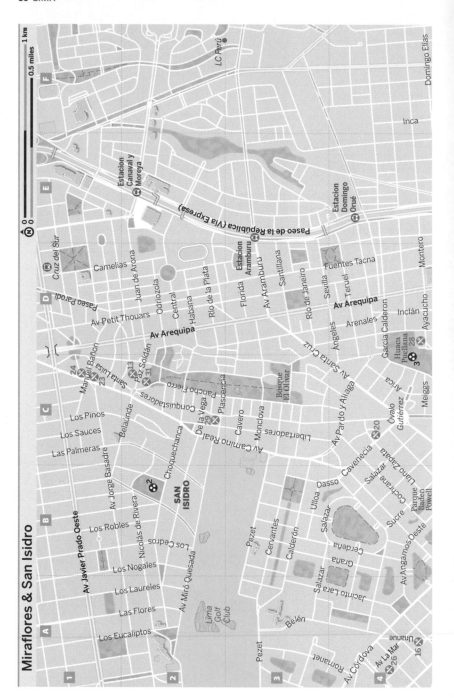

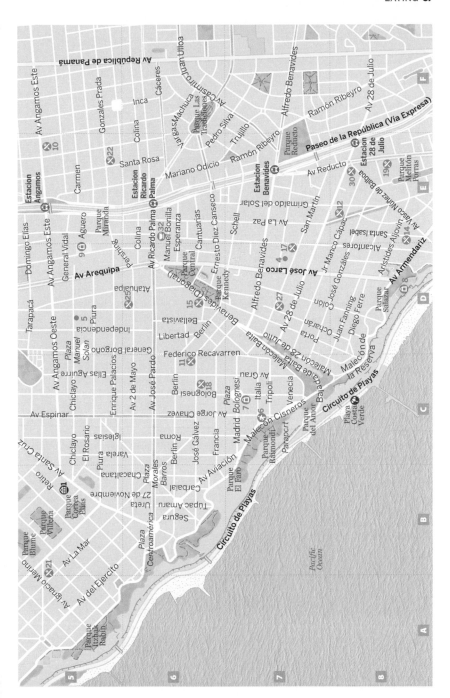

Miraflores & San Isidro

the last 100 years (the presidential palace is right across the street). Don't expect innovation here. It is known for its skillfully rendered *tacu tacu* (pan-fried rice and beans) and *butifarra* (French bread stuffed with country ham).

Domus   Peruvian $

(Map p52; ☑01-427-0525; Miró Quesada 410; 3-course menús S20; ☺7am-5pm Mon-Fri) A restored 19th-century mansion houses this modern-yet-intimate two-room restaurant that caters to journalists from the nearby offices of *El Comercio*. There is no à la carte dining, just a rotating daily list of well-executed Peruvian–Italian specialties that always includes a vegetarian option in the mix. Freshly squeezed juices accompany this well-tended feast. Excellent value.

Tanta   Cafe $$

(Map p52; ☑01-428-3115; Pasaje de los Escribanos 142, Lima Centro; mains S21-46; ☺9am-10pm Mon-Sat, to 6pm Sun) One of several informal bistros in the Gastón Acurio brand, Tanta serves Peruvian dishes, fusion pastas, heaping salads and sandwiches. It's a good bet in the city center where pickings are slim. The food is generally good but desserts shine: try the heavenly passionfruit cheesecake

mousse. There are other branches in **Miraflores** (☑01-447-8377; Av 28 de Julio 888) and **San Isidro** (☑01-421-9708; Pancho Fierro 115).

Wa Lok   Chinese $$

(Map p52; ☑01-447-1329, 01-427-2750; Paruro 878; mains S15-80; ☺9am-11pm Mon-Sat, to 10pm Sun) Serving seafood, fried rice as light and fresh as it gets, and sizzling meats that come on steaming platters, Wa Lok is among the best *chifas* (Chinese restaurants) in Chinatown. The 16-page Cantonese menu includes dumplings, noodles, stir-fries and a good selection of vegetarian options (try the braised tofu casserole). Portions are enormous; don't over-order.

L'Eau Vive   French $$

(Map p52; ☑01-427-5612; Ucayali 370; mains S25-35, 3-course menús S30-50; ☺12:30-3pm & 7:30-9:30pm Mon-Sat; ✳) In an 18th-century building, this very simple and unusual eatery is run by French Carmelite nuns. Expect French and other continental specialties (think *coquilles St Jacques*) with Peruvian influences. The food isn't jaw-dropping, but the real reason to come is to enjoy the strange serenade. Every night, after dinner (at around 9pm), the nuns gather to sing 'Ave Maria.'

San Isidro

Chic dining rooms, frothy cocktails and fusion haute cuisine: San Isidro is a bastion of fine dining – and not much else. Those on a budget may prefer to prepare their own meals, or head to nearby Miraflores, which is generally cheaper.

Al Toke Pez   Ceviche $

(Map p56; Av Angamos Este 886; mains S10-20; ⊙11:30am-3:30pm Tue-Sun) Before sunrise, chef Tomas Matsufuji hits the fish market for today's catch and filets it to serve as super fresh ceviche in his modest shop with a half-dozen stools lined at the counter on a busy avenue. His daily menu (S15) is a heaping plate of chicharron de marisco (fried seafood), ceviche and seafood rice done to perfection.

Segundo Muelle   Ceviche $$

(Map p56; ☑01-421-1206; www.segundomuelle. com; Conquistadores 490; mains S32-40; ⊙noon-5pm) 🥢 A mainstay of impeccable service and renowned ceviches with innovative twists. Try the *ceviche de mariscos a los tres ajíes,* a stack of mixed fish and shellfish bathed in three types of hot pepper sauce. The menu also features heaping rice and other seafood dishes, including a recommended *parrilla marina* (seafood grill).

Matsuei   Japanese $$

(Map p56; ☑01-422-4323; Manuel Bañon 260; maki S30-55; ⊙12:30-3:30pm & 7:30-11pm Mon-Sat) Venerated Japanese superchef Nobu Matsuhisa once co-owned this diminutive sushi bar. Don't let the modest appearance fool you: it serves some of the most spectacular sashimi and *maki* (sushi rolls) in Lima. A must-have: the *'acevichado,'* a roll stuffed with shrimp and avocado, then doused in a house-made mayo infused with ceviche broth. It makes your brain tingle.

La Balanza   Bistro $$

(Map p56; ☑01-222-2659; Cavenecia 162; mains S32-60; ⊙1-4pm & 7pm-midnight Mon-Sat; ☑) 🥢 A farm-to-table bistro serving satisfying meals, it's not surprising it's a hit with both families and couples on date night.

Free-range chicken, organic salads and wonders like beet gnocchi with blue cheese burst with flavor. Enjoy it with a glass of *chicha morada* (nonalcoholic purple maize drink) tinged with star anise. Green also permeates the ambience, with shelves of microgreens and cool recycled place mats.

Malabar   Fusion $$$

(Map p56; ☑01-440-5200; www.malabar.com.pe; Av Camino Real 101; mains S52-68; ⊙12:30-4pm & 7:30-11pm Mon-Sat) With an Amazonian bent, chef Pedro Miguel Schiaffino's seasonal menu features deftly prepared delicacies such as crisp, seared *cuy* and Amazonian river snails bathed in spicy chorizo sauce. Don't forego the cocktails (the chef's father, a noted pisco expert, consulted on the menu) or desserts – perhaps the lightest and most refreshing in Lima.

 Miraflores

By far the most varied neighborhood for eating, Miraflores carries the breadth and depth of Peruvian cooking at every price range imaginable, from tiny *comedores* with cheap lunchtime *menús* to some of the city's most revered gastronomic outposts. Pavement cafes are ideal for sipping pisco sours and people-watching.

Casual places with cheap *menús* abound on the tiny streets east of Av José Larco just off the Parque Kennedy.

Dédalo Arte y Cafe   Cafe $

(Map p56; Benavides 378; snacks S3-10; ⊙8am-9:30pm Mon-Sat; 🛜) Caffeine fiends find their way to this discreet cafe on Parque Kennedy where coffee is as serious as a sacrament. You'll find the usual suspects plus rarer *ristretto* and Australian takes like a flat white. It's owned by the same family as the tasteful Barranco home-decor and accessories shop.

Panchita   Peruvian $$

(Map p56; ☑01-242-5957; Av 2 de Mayo 298; mains S33-60; ⊙12:30-9pm Mon-Sat, to 5pm Sun) A Gastón Acurio homage to Peruvian street food in a contemporary setting ringed by folk art. *Anticuchos* are grilled

Causas (potato dish)

over an open flame to melt-in-your-mouth perfection, particularly the charred octopus. Another winner is the crisp suckling pig with *tacu tacu*. There's also a great salad bar. Portions are big and filling so don't come alone. With outstanding service.

Restaurant Huaca Pucllana
Peruvian $$

(Map p56; 📞01-445-4042; www.resthuacapucllana.com; Gral Borgoño cuadra 8; mains S24-60; ⊘12:30pm-midnight Mon-Sat, to 4pm Sun) Overlooking the illuminated ruins at Huaca Pucllana, this sophisticated establishment serves a skillfully rendered array of contemporary Peruvian dishes (from grilled *cuy* to seafood chowders), along with a smattering of Italian-fusion specialties. Portions are large. Save room for the pisco and lemon parfait come dessert.

El Punto Azul
Ceviche $$

(Map p56; 📞01-445-8078; San Martín 595; mains S22-40; ⊘noon-5pm) Awash in Caribbean blues, this pleasant family eatery dishes up fresh ceviches, *tiraditos* (Japanese-influenced versions of ceviche) and family-sized rice dishes. Try the risotto with shrimp, parmesan and *ají amarillo* (yellow chili) – and don't miss the line-up of beautiful desserts. It gets packed, so show up before 1pm if you want a table. Excellent value.

El Rincón del Bigote
Ceviche $$

(Map p56; José Galvez 529; mains S32-36; ⊘noon-4pm Tue-Sun) Go early. On weekends, locals and tourists line up for seating in this bare-bones ceviche house. The specialty is *almejas in su concha:* pair these marinated clams with a side of crisp yucca fries and a bottle of cold pilsner and you're in heaven.

AlmaZen
Vegetarian $$

(Map p56; 📞01-243-0474; Federico Recavarren 298; mains S30-40; ⊘9am-10pm Mon-Fri; 🌱) With soothing ambience, this vegetarian restaurant and teahouse offers a rotating daily selection of artfully prepared organic, vegan and gluten-free dishes. Its mango ceviche is second to none and juices, like *lulo* (a type of citrus), are delicious. Come only if you're not in a rush – the service is dead slow. Between lunch and dinner meal service stops but the cafe stays open.

Rafael
Novo Andino $$$

(Map p56; ☑01-242-4149; www.rafaelosterling. pe; San Martín 300; mains S39-78; ☺1-3pm & 8-11pm Mon-Wed, to midnight Thu-Sat) A consistent favorite of discerning palates, here Chef Rafael Osterling produces a panoply of fusion dishes, such as *tiradito* bathed in Japanese citrus or suckling goat stewed in Madeira wine. For slimmer budgets the crisp pizzas are divine. Make it past the generously poured cocktails and there's a decent and lengthy international wine list.

Fiesta
Peruvian $$$

(Map p56; ☑01-242-9009; www.restaurant fiestagourmet.com; Av Reducto 1278; mains S40-65; ☺noon-midnight Mon-Sat) The finest northern-Peruvian cuisine in Lima is served at this busy establishment on Miraflores' eastern edge. The *arroz con pato a la chiclayana* (duck and rice Chiclayo-style) is achingly tender and *ceviche a la brasa* gets a quick sear so it's lightly smoky, yet tender. It has to be eaten to be believed.

Pescados Capitales
Seafood $$$

(Map p56; ☑01-421-8808; www.pescadoscapital es.com; Av La Mar 1337; mains S35-65; ☺12:30-5pm) On a street once lined by clattering auto shops, this industrial-contemporary destination serves some of the finest ceviche around. Try the 'Ceviche Capital,' a mix of flounder, salmon and tuna marinated with red, white and green onions, bathed in a three-chili crème. A nine-page wine list offers a strong selection of Chilean and Argentinean vintages.

🗙 Barranco

Even as Barranco has gone upscale in recent years, with trendy restaurants serving everything fusion, the neighborhood still holds on to atmospheric, local spots where life is no more complicated than ceviche and beer.

A number of informal restaurants serving *anticuchos* and cheap *menús* line Av Grau around the intersection with Unión.

🍽 La Limeña

Many restaurants in Lima tone down the spices on some traditional dishes for foreign travelers. If you like your cooking spicy *(picante)*, tell them to turn up the heat by asking for your food *a la limeña* – Lima-style.

Chili peppers
AXEL FASSIO / GETTY IMAGES ©

Blu
Ice Cream $

(Map p62; ☑01-247-3791; Av 28 de Julio 202; cones S9; ☺noon-10pm Wed-Sat, to 8pm Sun) Creamy, dense chocolate, bright herbs, Madagascar vanilla or tart jungle fruit: this is Lima's best gelato, made fresh daily.

Cafe Bisetti
Cafe $

(Map p62; ☑01-713-9565; Av Pedro de Osma 116; coffee S8-16; ☺8am-9pm Mon-Fri, 10am-11pm Sat, 3-9pm Sun) Locals park their designer dogs out front of this roasting house with some of the finest lattes in town, well matched with fresh pastries or bitter chocolate pie. Check out the courses on roasting and tasting.

La 73
Bistro $$

(☑01-247-0780; Av El Sol Oeste 175; mains S29-45; ☺noon-midnight) ✐ Named for an iconic local bus, this contemporary bistro serves Peruvian-Mediterranean fare, with sustainable fish. Some dishes seem rushed, but standouts include homemade artichoke ravioli stuffed with goat cheese and duck risotto. The bar serves wine and pisco concoctions, or try the amazing *herba luisa* lemonade. To end on a sweet note, split the crisp, warm churros for dessert.

🍸 DRINKING & NIGHTLIFE

Lima is overflowing with establishments of every description, from rowdy beer halls to high-end lounges to atmospheric old bars. Downtown has the cheapest prices while San Isidro, Miraflores and Barranco feature trendier lounges serving premium cocktails.

The club scene gets started well after midnight and keeps going until the break of dawn. Barranco and Miraflores are the best neighborhoods to go clubbing, but spots come and go, so ask around before heading out. Music styles and cover charges vary depending on the night of the week. For other options, hit 'Pizza St' (Pasaje Juan Figari) in Miraflores, where a row of raucous clubs regularly spin their wares.

Cinemas, theaters, traveling art exhibits and concerts are covered in the daily *El Comercio*, with the most detailed listings found in Monday's 'Luces' section. The informational portal Living in Peru (www.livingin peru.com) maintains an up-to-date calendar

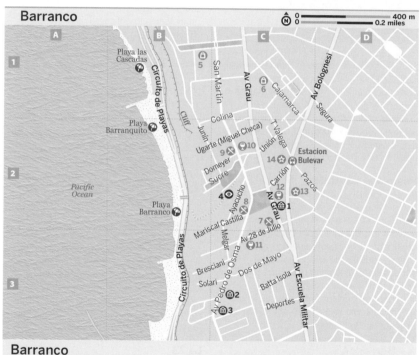

Barranco

of events. More youth oriented is *Oveja Negra* (ovejanegra.peru.com), a pocket-sized directory distributed free at restaurants and bars, which provides monthly listings of cultural and nightlife happenings.

Ayahuasca
Cocktail Bar

(Map p62; ☑01-247-6751; ayahuascarestobar. com; San Martín 130, Barranco; ☺8pm-close Mon-Sat) Lounge in a stunning restored *casona* full of Moorish architectural flourishes. Few actually admire the architecture, most guests are busy checking out everyone else. The hyper-real decor includes a dangling mobile made with costumes used in Ayacucho folk dances. There's a long list of contemporary pisco cocktails, like the tasty Ayahuasca sour made with jungle fruit *tambo* and coca leaves.

Museo del Pisco
Bar

(Map p52; ☑99-350-0013; www.museodelpisco. org; Jirón Junin 201; ☺10am-midnight) The 'educational' aspect of this wonderful bar might get you in the door, but it's the congenial atmosphere and outstanding original cocktails that will keep you here. We loved the *asu mare* – a pisco martini with ginger, cucumber, melon and basil. A sister bar to the popular original in Cuzco, this one occupies the Casa del Oidor, a 16th-century *casona*. At lunchtime there's a set menu. Watch the Facebook page for live-music news.

El Bolivarcito
Bar

(Map p52; ☑01-427-2114; Jirón de la Unión 958) Facing the Plaza San Martín from the Gran Hotel Bolívar, this frayed yet bustling spot is known as 'La Catedral del Pisco' for purveying some of the first pisco sours in Peru. Order the double-sized *pisco catedral* if your liver can take it.

Bar Piselli
Bar

(Map p62; ☑01-252-6750; Av 28 de Julio 297, Barranco; ☺10am-11pm Mon-Thu, to 3am Fri & Sat) This neighborhood bar reminiscent of old Buenos Aires beats all for ambience. There's live music on Thursdays provoking boisterous sing-alongs of Peruvian classics.

Café Bar Habana
Cafe

(Map p56; ☑01-446-3511; www.cafebarhabana. com; Manuel Bonilla 107; ☺6pm-late Mon-Sat) Boisterous Cuban proprietor Alexi García and his Peruvian wife, Patsy Higuchi, operate this homey establishment with delicious mojitos. The couple, both of whom are artists, sometimes display their works in the adjacent gallery.

Juanito's
Bar

(Map p62; Av Grau 274; ☺11:30am-2am Mon-Sat, noon-midnight Sun) This worn-in woody bar – it was a leftist hangout in the 1960s – is one of the mellowest haunts in Barranco. Decorated with a lifetime's worth of theater posters, this is where the writerly set arrives to swig *chilcano de pisco* (pisco cocktail with ginger ale) and deconstruct the state of humanity. There's no sign; look for the crowded room lined with wine bottles.

🟢 ENTERTAINMENT

Peruvian folk music and dance is performed on weekends at *peñas*. There are two main types of Peruvian music performed at these venues: *folklórica* and *criollo*. The first is more typical of the Andean highlands; the second, a coastal music driven by African-influenced beats.

Las Brisas del Titicaca
Traditional Music

(☑01-715-6960; www.brisasdeltiticaca.com; Wakuski 168, Lima Centro; from S30) A lauded *folklórica* show near Plaza Bolognesi downtown, in an enormous venue.

La Candelaria
Traditional Music

(Map p62; ☑01-247-1314; www.lacandelariaperu. com; Av Bolognesi 292, Barranco; from S35) In Barranco, a show that incorporates both *folklórica* and *criollo* music and dancing.

La Noche
Live Music

(Map p62; ☑01-247-1012; www.lanoche.com.pe; Av Bolognesi 307, Barranco) This well-known tri-level bar is *the* spot to see rock, punk and Latin music acts in Lima, though drinks could be better.

 What's On in Lima

The following festivals are unique to Lima but the city also celebrates nation-wide holidays.

Festival of Lima Celebrates the anniversary of Lima's founding on January 18.

Feria de Santa Rosa de Lima Held on August 30, this procession and feast honors Santa Rosa, the venerated patron saint of Lima and the Americas.

El Señor de los Milagros (Lord of Miracles) The city drapes itself in purple during this massive religious procession on October 18.

Traditional dancing, Lima
JOHN COLETTI / GETTY IMAGES ©

Teatro Segura Theatre
(Map p52; ☏01-426-7189; Huancavelica 265, Lima Centro) Built in 1909, the gorgeous Teatro Segura puts on opera, plays and ballet.

INFORMATION

DANGERS & ANNOYANCES

Like any large Latin American city, Lima is a land of haves and have-nots, which has made stories about crime here the stuff of legend. Yet the city has greatly improved since the lawless 1980s and most visitors have a safe visit. Nonetheless, stay aware.

The most common offense is theft, such as muggings. Do not resist robbery. You are unlikely to be physically hurt, but it is best to keep a streetwise attitude.

Increased police and private security in Miraflores and in the clifftop parks make them some of the city's safest areas. Barranco is mostly safe and pedestrian friendly but has seen a few evening robberies at a few restaurants and bars. Security may increase by the time you read this, but it doesn't hurt to go out with the minimum and leave the rest in a hotel safe. The most dangerous neighborhoods are San Juan de Lurigancho, Los Olivos, Comas, Vitarte and El Agustino.

Be skeptical of unaffiliated touts and taxi drivers who try to sell you tours or tell you that the hotel you've booked is closed or dodgy. Many of these are scam artists trying to steer you to places that pay them a commission.

EMERGENCY & IMPORTANT NUMBERS

Policía de Turismo (Tourist Police, Poltur; ☏01-225-8698; Av Javier Prado Este 2465, 5th fl, San Borja; ◷24hr) Main division of the Policía Nacional (National Police) at Museo de la Nación. English-speaking officers who can provide theft reports for insurance claims or traveler's-check refunds. In heavily touristed areas, it is easy to identify members of Poltur by their white shirts.

Policía Nacional Head Office (☏01-460-0921; Moore 268, Magdalena del Mar; ◷24hr)

MEDICAL SERVICES

There are a number of clinics with emergency service and some English-speaking staff. Consultations start in the vicinity of S80 and climb from there, depending on the clinic and the doctor. Treatments and medications attract an additional fee, and so do appointments with specialists.

Pharmacies abound in Lima. **Botica Fasa** (☏01-619-0000; www.boticafasa.com.pe; cnr Av José Larco 129-35, Miraflores; ◷24hr) and **Inka-Farma** (☏01-315-9000, deliveries 01-314-2020; www.inkafarma.com.pe; Alfredo Benavides 425, Miraflores; ◷24hr) is a well-stocked chain that is open 24 hours. It often delivers free of charge.

Clínica Anglo-Americana (☏01-436-9933; www.clinangloamericana.com.pe; Av La Fontana 362) A renowned (but expensive) hospital. There's a walk-in center in La Molina, near the US

Ayahuasca cocktail bar (p63), Barranco

embassy and a branch in **San Isidro** (☎616-8900; Salazar 350, San Isidro).

Clínica Good Hope (☎01-610-7300; www.good hope.org.pe, Malecón Balta 956) Quality care at good prices; there is also a dental unit.

MONEY

Banks are plentiful and most have 24-hour ATMs, which tend to offer the best exchange rates. For extra security use ATMs inside banks (as opposed to ones on the street or in supermarkets), cover the key pad as you enter passwords and graze the whole keypad to prevent infrared tracing of passwords. Avoid making withdrawals late at night.

TOURIST INFORMATION

The government's reputable tourist bureau, **iPerú** (☎01-574-8000; Aeropuerto Internacional Jorge Chávez), dispenses maps, offers good advice and can help handle complaints. The office in **Miraflores** (☎01-445-9400; LarcoMar; ☻11am-2pm & 3-8pm) is tiny but is highly useful on weekends. There's another branch in **San Isidro** (☎01-421-1627; Jorge Basadre 610; ☻9am-6pm Mon-Fri).

GETTING THERE & AWAY

AIR

Lima's **Aeropuerto Internacional Jorge Chávez** (☎01-517-3500, schedules 01-511-6055; www.lap. com.pe) is stocked with the usual facilities, plus a pisco boutique and car hire.

BUS

There is no central bus terminal; each company operates its ticketing and departure points independently. Some companies have several terminals, so always clarify from which point a bus leaves when buying tickets. The busiest times of year are Semana Santa (the week before Easter Sunday) and the weeks surrounding Fiestas Patrias (July 28–29), when thousands of *limeños* (inhabitants of Lima) make a dash out of the city and fares double. At these times, book well ahead.

The largest companies that are most popular for security and luxury are **Cruz del Sur** (www. cruzdelsur.com.pe; Av Javier Prado Este 1109) and **Ormeño** (☎01-472-1710; www.grupo-ormeno. com.pe; Av Javier Prado Este 1059). Both have a terminal in La Victoria.

GETTING AROUND

TO/FROM THE AIRPORT

The airport is in the port city of Callao, about 12km west of downtown or 20km northwest of Miraflores. As you come out of customs, inside the airport to the right is the official taxi service: **Taxi Green** (☏01-484-4001; www.taxigreen. com.pe). Allow 45/60 minutes to downtown/ Miraflores.

BUS

Metropolitano (www.metropolitano.com.pe), the new trans-Lima electric express-bus system, is the fastest and most efficient way to get into the city center. Routes are few, though coverage is expanding to the northern part of the city. Ruta Troncal (S2.50) goes through Barranco, Miraflores and San Isidro to Plaza Grau in the center of Lima. Users must purchase a *tarjeta intelligente* (cards S4.50) that can be credited for use.

Combis are traffic-clogging minivans that hurtle down the avenues with a *cobrador* (ticket taker) hanging out the door and shouting out the stops. Go by the destination placards taped to the windshield. Your best bet is to know the nearest major intersection or landmark close to your stop (eg Parque Kennedy) and tell that to the *cobrador* – he'll let you know whether you've got the right bus. *Combis* are generally slow and crowded, but startlingly cheap: fares run from S1 to S3, depending on the length of your journey.

The most useful **bus routes** link Central Lima with Miraflores along Av Arequipa or Paseo de la República. Minibuses along Garcilaso de la Vega (also called Av Wilson) and Av Arequipa are labeled 'Todo Arequipa' or 'Larco/Schell/ Miraflores' when heading to Miraflores and, likewise, 'Todo Arequipa' and 'Wilson/Tacna' when leaving Miraflores for Central Lima. Catch these buses along Av José Larco or Av Arequipa in Miraflores. To get to Barranco, look for buses along Av Arequipa labeled 'Chorrillos/ Huaylas/Metro' (some will also have signs that say 'Barranco'). You can also find these on the Diagonal, just west of the Parque Kennedy, in Miraflores.

TAXI

Lima's taxis lack meters, so negotiate fares before getting in. Fares vary depending on the length of the journey, traffic conditions, time of day (evening is more expensive) and your Spanish skills. Registered taxis or taxis hailed outside a tourist attraction charge higher rates. As a (very) rough guide, a trip within Miraflores costs around S5 to S10. From Miraflores to Central Lima is S10 to S15, to Barranco from S8 to S12, and San Isidro from S6 to S12. You can haggle fares – though it's harder during rush hour. If there are two or more passengers be clear on whether the fare is per person or for the car.

The majority of taxis in Lima are unregistered (unofficial); indeed, surveys have indicated that no less than one vehicle in seven here is a taxi. During the day, it's usually not a problem to use either. At night it is important to use registered taxis for your safety, which are traceable by the license number painted on the side. They should also have checkers, a rectangular authorization sticker with the word SETAME on the upper left corner of the windshield and may have yellow paint.

Registered taxis can be called by phone or found at taxi stands, such as the one outside the Sheraton in Central Lima or outside the LarcoMar shopping mall in Miraflores. Registered taxis cost about 30% more than regular street taxis but the security is worth it.

Easy Taxi (LarcoMar) Download the app for fast service from your smartphone or cost estimates.

Taxi Real (☏01-215 1414; www.taxireal.com)

Where to Stay

If arriving at night, it's worth contacting hotels in advance to arrange for airport pickup; even budget hostels can arrange this – sometimes for a few dollars less than the official airport service.

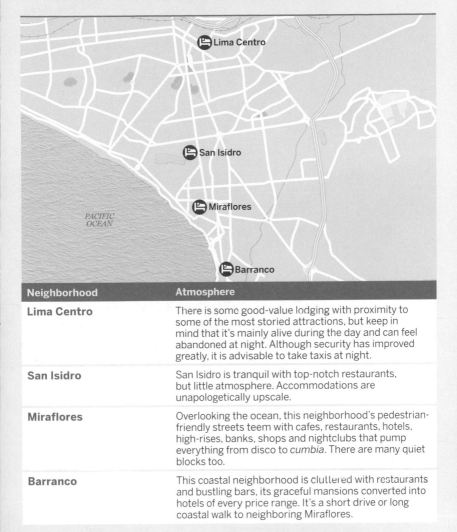

Neighborhood	Atmosphere
Lima Centro	There is some good-value lodging with proximity to some of the most storied attractions, but keep in mind that it's mainly alive during the day and can feel abandoned at night. Although security has improved greatly, it is advisable to take taxis at night.
San Isidro	San Isidro is tranquil with top-notch restaurants, but little atmosphere. Accommodations are unapologetically upscale.
Miraflores	Overlooking the ocean, this neighborhood's pedestrian-friendly streets teem with cafes, restaurants, hotels, high-rises, banks, shops and nightclubs that pump everything from disco to *cumbia*. There are many quiet blocks too.
Barranco	This coastal neighborhood is cluttered with restaurants and bustling bars, its graceful mansions converted into hotels of every price range. It's a short drive or long coastal walk to neighboring Miraflores.

ISLAS BALLESTAS

Islas Ballestas at a Glance...

Grandiosely nicknamed the 'poor man's Galápagos,' the Islas Ballestas nonetheless make for a memorable excursion. The only way to see them is on a boat tour – and while the tours do not disembark onto the islands (which are protected), they do get you startlingly close to the wildlife.

Islas Ballestas in One Day

Spend the day wildlife-spotting on a **boat tour** (p74) of Islas Ballestas. In the evening don't miss the local seafood at a restaurant such at **As de Oro's** (p77) in Pisco; or in El Chaco (Paracas) head to **Pisco and Olé** (p75) for the good food and cocktails at sunset.

Islas Ballestas in Two Days

The second day can be devoted to exploring the **Reserva Nacional de Paracas** (p74), the vast national park that spans the Península de Paracas. If you want to take it easy, you can simply explore the lively town of El Chaco (Paracas), or do sweet nothing on its long beaches.

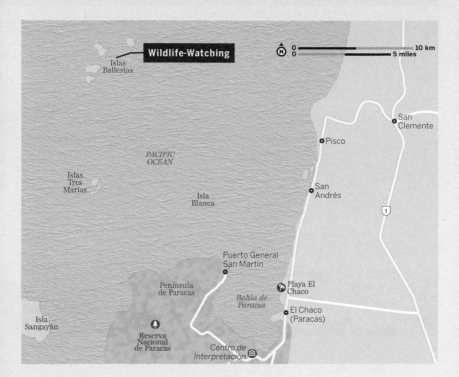

Wildlife-Watching

Islas Ballestas

PACIFIC OCEAN

Islas Tres Marías

Isla Blanca

Isla Sangayán

Península de Paracas

Bahía de Paracas

Reserva Nacional de Paracas

Centro de Interpretación

Puerto General San Martín

San Clemente

Pisco

San Andrés

Playa El Chaco

El Chaco (Paracas)

10 km
5 miles

Arriving in Islas Ballestas

Boat Tours (p72) The only way to get near the Islas Ballestas. Depart from El Chaco (Paracas).

Air The international airport in Pisco should have officially opened by the time you read this.

Bus A few buses run daily between Lima and Pisco or Paracas (the El Chaco beach district), some continuing to Nazca, Ica and Arequipa. Bus companies include Cruz del Sur (www.cruzdelsur.com.pe) and Oltursa (www.oltursa.com.pe).

Where to Stay

The evolving but rundown town of Pisco may tout itself as an alternative to the beach resort of El Chaco (Paracas), but the latter makes for a much better base for trips to the Reserva Nacional de Paracas and Islas Ballestas, with a better location and choice of facilities.

Candelabra geoglyph

Wildlife-Watching

Protruding out of the Pacific Ocean, the Islas Ballestas are home to an astonishing number of sea lions, birds and fish. A boat tour will bring you as close to the action as possible – dodging guano bombs is part of the fun.

Great For...

☑ **Don't Miss**

Pointing your eyes (and lens) down at crabs and starfish.

Mystery Glyph

On the outward boat journey to the Islas Ballestas, which takes about 30 minutes, you will stop just offshore to admire the famous three-pronged Candelabra geoglyph, a giant figure etched into the sandy hills in the distance, more than 150m high and 50m wide. No one knows exactly who made the glyph, or when, or what it signifies, but theories abound.

Birds & Dolphins

In general, a further hour is spent cruising around the islands' arches and caves and watching herds of noisy sea lions sprawl on the rocks. The most common guano-

Peruvian booby

PATRICK GIJSBERS / GETTY IMAGES ©

ⓘ Need to Know

Boat tours to Islas Ballestas depart from El Chaco on the Península de Paracas.

✕ Take a Break

Back on shore, grab a bite to eat at one of the many waterfront restaurants near the dock in El Chaco.

★ Top Tip

Although you can get close to the wildlife, some species, especially the penguins, are more visible with binoculars.

producing birds in this area are the guanay cormorant, the Peruvian booby and the Peruvian pelican, seen in boisterous colonies several thousand strong. You'll also see cormorants, Humboldt penguins and, if you're lucky, dolphins.

Preparation

None of the small boats have a cabin, so dress to protect against the wind, spray and sun. The sea can get rough, so sufferers of motion sickness should take medication before boarding. Wear a hat (cheap ones are sold at the harbor), as it's not unusual to receive a direct hit of guano (droppings) from the seabirds.

What's Nearby

At the southern tip of the Paracas peninsula, **Punta Arquillo** has a cliff-top lookout with grand views of the ocean and a sealion colony. Other seashore life around the reserve includes flotillas of jellyfish, some of which reach 70cm in diameter, with trailing stinging tentacles of 1m. They are often washed up on the shore, where they quickly dry to form mandala-like patterns on the sand. Beachcombers can also find sea hares, ghost crabs and seashells along the shoreline, and the Andean condor occasionally descends to the coast in search of rich pickings.

Tours of Islas Ballestas disembark back at the beach of El Chaco. From here take a three-hour tour (or taxi acting as a tour guide) of the Reserva Nacional de Paracas. At the southern end is Punta Arquillo.

El Chaco (Paracas)

The Paracas peninsula's main village, El Chaco – often referred to erroneously as 'Paracas' – is the primary embarkation point for trips to Islas Ballestas and the Reserva Nacional de Paracas. It's a fun place with a lively traveler scene. Its natural attractions and long beaches stand out from many south-coast destinations, and many travelers end up spending at least two or even three nights here, allowing for a day tour to the islands, beach time and an extended foray across the peninsula.

◎ SIGHTS

Reserva Nacional de Paracas   Park

(park entrance Islas Ballestas only S10, island & peninsula S15) This vast desert reserve occupies most of the Península de Paracas.

Centro de Interpretación   Museum

(⊙7am-6pm) FREE Located 1.5km south of the entry point to Reserva Nacional de Paracas, this modest center's displays kick off with a 12-minute rather twee video aimed, it would seem, at wide-eyed teenagers.

The subsequent exhibits on fauna, archaeology and geology are weightier and more inspiring. The bay in front of the complex is the best spot to view Chilean flamingos, and there's a walkway down to a *mirador* (lookout), from where these birds can best be spotted from June through August.

◷ ACTIVITIES

PeruKite   Kitesurfing

(☑99-456-7802; www.perukite.com; Paracas s/n, Paracas Restaurant) The area around Paracas offers pretty great kiteboarding with limited chop, easy shallow access and good winds. This operation does courses running one hour (US$60), three hours (US$175) and six hours (two days, US$320).

◷ TOURS

Prices and service for tours of Islas Ballestas and Reserva Nacional de Paracas are usually very similar. The better tours are es-

Peruvian pelican

corted by a qualified naturalist who speaks Spanish and English. Most island boat tours leave daily at 8am, 10am and noon, and cost around S35 per person. The number of tours and departure times varies, so it is recommended to reserve a day in advance.

Tours of the reserve can be combined with an Islas Ballestas tour to make a full-day excursion (S60). **Paracas Backpackers House** (☑056-53-5623; www.paracasbackpackershouse.com.pe; Av Los Libertadores; dm S17.50, s without bathroom S40, d with/without bathroom S80/45; 🛜) rents bikes for S30 per day.

Paracas Explorer   Tour

(☑056-53-1487; www.paracasexplorer.com; Paracas 9) This backpacker travel agency offers the usual island and reserve tours, as well as multiday trips that take you to Ica and Nazca (US$80 to US$90 per person).

Paracas Overland   Tour

(☑056-53-3855; www.paracasoverland.com.pe; San Francisco 111) Popular with backpackers, this agency offers tours of the Islas Ballestas with its own fleet of boats, as well as to the Reserva Nacional de Paracas and Tambo Colorado. It can also arrange sandboarding trips to nearby dunes.

EATING

Most of the action centers on the Malecón, where you'll find a pretty wide selection of restaurants and bars.

Punta Paracas   International $

(Blvd Turístico; mains S15-35; ⊙7am-10pm) Coffee and chocolate brownies hit the spot at this open-all-day cafe that remains lively after most other places have closed.

El Chorito   Peruvian $$

(Paracas; mains S20-30; ⊙noon-9pm) The Italians come to the rescue in the clean, polished Chorito – part of the Hostal Santa Maria – where a welcome supply of Illy coffee saves you from the otherwise-ubiquitous powdered Nescafé. The cooked-to-order fish dishes aren't bad either – all locally caught, of course.

Bird-Poo War

In the history of war, the 1864–66 skirmish between Spain and its former colonies of Peru and Chile might seem like a strange one: its primary motivation was guano, or, to put it less politely, bird poo. Although an unpleasant substance if dropped on your head, guano has long been a vital contributor to the Peruvian economy, and a resource worth protecting. In the early 19th century, German botanist Alexander von Humboldt sent samples of it to Europe, where innovative British farmers found it to be 30 times more efficient than cow dung as a fertilizer. By the 1850s a rapidly industrializing Britain was importing 200,000 tons of the crap annually. Suddenly the white droppings that covered Peru's bird-filled Pacific islands were worth the lion's share of the GDP. Spain understood as much in 1864 when, in an act of postcolonial petulance, it occupied the guano-rich Chincha Islands in an attempt to extract reparations from Peru over a small domestic incident in Lambayeque. Peru didn't hesitate to retaliate. A protracted naval war ensued that dragged in Chile, before the islands and their precious bird poo were wrenched back from Spain in 1866.

In the conflict-free present, the industry remains lucrative. Layers of sun-baked, nitrogen-rich guano still cover the Chincha Islands, as well as the nearby Islas Ballestas.

Pisco and Olé   Peruvian $$

(Malecón s/n; mains S25-35; 🛜) Tonier than the other spots on the Malecón, this friendly eatery offers a standard array of Peruvian seafood mash-ups. The only difference is the affable service and the slightly European styling. It's also a great sunset cocktail spot.

🍷 DRINKING & NIGHTLIFE

Misk'i Bar

(Calle 1; ◷6pm-close) Strong drinks and well-chilled vibes star at this back-to-basics tourist resto-bar that serves up plenty of international dishes and has a perpetual reggae soundtrack that will keep you skankin' it easy.

ℹ️ GETTING THERE & AWAY

A new international airport should have officially opened by the time you read this. Check to see if any of the Peruvian airlines are servicing the route.

A few buses run daily between Lima and the El Chaco beach district of Paracas (S40 to S55, 3½ hours) before continuing to other destinations south. These include Cruz del Sur (www. cruzdelsur.com.pe) and Oltursa (www.oltursa. com.pe); the latter also runs direct buses to Nazca, Ica, Arequipa and Lima from Paracas. Most agencies in El Chaco sell bus tickets, including Paracas Explorer (p75).

If arriving directly in El Chaco (Paracas), most hotels and hostels will pick you up from the bus terminal upon request.

Transportation from El Chaco to Pisco is possible via *combi* (S1.50, 30 minutes) or *colectivo* (shared transportation; S3 to S5, 20 minutes).

Pisco

Crushed by a 2007 earthquake that destroyed its infrastructure but not its spirit, Pisco is a town on the rebound, reinventing itself almost daily. Irrespective of the substantial damage, the town remains open for business, promoting itself, along with the nearby beach resort of El Chaco (Paracas), as a base for forays to the Reserva Nacional de Paracas and Islas Ballestas, although El Chaco trumps it in terms of location and choice of facilities.

The area is of historical and archaeological interest, having hosted one of the most highly developed pre-Inca civilizations – the Paracas culture from 700 BC until AD 400. Later it acted as a base for Peru's revolutionary fever in the early 19th century.

👁 SIGHTS

Tambo Colorado Archaeological Site

(admission S10; ◷dawn-dusk) This early Inca lowland outpost, about 45km northeast of Pisco, was named for the red paint that once completely covered its adobe walls. It's one of the best-preserved sites on the south coast and is thought to have served as an administrative base and control point for passing traffic, mostly conquered peoples.

From Pisco, it takes about an hour to get there by car. Hire a taxi for half a day (S50) or take a tour from Pisco (S60, two-person minimum). A *combi* through the village of Humay passes Tambo Colorado 20 minutes beyond the village; it leaves from the Pisco market early in the morning (S8, three hours). Once there, ask the locals about when to expect a return bus, but you could get really stuck out there, as transportation back to Pisco is infrequent and often full.

🎫 TOURS

It is still perfectly viable to use Pisco as a base for tours of the Península de Paracas and the Islas Ballestas. Various agencies dot the central area.

Aprotur Pisco Tour

(056-50-7156; aproturpisco@hotmail.com; San Francisco 112) This laid-back but business-like travel company organizes trips to all the local sights, including Islas Ballestras (S70) and even the Nazca Lines (US$140). Guides speak six languages, including Hebrew.

🍴 EATING

Only a few cafes in Pisco open early enough for breakfast before an Islas Ballestas tour, so many hotels include breakfast in their rates.

**La Concha de
Tus Mares** Peruvian $$

(Calle Muelle 992; mains S15-25) Old pictures of what Pisco used to look like pre-2007 adorn the walls of this nostalgic place next to the Colegio Alexander Von Humboldt about 1km south of the center. The fish comes in big portions and is lauded by the locals.

As de Oro's   Peruvian $$$

(www.asdeoros.com.pe; San Martín 472; mains S30-50; ⊙noon-midnight Tue-Sun) Talk about phoenix from the flames; the plush As de Oro serves up spicy mashed potato with octopus, plaice with butter and capers, and grilled prawns with fried yucca and tartare sauce overlooking a small swimming pool, as the rest of the town struggles back to its feet.

🍷 DRINKING & NIGHTLIFE

Pisco shares its name with the national beverage, a brandy that is made throughout the region.

Taberna de Don Jaime   Bar

(☎056-53-5023; San Martín 203; ⊙4pm-2am) This clamorous tavern is a favorite with locals and tourists alike. It is also a showcase for artisanal wines and piscos. On weekends, the crowds show up to dance to live Latin and rock tunes into the small hours.

INFORMATION

There's no tourist office in Pisco, but travel agencies on the main plaza and the local **police** (☎056-53-2884; San Francisco 132; ⊙24hr) help when they can. Everything else you'll need is found around the Plaza de Armas, including internet cafes.

GETTING THERE & AWAY

Pisco is 6km west of Panamericana Sur, and only buses with Pisco as the final destination actually go there. **Ormeño** (☎056-53-2764; San Francisco), **Flores** (☎056-79-6643; San Martín) and **Soyuz** (www.soyuz.com.pe; Av Ernesto R Diez Canseco 4) offer multiple daily departures north to Lima and south to Ica and Arequipa. There's no direct service from Pisco to Nazca; you'll need to leave from El Chaco (Paracas) or change buses in Ica.

Transportation from Pisco to El Chaco (Paracas) is possible via *combi* (S1.50, 30 minutes), or *colectivo* (20 minutes), which leave frequently from near Pisco's central market (S3) or the center (S4 to S5).

Sea lion colony

WILDNEROPIX / SHUTTERSTOCK ©

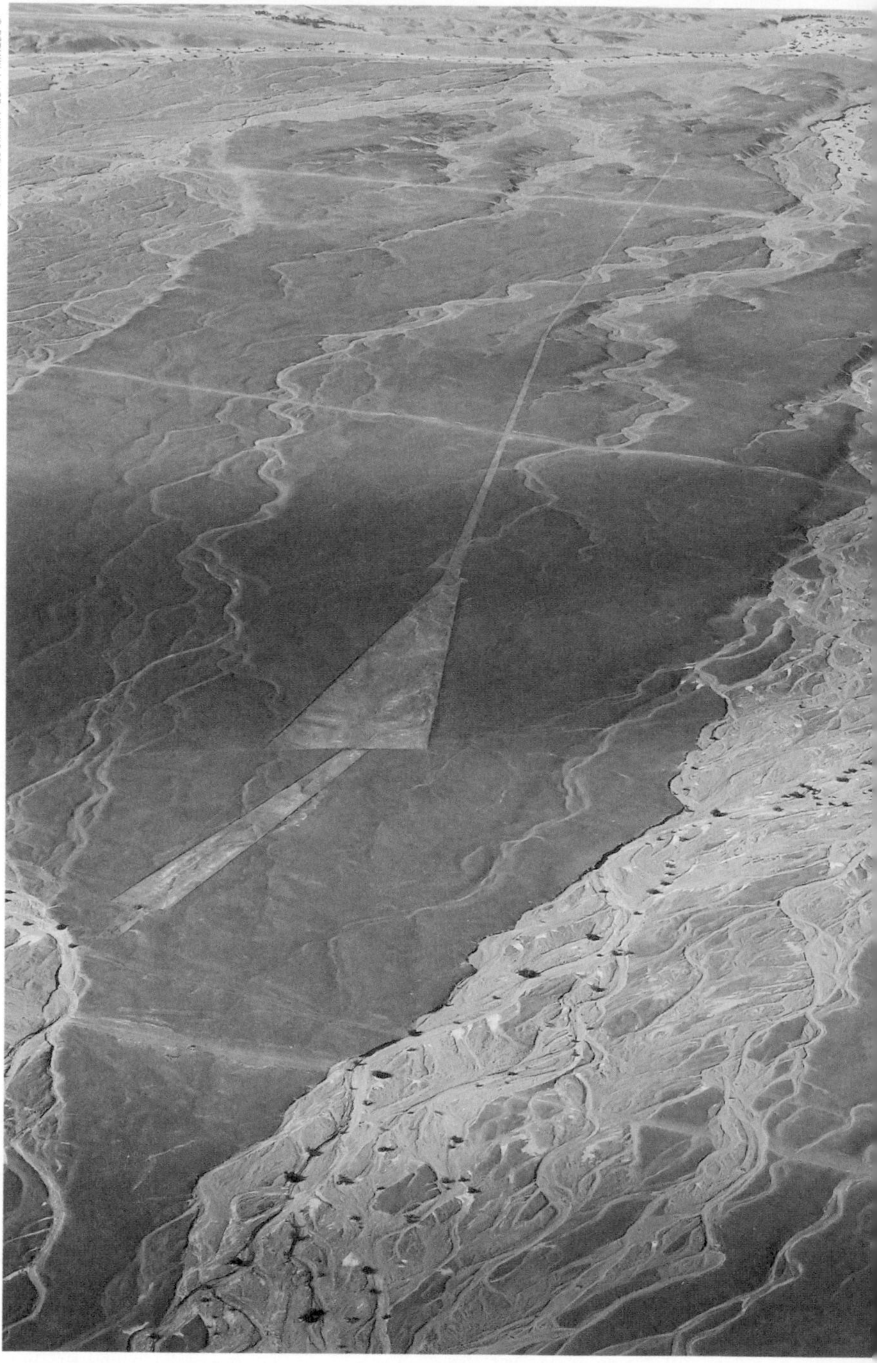

NAZCA

Nazca at a Glance...

It's hard to say the word 'Nazca' without following it immediately with the word 'Lines,' a reference not just to the ancient geometric lines that crisscross the Nazca desert, but to the enigmatic animal geoglyphs that accompany them. Like all great unexplained mysteries, these immense etchings on the pampa, thought to have been made by a pre-Inca civilization between AD 450 and 600, attract a variable fan base of archaeologists, scientists, history buffs, New Age mystics, curious tourists, and pilgrims on their way to (or back from) Machu Picchu.

Documented for the first time by North American scientist Paul Kosok in 1939 and declared a Unesco World Heritage site in 1994, the lines today are the south coast's biggest tourist attraction.

Nazca in One Day

Start the day with just a snack for breakfast – your stomach will thank you once you hit the dips and turns on the flights over the **Nazca Lines** (p82). Have brunch proper from one of the many international options in Nazca, then spend the afternoon with the fascinating archaelogical finds at the **Museo Didáctico Antonini** (p84). In the evening see the Nazca Lines explained in a projection on the dome of the **Nazca Planetarium** (p85).

Nazca in Two Days

On the second day, see more geoglyphs without the rush at the **Palpa Lines** (p86), the more abundant, but less famous cousin of the Nazca Lines. See them from a lookout, no overflight needed, then head further to the **Chauchilla Cemetery** (p85) to finish the afternoon getting close to ancient skeletons and mummies of the local desert from AD 1000.

Nazca Map (p86)

Arriving in Nazca

Maria Reiche Neuman Airport A taxi from the airport to central Nazca, 4km away, costs about S4.

Bus Companies cluster at the west end of Calle Lima, near the *óvalo* (main roundabout) and about a block toward town on the same street.

Where to Stay

There are lots of hotels (and restaurants) in and around Callao and Bolognesi to the streets west of the Plaza de Armas.

Prices drop by up to 50% outside of peak season, which runs from May until August.

Monkey biomorph

Nazca Lines

The Nazca Lines – a set of carved glyphs so massive they can only be seen from the air – have long captured travelers' imaginations with their precision and scale.

Great For...

☑ Don't Miss

The intriguing owl-headed geoglyph, often referred to as an astronaut because of its goldfish-bowl-shaped head.

Design

Spread over 500 sq km (310 sq miles) of arid, rock-strewn plain in the Pampa Colorada (Red Plain), the Nazca Lines are one of the world's great archaeological mysteries. Comprising over 800 straight lines, 300 geometric figures (geoglyphs) and 70 animal and plant drawings (biomorphs), the lines are almost imperceptible on the ground. From above, they form a striking network of stylized figures and channels, many of which radiate from a central axis.

The lines were made by the simple process of removing the dark sun-baked stones from the surface of the desert and piling them up on either side of the lines, thus exposing the lighter, powdery gypsum-laden soil below.

The figures are mostly etched out in single continuous lines, while the encom-

Owl-headed 'astronaut' geoglyph

Scenic-flight airplane, Maria Reiche Neuman Airport

❶ Need to Know

Choose safety first – question any operator who charges less than US$80 for the standard 30-minute overflight.

✕ Take a Break

Eat after, not before, an overflight, as some twisting and turning is tummy challenging.

★ Top Tip

Morning overflights are best because the air is less turbulent.

passing geoglyphs form perfect triangles, rectangles or straight lines running for several kilometers across the desert.

The most elaborate designs represent animals, including a hummingbird, a spider, a 180m-long lizard, a monkey with an extravagantly curled tail, and a condor with a 130m (426ft) wingspan.

Mystery

Endless questions remain. Who constructed the lines and why? And how did they know what they were doing when the lines can only be properly appreciated from the air? Maria Reiche (1903–98), a German mathematician and long-time researcher of the lines, theorized that they were made by the Paracas and Nazca cultures between 900 BC and AD 600, with some additions by the Wari settlers from the highlands

in the 7th century. She also claimed that the lines were an astronomical calendar developed for agricultural purposes, and that they were mapped out through the use of sophisticated mathematics (and a long rope).

A slightly more surreal suggestion from explorer Jim Woodman was that the Nazca people knew how to construct hot-air balloons and that they did, in fact, observe the lines from the air.

Water Worship

A more down-to-earth theory, given the value of water in the sun-baked desert, was suggested by anthropologist Johann Reinhard, who believed that the lines were involved in mountain worship and a fertility/water cult. Recent work by the Swiss-Liechtenstein Foundation (SLSA; www.slsa.ch) agrees that they were dedicated to the worship of water, and it is thus ironic that their theory about the demise of the Nazca culture suggests that it was due not to drought, but to destructive rainfall caused by a phenomenon such as El Niño.

◎ SIGHTS

As the hub of one of Peru's biggest tourist attractions, the small and otherwise-insignificant desert town of Nazca can be a bit of a circus.

Mirador   Viewpoint
(admission S2) You'll get only a sketchy idea of the Lines at this lookout on the Panamericana Sur 20km north of Nazca, which has an oblique view of three figures: the lizard, tree and hands (or frog, depending on your point of view). It's also a lesson in the damage to which the Lines are vulnerable. The Panamericana Sur runs smack through the tail of the lizard, which from nearby seems all but obliterated.

Signs warning of landmines are a reminder that walking on the Lines is strictly forbidden. It irreparably damages them, and besides, you can't see anything at ground level. To get to the observation tower from Nazca, catch any bus or *colectivo* northbound along Panamericana Sur (S1.50, 30 minutes). Some tours (from S50 per person) also combine a trip to the *mirador* with visits to another natural viewpoint and the Museo Maria Reiche. About 1km south of the man-made *mirador* (lookout) there is a **Mirador Natural** (free) on a small knoll-like hill with a close up view of one of the geometric lines made by removing reddish pebbles from the grey earth.

Museo Maria Reiche   Museum
(admission S25; ◎9am-6pm) When Maria Reiche, the German mathematician and long-term researcher of the Nazca Lines, died in 1998, her house, which stands 5km north of the *mirador* along Panamericana Sur, was made into a small museum. Though disappointingly scant on information, you can see where she lived, amid the clutter of her tools and obsessive sketches.

Museo Didáctico Antonini   Museum
(☏056-52-3444; Av de la Cultura 600; admission S20, plus camera S5; ◎9am-7pm) On the east side of town, this excellent archaeological

Hummingbird biomorph

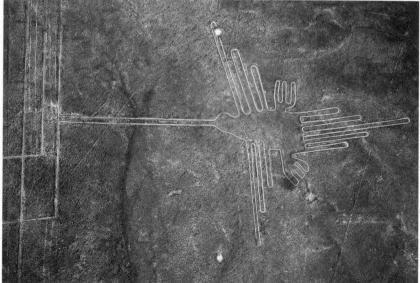

museum has an aqueduct running through the back garden, as well as interesting reproductions of burial tombs, a valuable collection of ceramic pan flutes and a scale model of the Lines.

You can get an overview of both the Nazca culture and a glimpse of most of Nazca's outlying sites here. Though the exhibit labels are in Spanish, the front desk lends foreign-language translation booklets for you to carry around. To get to the museum follow Bolognesi to the east out of town for 1km, or take a taxi (S2).

Nazca Planetarium
Planetarium

(☑056-52-2293; Nazca Lines Hotel, Bolognesi 147; admission S20; ☺in English 7pm, in Spanish 8:15pm) This small planetarium is in the Nazca Lines Hotel and offers scripted evening lectures on the Lines with graphical displays on a domed projection screen that last approximately 45 minutes. Call ahead or check the posted schedules for show times.

Chauchilla Cemetery
Archaeological Site

(admission S7.50; ☺8am-2pm) The most popular excursion from Nazca, this cemetery, 30km south of Nazca, will satisfy any urges you have to see ancient bones, skulls and mummies. Dating back to the Ica-Chincha culture around AD 1000, the mummies were, until recently, scattered haphazardly across the desert, left by ransacking tomb-robbers.

Now they are seen carefully rearranged inside a dozen or so tombs, though cloth fragments and pottery and bone shards still litter the ground outside the demarcated trail. Organized tours last three hours and cost US$10 to US$35 per person.

Cahuachi
Ruin

(☺9am-4pm) **FREE** A dirt road travels 25km west from Nazca to Cahuachi, the most important known Nazca center, which is

Greenpeace Did What to the Nazca Lines?

The earth does deserve a voice, but for many Peruvians, and world citizens, the Greenpeace action on December 8, 2014 that placed a message – 'Time For Change! The Future is Renewable. Greenpeace' – in large yellow letters next to the iconic hummingbird biomorphic geoglyph in the Nazca Lines was an act of vandalism, causing irreparable damage to a World Heritage site.

Since the action, which was designed to call the attention of world leaders attending a UN Climate Summit in Lima, Greenpeace has issued apologies, and three of the 20 people taking part have been publicly accused (with Greenpeace releasing the names of four more participants), with criminal proceedings ongoing.

Because of the delicate nature of these mysterious formations, nobody is permitted to walk on the Nazca Lines complex (these rules apply to everyone from backpackers to presidents). Only using special weight-dispersing padded shoes do archaeologists enter the site. And while Greenpeace points out that activists did not walk on the geoglyph itself, they did overturn rocks. Recent drone flights reveal disrupted areas where the activists entered the site, and the Peruvian government is now looking at ways to restore the area.

still undergoing excavation. It consists of several pyramids, a graveyard and an enigmatic site called Estaquería, which may have been used as a place of mummification. Tours from Nazca take three hours, cost US$15 to US$50 per person, and may include a side trip to Pueblo Viejo, a nearby pre-Nazca residential settlement.

Palpa Lines   Archaeological Site

Like Nazca, Palpa is surrounded by perplex-
ing geoglyphs, the so-called Palpa Lines,
which are serially overshadowed by the
more famous, but less abundant, Nazca
Lines to the south. The Palpa Lines display
a greater profusion of human forms, including the Familia Real de Paracas, a group of
eight figures on a hillside.

Due to their elevated position, the figures
are easier to view from terra firma at a
mirador 8km south of the town. A small
museum hut on-site offers further explanations in English and Spanish. The best way
to see more of these lines is on a combined
overflight from Nazca.

🖙 TOURS

Most people fly over the lines (US$80)
then leave, but there's more to see around
Nazca. If you take one of the many local
tours, it will typically include a torturously
long stop at a potter's and/or gold-miner's
workshop for a demonstration of their
techniques (tips for those who show you
their trade are expected too).

Hotels tirelessly promote their own
tours. Nazca Lines Hotel and Casa Andina
are good options.

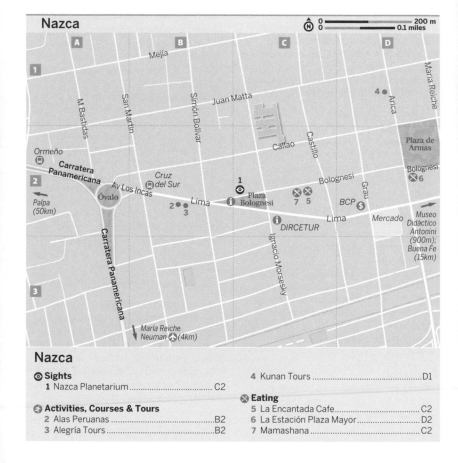

Nazca

Alegría Tours   Adventure Tour

(☏056-52-3775; www.alegriatoursperu.com; Hotel Alegría, Lima 168) Behemoth agency that offers all the usual local tours, plus off-the-beaten-track and sandboarding options. The tours are expensive for one person, so ask to join up with other travelers to receive a group discount. Alegría can arrange guides in Spanish, English, French and German in some cases.

Kunan Tours   Tour

(☏056-52-4069; www.kunantours.com; Arica 419) Based out of the Kunan Wasi Hotel, this comprehensive travel company offers all the Nazca tours, plus excursions to Islas Ballestas, Huacachina and Chincha.

Alas Peruanas   Scenic Flights

(☏056-52-2444; www.alasperuanas.com) Nazca Lines flightseeing.

🅧 EATING

West of the Plaza de Armas, Bolognesi is stuffed full of foreigner-friendly pizzerias, restaurants and bars.

Mamashana   International $$

(☏056-21-1286; www.mamashana.com; Bolognesi 270; mains S20-35; ⊙10am-11pm; �) Head upstairs to take advantage of bird's-eye views of the street below at this international-traveler-set favorite. The food is quite good, and prepared with a worldwide audience in mind. Choose from steaks and seafood, to lasagna and hamburgers. The cane-thatched room and exposed wood lend a South American air.

La Encantada Cafe   International $$

(www.hotellaencantada.com.pe; Bolognesi 282; mains S20-40) A top spot on the 'Boulevard' (Bolognesi), La Encantada sparkles in Nazca's dusty center with well-placed wine displays, great coffee, and courteous and friendly wait staff. The extensive menu mixes European flavors (pasta etc) with Peruvian favorites.

La Estación Plaza Mayor   Steak $$

(cnr Calle Bolognesi & Arica; meals S15-25) This longstanding spot has a coal grill with a rustic wood-and-bamboo mezzanine seating area overlooking Plaza de Armas; barbecued meats dominate.

ℹ INFORMATION

It pays to put safety before price when choosing your overflight company. Question anyone who offers less than US$80 for the standard 30-minute excursion and don't be afraid to probe companies on their safety records and flight policies.

If you do opt for a flight, bear in mind that, because the small aircraft bank left and right, it can be a stomach-churning experience, so motion-sickness sufferers should consider taking medication. Looking at the horizon may help mild nausea.

BCP (Lima 495) Has a Visa/MasterCard ATM and changes US dollars.

DIRCETUR (Parque Bolognesi, 3rd fl) Government-sponsored tourist information office; can recommend local tour operators. There is also a regularly staffed tourist information booth in Plaza Bolognesi.

ℹ GETTING THERE & AWAY

Nazca is a major destination for buses on the Panamericana Sur and is easy to get to from Lima, Ica or Arequipa. Bus companies cluster at the west end of Calle Lima, near the *óvalo* (main roundabout) and about a block toward town on the same street.

Most long-distance services leave in the late afternoon or evening. **Cruz del Sur** (☏0801-11111; www.cruzdelsur.com.pe; Av Los Incas) and **Ormeño** (☏056-52-2058; www.grupo-ormeno.com.pe; Av Los Incas) have a few luxury buses daily to Lima.

To go direct to Cuzco, several companies, including Cruz del Sur, take the paved road east via Abancay. Alternatively, some companies also offer direct buses to Cuzco via Arequipa.

A taxi from central Nazca to **Maria Reiche Neuman Airport**, 4km away, costs about S4. The airport normally charges a departure tax of S20.

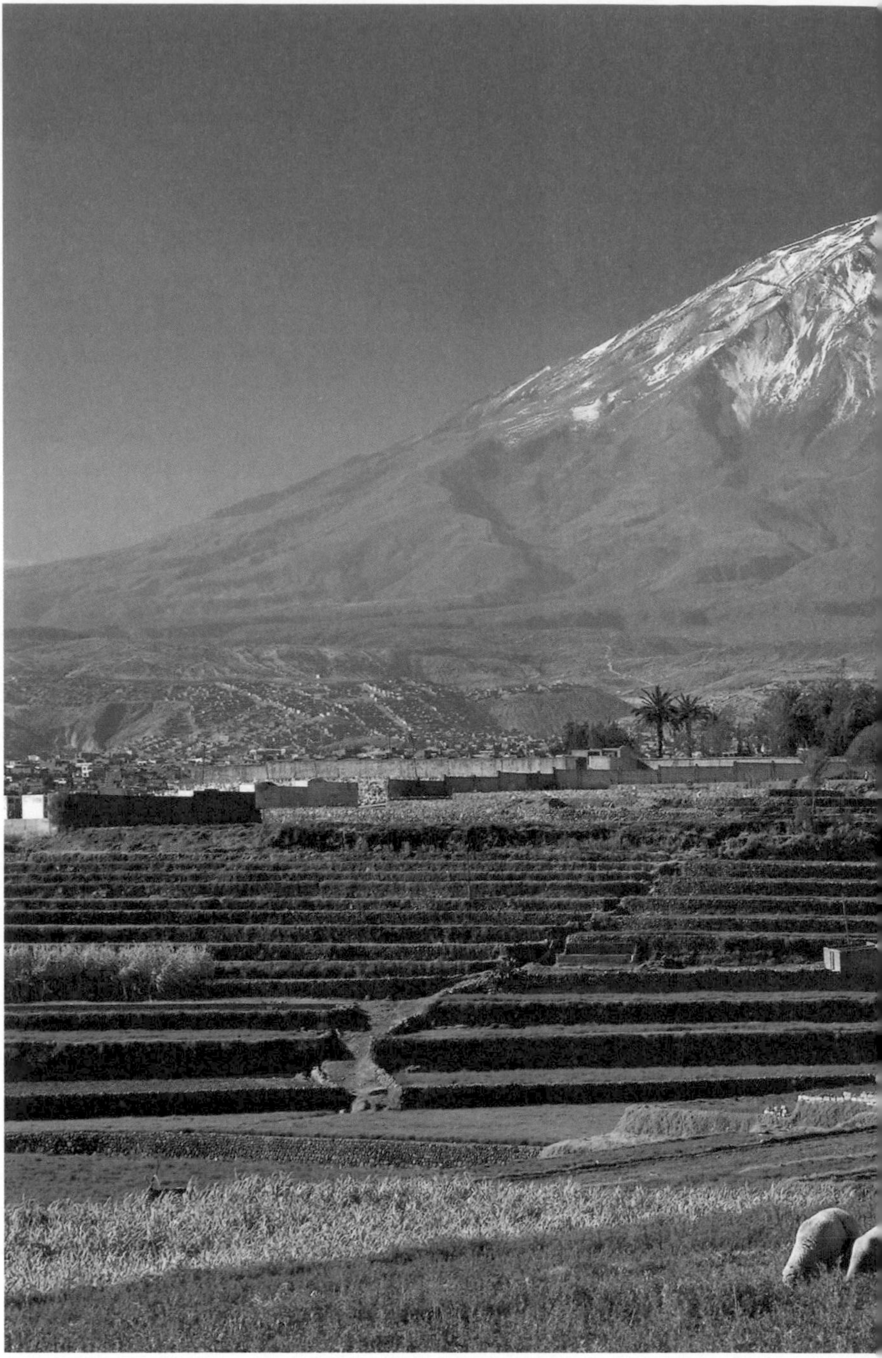

AREQUIPA

Arequipa at a Glance...

Peru's second-largest city is only one-tenth of Lima's size, but pugnaciously equal to it in terms of cuisine, historical significance and confident self-awareness. Guarded by three volcanoes, the city enjoys a resplendent, if seismically precarious setting. Fortunately, the city's architecture, an ensemble of baroque buildings grafted out of the sillar (white volcanic rock), has so far withstood most of what nature has thrown at it.

In 2000 the city earned a well-deserved Unesco World Heritage listing, and the sight of the gigantic cathedral, with ethereal El Misti rising behind it, is worth a visit alone.

Arequipa in Two Days

Spend the morning discovering the *sillar* (white volcanic rock) wonders of **La Catedral** (p98) and the buildings around the **Plaza de Armas** (p98). Make plans for your tour of El Misti with one of ample tour operators nearby, then walk the narrow corridors of **Monasterio de Santa Catalina** (p94). Day two is all about climbing **El Misti** (p92).

Arequipa in Four Days

Start day three in nearby **Yanahuara** (p93) and its *picanterías* (local restaurants), spy El Misti from afar at the *mirador* (lookout), and stop for a pisco at a bar along Calle San Francisco. On day four, see 'Juanita, the Ice Maiden' at **Museo Santuarios Andinos** (p98), then blur the lines between shopping and sightseeing at the **Claustros de la Campañía** (p101). Finish on a high with top-notch nouveau Peruvian cuisine.

Arequipa Map (p100)

Arriving in Arequipa

Rodríguez Ballón International Airport Located about 8km northwest of the city center.

Terminal terrestre The main bus terminal, located on Av Andrés, under 3km south of the city center.

Terrapuerto bus terminal The smaller of the two bus terminals is next door to the main terminal, also on Av Andrés.

Where to Stay

Anywhere within about three blocks of the Plaza de Armas is convenient for exploring the city, especially north, nearest Monasterio de Santa Catalina.

Converted *casonas* (stately homes) are beautiful and have thick, sound-insulated walls along with inner courtyards to cushion you from street noise and car exhaust. Even more peaceful, San Lazaro, on the western end of Calle Llosa, has a cute square, slick places to eat and drink, and a village vibe, yet is still within strolling distance of Calle San Francisco.

There are plenty of budget options along Av Puente Grau near the corner with Calle Jerusalén.

CHRISTIAN KOBER / ROBERTHARDING / GETTY IMAGES ©

El Misti

Looming 5822m (19,101ft) above Arequipa, the city's guardian volcano is the most popular climb in the area. Misti's sulfurous crater hisses gas, and there are spectacular views from the summit.

Great For...

☑ Don't Miss

Lingering in Reserva Nacional Salinas y Aguada Blanca (p116) to spot vicuñas and trek old Inca trails.

El Misti is within one of southern Peru's finest protected reserves, Reserva Nacional Salinas y Aguada Blanca, along with Chachani mountain and the volcano Pichu Pichu. El Misti is technically one of the easiest ascents of any mountain of this size in the world, but it's hard work nonetheless and you normally need an ice ax and, sometimes, crampons. The view from the summit makes it worth it. On a clear day you can see as far out as the Pacific Ocean.

Routes

The ascent can be approached by many routes, some more worn in than others, most of which can be done in two days, to allow enough time to acclimatize to the altitude. No route is clearly marked and at least one (notably the Apurímac route) is

El Misti towers over Arequipa and its surrounds

❶ Need to Know

Misti is best climbed between July and November, with the later months being the least cold.

✕ Take a Break

Although most guides provide meals, come prepared with plenty of water and snacks.

★ Top Tip

El Misti showed signs of reawakening in 2016. Check its webcam (http://ovi. ingemmet.gob.pe/visual/misti) for live updates.

What's Nearby?

If you're more interested in photo ops of El Misti without the huff and puff, the peaceful neighborhood of **Yanahuara** makes a diverting excursion from Arequipa's city center. The plaza there has a *mirador* (lookout) with excellent views of El Misti and Arequipa, optionally glimpsed through stone arches inscribed with poetry. Yanahuara is walking distance: go west on Av Puente Grau over the Puente Grau bridge, and continue on Av Ejército for half a dozen blocks. Turn right on Av Lima and walk five blocks to the small plaza.

notorious for robberies, so taking a guide is highly recommended. A two-day trip will usually cost from US$50 to US$70 per person.

One popular route, starting from **Chiguata**, is an eight-hour hard up-hill slog on rough trails to base camp (4500m/14,763ft); from there to the summit and back takes eight hours, while the sliding return from base camp to Chiguata takes three hours or less. The most common method to reach the mountain is hiring a driver in a 4WD for around S250, who will take you up to 3300m and pick you up on the return.

The Aguada Blanca route is restricted to a handful of official tour operators and allows climbers to arrive at 4100m before starting to climb.

OSTILL / SHUTTERSTOCK ©

Monasterio de Santa Catalina

Even if you've overdosed on colonial edifices, this convent shouldn't be missed. Occupying a whole block and guarded by imposing high walls, it is one of the most fascinating religious buildings in Peru.

Great For...

☑ Don't Miss

Climbing the narrow stairs next to Zocodober Sq for a rooftop view of El Misti and Arequipa.

Santa Catalina is not just a religious building, the 20,000-sq-meter complex is almost a citadel within the city. It was founded in 1580 by a rich widow, doña María de Guzmán.

The best way to visit is to hire a guide, available for S20 from inside the entrance (in the southeast corner). Guides speak Spanish, English and other languages. The tours last about an hour, after which you're welcome to keep exploring by yourself, until the gates close. Alternatively, you can wander around on your own without a guide, soaking up the meditative atmosphere and getting slightly lost. A helpful way to begin is to focus a visit on the three main cloisters.

Novice Cloister

After passing under the *silencio* (silence) arch you will enter the Novice Cloister, marked by a courtyard with a rubber tree

MATTHEW WILLIAMS-ELLIS / GETTY IMAGES ©

❶ Need to Know

📞054-22-1213; www.santacatalina.org.pe; Santa Catalina 301; admission S40; ⏰8am-5pm, to 8pm Tue & Thu, last entry 1hr before closing

✕ Take a Break

Stop by next door for Italian specialties at **La Trattoria del Monasterio** (📞054-20-4062; www.latrattoriadelmonasterio.com; Santa Catalina 309; mains S21-46; ⏰lunch from noon daily, dinner from 7pm Mon-Sat).

★ Top Tip

Catalina opens two evenings a week for traipsing through the shadowy grounds by candlelight.

at its center. After passing under this arch, novice nuns were required to zip their lips in a vow of solemn silence and resolve to a life of work and prayer for four years, during which time their wealthy families were expected to pay a dowry of 100 gold coins per year. Afterwards they could choose between taking their vows and entering into religious service, or leaving the convent – although the latter would have brought shame upon their family.

Orange Cloister

Graduated novices passed onto the Orange Cloister, named for the orange trees clustered at its center that represent renewal and eternal life. This cloister allows a peek into the Profundis Room, a mortuary where dead nuns were mourned. Paintings of the deceased line the walls.

Continuing, Córdova St is flanked by cells that served as living quarters, housing one or more nuns, along with a handful of servants. Toledo St leads you to the communal washing area where servants washed in mountain runoff.

Great Cloister

Heading down Burgos St toward the cathedral's sparkling *sillar* tower, visitors may enter the musty darkness of the communal kitchen.

Just beyond, Zocodober Sq was where nuns gathered on Sundays to exchange handicrafts such as soaps and baked goods. Continuing on, to the left is the cell of legendary Sor Ana, a nun renowned for her eerily accurate predictions about the future.

Finally, the Great Cloister is bordered by the chapel on one side and the art gallery, which used to serve as a communal dormitory, on the other.

Architecture Walking Tour

The star of the Arequipa's architecture may be its unique *sillar* white volcanic rock, but it isn't the only feature. Jump from baroque to *churrigueresque* (an elaborate and intricately decorated Spanish style).

Start Plaza de Armas
Distance 1km
Duration 3 hours

Take a Break... Chicha (p103) Innovative Inca-Spanish cuisine

5 Pass treasure-laden antique stores on the way to **Monasterio de Santa Catalina** (p94) and its fascinating, sprawling interior.

4 Head back behind La Catedral. Turn right on Calle Santa Catalina and then take the first left down Moral to the baroque **Casa de Moral** (p99).

Classic Photo of La Catedral with El Misti in the background

1 Start in the **Plaza de Armas** (p98), Arequipa's main square. Its centerpiece is **La Catedral** (p98), Peru's widest cathedral.

Bolívar

Moral

Santa Catalina

Moral

San Agustín

La Merced

START

Plaza de Armas

La Merced

Palacio Viejo

Álvarez Thomas

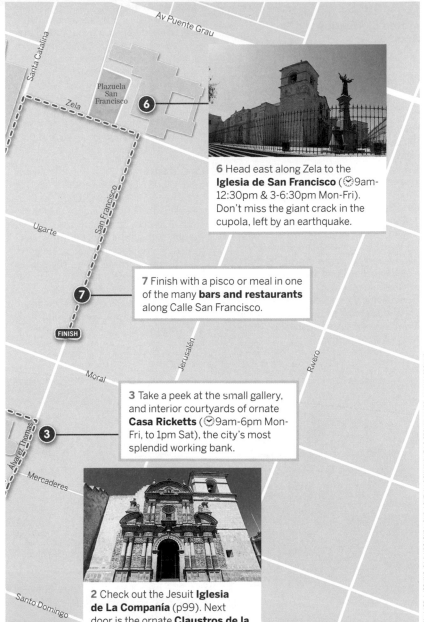

6 Head east along Zela to the **Iglesia de San Francisco** (⊙9am-12:30pm & 3-6:30pm Mon-Fri). Don't miss the giant crack in the cupola, left by an earthquake.

7 Finish with a pisco or meal in one of the many **bars and restaurants** along Calle San Francisco.

3 Take a peek at the small gallery, and interior courtyards of ornate **Casa Ricketts** (⊙9am-6pm Mon-Fri, to 1pm Sat), the city's most splendid working bank.

2 Check out the Jesuit **Iglesia de La Compañía** (p99). Next door is the ornate **Claustros de la Campañía** (p101), an outdoor museum with boutique shops.

FINISH

0 — 100 m
0 — 0.05 miles

◎ SIGHTS

Museo Santuarios Andinos
Museum

(☑054-20-0345; www.ucsm.edu.pe/santury; La Merced 110; admission S20; ☺9am-6pm Mon-Sat, to 3pm Sun) There's an escalating drama to this theatrically presented museum, dedicated to the preserved body of a frozen 'mummy,' and its compulsory guided tour (free, but a tip is expected at the end). Spoiler: the climax is the vaguely macabre sight of poor Juanita, the 12-year-old Inca girl sacrificed to the gods in the 1450s and now eerily preserved in a glass refrigerator. Tours take about an hour and are conducted in Spanish, English and French.

Before presenting Juanita herself, well-versed student guides from the university lead you through a series of atmospheric, dimly lit rooms filled with artifacts from the expedition that found the 'mummy.' There is a beautifully shot 20-minute film about how Juanita, the so-called 'Ice Maiden,' was unearthed atop Nevado Ampato in 1995. From January to April, Juanita is switched for a different 'mummy.'

Plaza de Armas
Square

Arequipa's main plaza, unblemished by modern interference, is a museum of the city's *sillar* architecture – white, muscular and aesthetically unique. Impressive colonnaded balconies line three sides. The fourth is given over to Peru's widest cathedral, a humongous edifice with two soaring towers. Even this is dwarfed by the duel snowcapped sentinels of El Misti and Chanchani, both visible from various points in the central park.

La Catedral
Cathedral

(☑054-23-2635; ☺7-11:30am & 5-7:30pm Mon-Sat, 7am-1pm & 5-7pm Sun) **FREE** On the Plaza de Armas, this building stands out for its stark white *sillar* and massive size – it is the only cathedral in Peru that stretches the length of a plaza. It also has a history of stretching up from the ashes. The original structure, dating from 1656, was gutted by fire in 1844. Consequently rebuilt, it was then flattened by the 1868 earthquake. Most of what you see now has been rebuilt since then.

Plaza de Armas and La Catedral

MATTHEW WILLIAMS-ELLIS / GETTY IMAGES ©

An earthquake in 2001 toppled one enormous tower, and made the other slump precariously, yet by the end of the next year the cathedral looked as good as new.

The interior is simple and airy, with a luminous quality, and the high vaults are uncluttered. It also has a distinctly international flair; it is one of fewer than 100 basilicas in the world entitled to display the Vatican flag, which is to the right of the altar. Both the altar and the 12 columns (symbolizing the 12 Apostles) are made of Italian marble. The huge Byzantine-style brass lamp hanging in front of the altar is from Spain and the pulpit was carved in France. In 1870 Belgium provided the impressive organ, said to be the largest in South America, though damage during shipping condemned the devout to wince at its distorted notes for more than a century.

Iglesia de La Compañía   Church

(⊘9am-12:30pm & 3-6pm Sun-Fri, 11:30am-12:30pm & 3-6pm Sat) **FREE** If Arequipa's cathedral seems *too* big, an interesting antidote (proving that small can be beautiful) is this diminutive Jesuit church on the southeast corner of the Plaza de Armas. The facade is an intricately carved masterpiece of the *churrigueresque* style (think baroque and then some – a style hatched in Spain in the 1660s). The equally detailed altar, completely covered in gold leaf, takes the style further and will be eerily familiar to anyone who has visited Seville cathedral in Spain.

To the left of the altar is the **San Ignacio Chapel** (admission S4; ⊘9am-12:30pm & 3-6pm Sun-Fri, 11:30am-12:30pm & 3-6pm Sat), with a polychrome cupola smothered in unusual junglelike murals of tropical flowers, fruit and birds, among which mingle warriors and angels.

Casa de Moral   Historic Building

(☏054-21-4907; Moral 318; admission S5; ⊘9am-5pm Mon-Sat) Built in 1730, this stylized baroque house is named after the

Juanita – the Ice Maiden

In 1992 local climber Miguel Zárate was guiding an expedition on Nevado Ampato (6288m) when he found curious wooden remnants, suggestive of a burial site, exposed near the icy summit. In September 1995 he returned with American mountaineer and archaeologist Johan Reinhard and together they discovered a statue and other offerings and, some distance from the collapsed burial site, the bundled mummy of an Inca girl.

The girl had been wrapped and almost perfectly preserved by the icy temperatures for about 500 years. It was apparent from the remote location of her tomb and from the care and ceremony surrounding her death (as well as the crushing blow to her right eyebrow) that this 12- to 14-year-old girl had been sacrificed to the gods at the summit. For the Incas, mountains were gods who could kill by volcanic eruption, avalanche or climatic catastrophes. These violent deities could only be appeased by sacrifices from their subjects, and the ultimate sacrifice was that of a child.

After being carried down the mountain and undergoing a battery of scientific examinations at the Universidad Católica in Arequipa, the mummy (dubbed 'Juanita, the Ice Maiden') was given her own museum, Museo Santuarios Andinos, in 1998.

200-year-old mulberry tree in its central courtyard. Owned by BCP (a bank) since 2003, it is now a museum notable for its antique maps, heavy furniture, religious art, and extensive Peruvian coin and banknote collection (courtesy of BCP). Explanations are in Spanish and English.

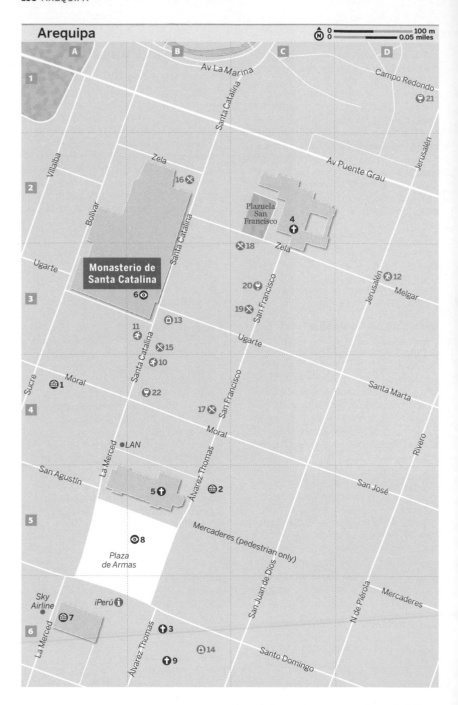

Arequipa

N

0 ——————— 100 m
0 ——————— 0.05 miles

Av La Marina

Campo Redondo

21

Villalba

Zela

Av Puente Grau

Jerusalén

Santa Catalina

16

Bolívar

Plazuela
San
Francisco

4

Zela

18

Jerusalén

12

Melgar

Ugarte

**Monasterio de
Santa Catalina**

6

San Francisco

20

19

13

Ugarte

Santa Marta

11

15

10

Sucre

Moral

1

22

San Francisco

17

Moral

Rivero

Santa Marta

San Agustín

LAN

La Merced

Álvarez Thomas

5

2

San José

8

Mercaderes (pedestrian only)

Plaza
de Armas

San Juan de Dios

N de Piérola

Mercaderes

Sky
Airline

iPerú

7

3

14

9

Santo Domingo

La Merced

Álvarez Thomas

Arequipa

ACTIVITIES

Carlos Zárate Adventures
Adventure Sports

(☏054-20-2461; www.zarateadventures.com; Santa Catalina 204, Oficina 3) This highly professional company was founded in 1954 by Carlos Zárate, the great-grandfather of climbing in Arequipa. One of Zárate's sons, Miguel, was responsible, along with archaeologists, for unearthing Juanita 'the Ice Maiden' (p99) atop Nevado Ampato in 1995. Now run by another son, experienced guide Carlos Zárate Flores, it offers various treks, and climbs all the local peaks.

Prices depend on group size and transportation method. It charges from US$250 per person for a group of four to climb El Misti, and US$220 for a three-day trek in the Cañón del Colca, both with private transport, guide, meals and all equipment.

Zárate's guides generally speak Spanish or English, but are also available in French when prearranged. It also rents all kinds of gear to independent climbers and hikers, including ice axes, crampons and hiking boots.

Naturaleza Activa
Adventure Sports

(☏96-896-9544; naturactiva@yahoo.com; Santa Catalina 211) A favorite of those seeking adventure tours, and offering a full range of trekking, climbing and mountain-biking options. A major advantage over going to

an agency is that the people you speak to at Naturaleza Activa are actually the qualified guides, not salespeople, so can answer your questions with genuine knowledge. Guides speak English, French and German.

Pablo Tour
Adventure Sports

(☏054-20-3737; www.pablotour.com; Jerusalén 400 AB-1) Consistently recommended by readers, Pablo Tour's guides are experts in trekking and cultural tours in the region, and can furnish trekkers with all the necessary equipment and topographical maps.

SHOPPING

Arequipa overflows with antique and artisan shops, especially on the streets around Monasterio de Santa Catalina. High-quality leather, alpaca and vicuña (threatened wild relative of alpacas) goods, and other handmade items, are what you'll most often see being sold.

Claustros de la Campañía
Shopping Center

(Santo Domingo) This is one of South America's most elegant shopping centers. Its ornate double courtyard is ringed by cloisters held up by *sillar* columns, etched with skillful carvings. You'll find a wine bodega, an ice-cream outlet, numerous alpaca-wool shops and a couple of elegant cafes on the

Taste it, Cook it

If you recognize the name Gastón Acurio and concur that Peru is the gastronomical capital of Latin America, you may be inspired to enroll in an Arequipa **cooking course**. Local guide and qualified chef Miguel Fernández, who runs Al Travel, organizes **Peru Flavors**, a four-hour cooking course (S100, minimum two people) where you will learn to prepare a trio of appetizers and mains from the three different geographical regions of Peru: Amazonia, the Andes and the coast. Dishes include *rocoto relleno* (stuffed peppers), *lomo saltado* (strips of beef stir-fried with onions, tomatoes, potatoes and chili) and *chupe de camerones* (shrimp chowder).

Another popular option is the **Peruvian Cooking Experience** (☑054-213-177; www.peruviancookingexperience.com; San Martín 116, Val), based at the Casa de Avila hotel, four blocks southwest of Plaza de Armas. Three-hour courses (11am to 2pm; S65) run Monday to Saturday. You can study the art of ceviche preparation or even opt for vegetarian recipes. Courses are available in Spanish and English. Maximum group size is six.

Chicharrón (deep-fried pork with potato and onion)
MIRCEADOBRE / GETTY IMAGES ©

courtyard. Young couples dot the upper levels enjoying the romantic setting and southerly views.

Casona Santa Catalina
Clothing, Souvenirs

(☑054-28-1334; www.santacatalina-sa.com.pe; Santa Catalina 210; ⊗most shops 10am-6pm) Inside this polished tourist complex, you'll find a few shops of major export brands, such as Sol Alpaca and Biondi Piscos.

🗱 EATING

Hunker down. If you want to truly 'get' Arequipa, you have some serious food sampling to enjoy. Start with the basics: *rocoto relleno* (stuffed spicy red peppers) and *chupe de camarones* (prawn chowder) and work up to the stuff you'll never find east of the Amazon (at least on a dinner plate) – guinea pig, anyone? Upscale restaurants are leading a Peruvian gastronomical renaissance along Calle San Francisco north of the Plaza de Armas, while touristy outdoor cafes huddle together on Pasaje Catedral, behind the cathedral and away from the plaza.

Crepisimo
Cafe, Creperie $

(www.crepisimo.com; Alianza Francesa, Santa Catalina 208; mains S7-16; ⊗8am-11pm Mon-Sat, noon-11pm Sun; 🛜) All the essential components of a great cafe – food, setting, service, ambience – come together at Crepisimo in the French cultural center. In this chic colonial setting, the simple crepe is offered with 100 different types of filling, from Chilean smoked trout to exotic South American fruits, while casual wait staff serve you Parisian-quality coffee.

Zingaro
Peruvian $$

(www.zingaro-restaurante.com; San Francisco 309; mains S30-49; ⊗noon-11pm Mon-Sat) In an old *sillar* building with wooden balconies, stained glass and a resident pianist, culinary legends are made. Zingaro is a leading font of gastronomic innovation, meaning it's an ideal place to try out nouveau renditions of Peruvian standards including alpaca ribs, ceviche, or perhaps your first *cuy* (guinea pig).

Two doors down (San Francisco 315), sister restaurant **Parrilla de Zingaro** specializes in Argentinian-style meats with equally splendid results.

Zig Zag Peruvian $$

(☎054-20-6020; www.zigzagrestaurant.com; Zela 210; mains S33-45; ☺noon-midnight) Upscale but not ridiculously pricey, Zig Zag is a Peruvian restaurant with European inflections. It inhabits a two-story colonial house with an iron stairway designed by Gustave Eiffel. The menu classic is a meat selection served on a volcanic stone grill. The fondues are also good. Some heretics claim it's even better than Peruvian chef Gastón Acurio's Chicha. The lunch *menús* (set meals; from S45) are an accessible way to taste-test.

Nina-Yaku Peruvian, Fusion $$

(☎054-28-1432; San Francisco 211; menús S28, mains S28-38; ☺11am-11pm) Escaping the tumult of Calle San Francisco, Nina Yaku offers an atmosphere of whispered refinement along with affordable Arequipan specialties such as broccoli soufflé, potatoes in Huatacay sauce, and fettuccine pesto with alpaca.

La Nueva Palomino Peruvian $$

(Leoncio Prado 122; mains S14-29; ☺noon-6pm) Definitely the local favorite, the atmosphere at this *picantería* (local restaurant)

is informal and can turn boisterous even during the week when groups of families and friends file in to eat local specialties and drink copious amounts of *chicha de jora* (fermented corn beer). The restaurant is in the Yanahuara district (2km northwest of the city center), east of the *mirador*.

El Tío Dario Seafood $$

(☎054-27-0473; Callejon de Cabildo 100, Yanahuara; mains S27-45) Like fish? Like intimate secret-garden settings? Then grab a taxi (or walk) out to the pleasant Yanahuara district for the ultimate in ceviches or grilled-fish dishes served in a flower-rich garden that frames superb volcano views. Tío Dario is through the charming archway to the left of Yanahuara *mirador*.

Chicha Peruvian, Fusion $$$

(☎054-28-7360; www.chicha.com.pe; Santa Catalina 210; mains S28-49; ☺noon-midnight Mon-Sat, to 9pm Sun) Gastón Acurio, Peru's most famous chef, owns this wildly experimental place where the menu never veers far from Peru's Inca-Spanish roots. River prawns are a highlight in season (April to

Traditional dishes including *rocoto relleno* (stuffed pepper)

From left: Juice stalls; Calle Cordoba at Monasterio de Santa Catalina (p94); Fruit seller in Calle San Francisco

December), but Acurio prepares Peruvian staples with equal panache, along with tender alpaca burgers and earthy pastas.

Try the *tacu-tacu* (a Peruvian fusion dish of rice, beans and a protein), *lomo saltado* (strips of beef stir-fried with onions, tomatoes, potatoes and chili) or ceviche. Like many 'celeb' places, Chicha divides opinion between food snobs and purists. Step inside its fine colonial interior and join the debate.

🍷 DRINKING & NIGHTLIFE

The nocturnal scene in Arequipa takes off on weekends, especially on Calle San Francisco. The block between Ugarte and Zela has the highest concentration of places to compare fashion notes.

Museo del Pisco   Cocktail Bar
(http://museodelpisco.org; cnr Santa Catalina & Moral; drinks S16-32, degustation for 1/2 people S45/60; ☉noon-midnight) The name says museum, but the designer slabs of stone and glass, plus the menu of more than 100 piscos, says cocktail bar. Pick a favorite with a pisco degustation, which includes

three mini craft piscos with an explanation in English by knowledgeable bar staff. Then mix your own (S30). Pace yourself with gourmet burgers and hummus.

Chelawasi
Public House   Microbrewery
(Campo Redondo 102; beer S12; ☉4pm-midnight Thu-Sat, to 10pm Sun) New to craft beer? The friendly Canadian-Peruvian owners will step you through the best beers from Peru's microbreweries, with bonus local travel advice. Arequipa's first craft-beer bar is a modern but unpretentious pub in the village-like San Lázaro area.

Casona Forum   Club
(www.casonaforum.com; San Francisco 317) A five-in-one excuse for a good night out in a *sillar* building incorporating a pub (Retro), pool club (Zero), sofa bar (Chill Out), nightclub (Forum) and restaurant (Terrasse).

❶ INFORMATION

iPerú (☎054-22-3265; iperuarequipa@ promperu.gob.pe; Portal de la Municipalidad 110, Plaza de Armas; ☉9am-6pm Mon-Sat, to 1pm

Sun) Government-supported source for objective information on local and regional attractions. There is also an office at the **airport** (☑054-44-4564; 1st fl, Main Hall, Aeropuerto Rodríguez Ballón; ☺10am-7:30pm).

ⓘ GETTING THERE & AWAY

AIR

Arequipa's **Rodríguez Ballón International Airport** (AQP; ☑054-44-3458) is about 8km northwest of the city center.

LAN (p309) has daily flights to Lima and Cuzco. **LCPerú** (p309) also offers daily flights to Lima. **Sky Airline** (☑054-28-2899; www.skyairline.cl; La Merced 121) flies to Santiago in Chile.

BUS

Most bus companies have departures from the *terminal terrestre* or the smaller Terrapuerto bus terminal; both are together on Av Andrés Avelino Cáceres, less than 3km south of the city center (take a taxi for S8). Check in advance which terminal your bus leaves from and keep a close watch on your belongings while you're waiting there. Both terminals have shops, restaurants and left-luggage facilities. The more chaotic

terminal terrestre also has a global ATM and a tourist information office.

Dozens of bus companies have desks at the *terminal terrestre*, including superluxury **Cruz del Sur** (☑054-42-7375; www.cruzdelsur.com.pe) and **Ormeño** (☑054-42-3855), with 180-degree reclining 'bed' seats.

ⓘ GETTING AROUND

TO/FROM THE AIRPORT

There are no airport buses or shared taxis. An official taxi from downtown Arequipa to the airport costs around S25.

TAXI

You can often hire a taxi with a driver for less than renting a car from a travel agency. Local taxi companies include **Tourismo Arequipa** (☑054-45-8888) and **Taxitel** (☑054-45-2020). A short ride around town costs about S4, while a trip from the Plaza de Armas out to the bus terminals costs about S8. Whenever possible, try to call a recommended company to ask for a pickup as there have been numerous reports of travelers being scammed or assaulted by taxi drivers.

CAÑÓN DEL COLCA

Cañón del Colca at a Glance...

It's not just the vastness and depth of the Colca that make it so fantastical, it's the shifts in its scenery, from the ancient terraced farmland of Yanque and Chivay into the steep-sided canyon proper beyond Cabanaconde.

Of course one shouldn't turn a blind eye to the vital statistics. The Colca is the world's second-deepest canyon, a smidgen shallower than the Cotahausi, and twice as deep as the more famous Grand Canyon in the US. But, more than that, it is replete with history, culture, ruins, tradition and – rather like Machu Picchu – intangible Peruvian magic.

Cañón del Colca in Two Days

The *classico* tour from Arequipa stops to spot wild vicuñas and lofty mountain peaks, then finishes in **Chivay** (p118), with restaurant performances. Day two starts early to catch kids dancing in the square at **Yanque**, making stops to wonder at **Cañón del Colca** and visiting **Cruz del Cóndor** (p113) to see the condors glide over the canyon.

Cañón del Colca in Four Days

With more time, continue from Cruz del Cóndor to the true canyon experience of **Cabanaconde** (p120). Descend on a two-hour hike to the greenery of **Sangalle** (p120), cooling off with a swim at the pools, then spending the night at some simple lodgings under a blanket of stars. On day four, hike back up and return to Chivay.

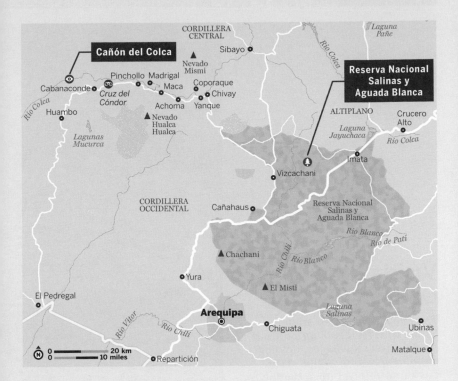

Arriving in Cañón del Colca

Bus and Car Chivay is the gateway (and resting point) to the region on most standard *classico* tours from Arequipa.

Where to Stay

Though it's a tiny town, Chivay has plenty of budget guesthouses to choose from. The most convenient are on Siglo XX, off the plaza.

In Yanque, a number of simple, family-run guesthouses have joined together in a local development project; they are scattered around town, and offer lodging from S15 per night.

Accommodations options are limited in Cabanaconde.

Llama herder and flock, Chivay

Visiting the Canyon

The canyon has been embel-lished with terraced agricultural fields, pastoral villages, colonial churches, and ruins that date back to pre-Inca times. Hike it, bike it, raft it or zip-line it, just keep your eyes peeled for its emblematic condors.

Cañón del Colca

Nevado Coropuna

Río Colca

Chivay

Huambo

Lagunas Mucurca

Río Majes

Reserva Nacional Salinas y Aguada Blanca

Arequipa

Great For...

ⓘ Need to Know

June to September is your best chance of seeing Andean condors gliding above the canyon.

★ **Top Tip**
Locals bearing birds or llamas, urging you to take photos, expect a S1 tip.

Despite its depth, the Cañón del Colca is geologically young. The Río Colca has cut into beds of mainly volcanic rocks, which were deposited less than 100 million years ago along the line of a major fault in the earth's crust. Though cool and dry in the hills above, the deep valley and generally sunny weather produce frequent updrafts on which soaring condors often float by at close range.

Viscachas (burrowing rodents closely related to chinchillas) are also common around the canyon rim, darting furtively among the rocks. Cacti dot many slopes and, if they're in flower, you may be lucky enough to see tiny nectar-eating birds braving the spines to feed. In the depths of the canyon it can be almost tropical, with palm trees, ferns, and even orchids in some isolated areas.

Boleto Turístico

To access sites in the Cañón del Colca you need to purchase a *boleto turístico* (tourist ticket; S70) from a booth on the Arequipa road just outside Chivay. If you are taking an organized tour, the cost of the tour usually does not include this additional fee, and you will be asked for this in cash by your guide at the booth.

Half of the proceeds from this ticket go to Arequipa for general maintenance and conservation of local tourist attractions, while the other half goes to the national agency of tourism.

Coporaque's colonial church

Hualca Hualca

Pinchollo, about 30km from Chivay, is one of the valley's poorer villages. From here, a trail climbs toward Hualca Hualca (a snowcapped volcano of 6025m) to an active geothermal area set amid wild and interesting scenery. Though it's not very clearly marked, there's a rough four-hour trail up to a bubbling geyser that used to erupt dramatically before an earthquake contained it.

☑ Don't Miss

Noncommercialized Coporaque, which has the valley's oldest church and gorgeous views of canyon slopes covered in terraced fields.

RAFAL CICHAWA / GETTY IMAGES ©

Cruz del Cóndor

Some much hyped travel sights are anti-climactic in the raw light of day, but this is *not* one of them. No advance press can truly sell the **Cruz del Cóndor** (Chaq'lla; admission with boleto turístico), a famed viewpoint, also known locally as Chaq'lla, about 50km west of Chivay. A large family of Andean condors nests by the rocky outcrop and, weather and season permitting, they can be seen between approximately 8am and 10am gliding effortlessly on thermal air currents rising from the canyon, swooping low over onlookers' heads. It's a mesmerizing scene, heightened by the spectacular 1200m drop to the river below and the sight of **Nevado Mismi** reaching over 3000m above the canyon floor on the other side of the ravine.

Recently it has become more difficult to see the condors, mostly due to air pollution, including from travelers' campfires and tour buses. The condors are also less likely to appear on rainy days, so it's best to visit during the dry season; they are unlikely to emerge at all in January and February. You won't be alone at the lookout; expect a couple of hundred people for the 8am 'show' in season. Afterwards, it is possible to walk 12.5km from the viewpoint to Cabanaconde.

Cabanaconde

Only approximately 20% of Cañón del Colca visitors get as far as ramshackle Cabanaconde (most organized itineraries turn around at the Cruz del Cóndor). For those who make it, the attractions are obvious – less people, more authenticity and greater tranquility. Welcome to the *true* canyon experience. The Colca is significantly deeper here, with steep, zigzagging paths tempting the fit and the brave to descend 1200m to the eponymous river.

Paso de Patopampa

The highest point on the road between Arequipa and Chivay is this almost lifeless pass which, at 4910m, is significantly higher than Europe's Mt Blanc and anywhere in North America's Rocky Mountains. If your red blood cells are up to it, disembark into the rarefied air at the **Mirador de los Volcanes** to view a muscular consortium of eight snowcapped volcanoes: Ubinas (5675m), El Misti (5822m), Chachani (6075m), Ampato (6310m), Sabancaya (5976m), Huaca Huaca (6025m), Mismi (5597m) and Chucura (5360m).

Less spectacular but no less amazing is the scrubby *yareta*, one of the few plants that can survive in this harsh landscape. *Yaretas* can live for several millennia and their annual growth rate is measured in millimeters rather than centimeters. Hardy ladies in traditional dress discreetly ply their wares at the *mirador* (lookout) during the day – this must be the world's highest shopping center.

Pampa de Toccra

Pampa de Toccra, a high plain (pampa) that lies between El Misti/Chachani and the Cañón del Colca has an average height of around 4300m and supports plentiful bird and animal life. You're almost certain to see vicuñas roadside in the Zona de Vicuñas on the approach to **Patahuasi**. At a boggy and sometimes-icy lake, waterfowl and flamingos reside in season. Nearby is a bird-watching *mirador*.

The **Centro de Interpretación de la Reserva Nacional Salinas** (⏱9am-5pm) has detailed notes in English and Spanish about the area's geology and fauna. All four members of the South American camelid family thrive at the pampas in this region: the domesticated llama and alpaca, and the wild vicuña and (timid and rare) guanaco.

'El Clásico' Trek

Short on time? Confused by the complicated web of Colca paths? Couldn't stand the crowds on the Inca Trail? What you need is 'El Clásico,' the unofficial name for a circular two- to three-day hike that incorporates the best parts of the mid-lower Cañón del Colca below the Cruz del Cóndor and Cabanaconde.

Start by walking out of Cabanaconde on the Chivay road. At the San Miguel viewpoint, start a long 1200m descent into the canyon on a zigzagging path. Cross the Río Colca via a bridge and enter the village of **San Juan de Chuccho**. Bungalow accommodations with warm water and a

Condor monument, Cabanaconde (p113)

simple restaurant are available here. Alternatively, you can ascend to the charming village of **Tapay**. On day two descend to the **Cinkumayu Bridge** before ascending to the villages of **Coshñirwa** and **Malata**. The latter has a tiny **Museo Familiar**, basically a typical local home where the owner will explain about the Colca culture. From Malata, descend to the beautiful **Sangalle** oasis (crossing the river again), with more overnight options, before ascending the lung-stretching 4km trail back to Cabanaconde (1200m of ascent).

Though it's easy to do solo, this classic trek can be easily organized with any reputable Arequipa travel agency.

❶ Did You Know?

The wingspan of an Andean Condor can measure up to 3.3m.

✖ Take a Break

Small towns and Cruz del Cóndor itself have home-cooked meals, as well as coca-leaf tea to help with the altitude.

DANIELE FALLETTA / ALAMY STOCK PHOTO ©

Reserva Nacional Salinas y Aguada Blanca

There is an otherworldly beauty to the odd wildlife and plant life that survives here at such high altitudes among the bizarrely eroded rock formations.

The trouble with all those organized Cañón del Colca tours is that they rush through one of southern Peru's finest protected reserves, Reserva Nacional Salinas y Aguada Blanca, a vast Andean expanse of dozing volcanoes and brawny wildlife forging out an existence against the odds several kilometers above sea level. Drives here take you up to an oxygen-deprived 4910m where, in between light-headed gasps for air, you can ponder weird wind-eroded rock formations, trek on old Inca trails and watch fleet-footed vicuñas (wild relatives of alpacas) run across the desolate pampa at speeds of up to 85km/h.

Great For...

☑ Don't Miss

Chewing coca leaves en route. Not only does it help combat the high altitudes, it's a traditional experience.

Llamas

CULTURA RM EXCLUSIVE / MATT DUTILE / GETTY IMAGES ©

ⓘ Need to Know

Administrative Headquarters ☎054-25-7461; reserve ⊙24hr

✕ Take a Break

Be sure to stock up snacks and water as stops are few and far between.

★ Top Tip

Vicuñas are unmissable, but startle easily, so you'll need a camera with a good zoom.

Wildlife

As a national reserve, Salinas y Aguada Blanca enjoys better protection than the Cañón del Colca, primarily because no one lives here bar the odd isolated llama-herder. Its job is to protect a rich raft of high-altitude species such as the vicuñas, *tarucas envinados* (Andean deer), guanacos (camelids that are related to llamas) and various birds, most notably flamingos. Both El Misti and Chachani volcanoes are part of the reserve.

Chachani

One of the easiest 6000m peaks in the world is Chachani (6075m), which is as close to Arequipa as El Misti. You will need crampons, an ice ax and good equipment. There are various routes up the mountain, one of which involves going by 4WD to Campamento de Azufrera at 4950m. From there you can reach the summit in about nine hours and return in under four hours. Alternatively, for a two-day trip, there is a good spot to camp at 5200m. Other routes take three days, but are easier to get to by 4WD (US$125 to US$180).

El Misti

El Misti volcano is also part of the reserve but is easier to visit from Arequipa (p89), one hour away.

Chivay

The unashamedly disheveled nexus of the canyon, Chivay is a traditional town that has embraced tourism without (so far) losing its unkempt high-country identity. The town affords enchanting views of snowcapped peaks and terraced hillsides, and serves as a logical base from which to explore smaller towns further up the valley.

◉ SIGHTS

Astronomical Observatory   Observatory

(Planetario; ☏054-53-1020; Huayna Cápac; admission S25; ☺Apr-Dec) No light pollution equals excellent Milky Way vistas. The Casa Andina hotel has a tiny observatory which holds nightly sky shows in Spanish and English. The price includes a 30-minute explanation and chance to peer into the telescope. It is closed between January and March as it is hard to catch a night with clear skies.

✪ ACTIVITIES

Chivay is a good starting point for canyon hikes, both short and long.

La Calera Hot Springs   Thermal Baths

(admission S15; ☺4:30am-7pm) If you've just bussed or driven in from Arequipa, a good way to acclimatize is to stroll 3km to La Calera Hot Springs and examine the canyon's (surprisingly shallow) slopes alfresco while lying in the naturally heated pools. The setting is idyllic and you'll be entertained by the whooping zip-liners as they sail overhead. *Colectivos* (shared transportation) from Chivay cost S1 to S2.

Colca Zip-Lining   Adventure Sports

(☏95-898-9931; www.colcaziplining.com; 2/4 rides S50/100; ☺from 9am Mon-Sat, from 10.30am Sun) You can dangle terrifyingly

> *the town affords enchanting views of snow-capped peaks and terraced hillsides*

Reserva Nacional Salinas y Aguada Blanca (p116)

SLONEG / GETTY IMAGES ©

over the Río Colca while entertaining bathers in La Calera Hot Springs (who relax below) doing the canyon's most modern sport – zip-lining. The start point is just past La Calera Hot Springs, 3.5km from Chivay. Four-ride sessions last one hour.

BiciSport Bicycle Rental

(☑95-880-7652; Zaramilla 112; ☉9am-6pm) Mountain bikes in varying condition can be readily hired from BiciSport behind the market for about S5 per day.

EATING

Innkas Café Peruvian $

(Plaza de Armas 705; mains S12-20; ☉7am-10pm) An old building with cozy window nooks warmed by modern gas heaters (and boy do you need 'em). Maybe it's the altitude, but the *lomo saltado* (strips of beef stir-fried with onions, tomatoes, potatoes and chili) tastes Gastón Acurio–good here. The sweet service is backed up by even sweeter cakes and coffee.

INFORMATION

There's a helpful **information office** (☑054-53-1143; Plaza de Armas 119; ☉8am-1pm & 3-7pm) right on the main plaza. The police station is next to the *municipalidad* (town hall) on the plaza.

GETTING THERE & AWAY

Most visitors arrive in Chivay with a hired driver or via organized tours.

The bus terminal is a 15-minute walk from the plaza. There are nine daily departures to Arequipa (S15, three hours) and four daily to Cabanaconde (S5, 2½ hours), stopping at towns along the southern side of the canyon and at Cruz del Cóndor.

You can arrange a private taxi to the surrounding villages.

To get to Puno, take a direct tourist bus from Chivay with **4M Express** (☑95-974-6330; www.4m-express.com; Chivay to Puno US$45)

People of the Canyon

The local people are descendants of two conflicting groups that originally occupied the area, the Cabanas and the Collagua. These two groups used to distinguish themselves by performing cranial deformations, but nowadays use distinctively shaped hats and intricately embroidered traditional clothing to denote their ancestry. In the Chivay area at the east end of the canyon, the white hats worn by women are usually woven from straw and are embellished with lace, sequins and medallions. At the west end of the canyon, the hats have rounded tops and are made of painstakingly embroidered cotton.

Around the market area and in the main square are good places to catch a glimpse of the decorative clothing worn by local Colca women.

or **Rutas del Sur** (☑95-102-4754; chivay@rutasurperu.com; Av 22 de Agosto s/n; Chivay to Puno US$35), both leaving near Chivay's plaza at 1:30pm and arriving at Puno's plaza at 7:30pm.

Yanque

Of the canyon's dozen or so villages, Yanque, 7km west of Chivay, has the prettiest and liveliest main square, and sports its finest church (from the exterior, at least), the **Iglesia de la Inmaculada Concepción**, the ornate baroque doorway of which has an almost *churrigueresque* (an elaborate and intricately decorated Spanish style) look. Local children in traditional costume dance to music in the main square most mornings at around 7am, catching tourists on their way to the Cruz del Cóndor.

SIGHTS & ACTIVITIES

Museo Yanque   Museum

(http://yanqueperu.com; admission S5; ⊘9am-6:30pm) Opposite the church on the plaza sits this university-run museum, unexpectedly comprehensive for a small village, which explains the culture of the Cañón del Colca in conscientious detail. Exhibits include information on Inca fabrics, cranial deformation, local agriculture, ecclesial architecture and a miniexpose on Juanita, the 'Ice Maiden' (p99).

Baños Chacapi   Thermal Baths

(admission S10; ⊘4am-7pm) From the plaza, a 30-minute walk down to the river brings you to these hot springs, a kind of poor man's La Calera. The early-bird opening time is mainly for locals, many of whom don't have hot water in their houses.

Cabanaconde

You've only half-experienced Colca if you haven't descended into the canyon by foot (the only method anywhere west of Madrigal). The shortest way in is via the spectacular two-hour hike from Cabanaconde down to the flower-filled greenery of **Sangalle** (per person S5), also popularly known as 'the oasis', at the bottom of the canyon. The mountain walls create a tranquil oasis indeed, topped with a blanket of stars at night.

Here four sets of basic bungalows and camping grounds have sprung up. There are two natural pools for swimming. Do not light campfires as almost half of the trees in the area have been destroyed in this manner, and cart all trash out with you. The return trek to Cabanaconde is a stiff climb and thirsty work; allow 1½ hours (superfit), two to 2½ hours (fit) or three hours plus (average fitness). There's food and drink available in Sangalle.

EATING

Most people eat where they're sleeping, although there are a couple of cheap local restaurants near or on the main plaza.

Restaurante
Las Terrazas   International $

(☑95-810-3553; www.villapastorcolca.com; Plaza de Armas s/n; snacks S10-15) Pizza, pasta, sandwiches and cheap Cuba Libres are offered here overlooking the main square and its bucolic donkey traffic. There's also a computer terminal charitably offering free internet. Rooms are available.

INFORMATION

There are no ATMs in Cabanaconde, so stash some cash.

ⓘ GETTING THERE & AWAY

If not on an organized tour, buses for Chivay and Arequipa via Cruz del Cóndor leave Cabanaconde from the main plaza seven times per day with four companies, including **Andalucía** (☑054-44-5089) and **Reyna** (☑054-43-0612). All buses stop upon request at towns along the main road on the southern side of the canyon.

Clockwise from top: Alpaca herd, Reserva Nacional Salinas y Aguada Blanca (p116); view over the Colca valley; condors

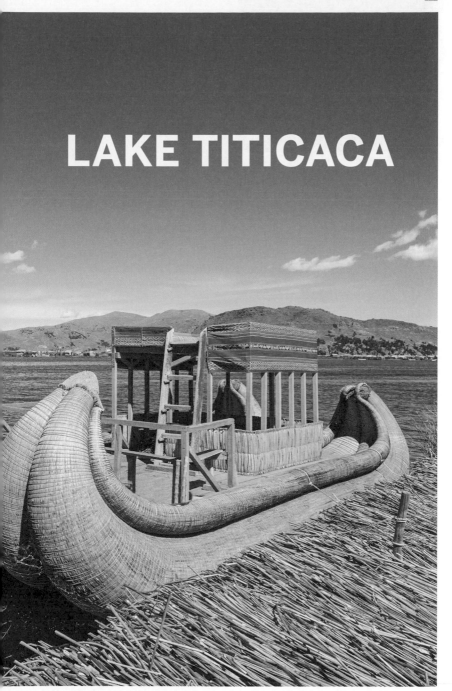

LAKE TITICACA

Lake Titicaca at a Glance...

In Andean belief, Titicaca is the birthplace of the sun. In addition, it's the largest lake in South America and the highest navigable body of water in the world. Enthralling, and in many ways singular, the shimmering deep-blue Lake Titicaca is the longtime home of highland cultures steeped in the old ways. Pre-Inca Pukara, Tiwanaku and Collas all left a mark on the landscape.

Today, the region is a mix of crumbling cathedrals, desolate altiplano and checkerboard fields backed by rolling hills and high Andean peaks. The area might at first appear austere, but ancient holidays are marked with riotous celebrations where elaborately costumed processions and brass bands start a frenzy that lasts for days.

Lake Titicaca in Two Days

Spend the first day exploring the floating reed islands of **Islas Uros** (p126), continue on to some great walks on **Isla Taquile** (p130), then head back to Puno to check out **Catedral de Puno** (p132), and have dinner nearby.
Spend day two exploring the *chullpas* (funerary towers) at **Sillustani** (p128) and visiting a local home as evening falls.

Lake Titicaca in Four Days

On the third day head along the road toward Bolivia and stay in a homestay at a south-shore community of Lake Titicaca, such as **Luquina Chico** (p140). Explore the miniature funerary towers there in the late afternoon. On the fourth day you can continue on to Bolivia or head back to Puno to visit the late-opening **Coca Museum** (p132).

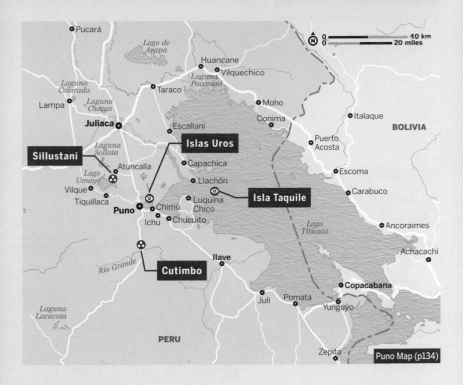

Arriving in Lake Titicaca

Aeropuerto Internacional Inca Manco Cápac The region's only airport is one hour from Puno, the gateway to Titicaca.

Bus and car Overland crossings from the southeast side of the lake are usually through Copacabana in Bolivia to the border post at Yunguyo.

Where to Stay

In Puno, pedestrianised Calle Lima between Parque Pino and Plaza de Armas is the most active and safest street. Staying anywhere within three blocks of here is the most convenient and secure. Calle Lima and Arequipa can suffer from nighttime bar or traffic noise, so try to avoid street-facing rooms.

There are homestays on many of the islands, which include the option of a home-cooked meal while staying with a local family.

If you get stuck in Pucará, there are some simple accommodations near the bus stop.

Reed boats, Islas Uros

SAIKO3P / GETTY IMAGES ©

Islas Uros

These extraordinary floating islands are Lake Titicaca's top attraction. Their uniqueness is due to their construction, created entirely with the buoyant **totora** *reeds that grow abundantly in the shallows of the lake.*

Great For...

☑ **Don't Miss**

A taste test of the reeds, which resemble sugarcane without any sweetness.

The lives of the Uros people are interwoven with *totora* reeds. Partially edible (tasting like nonsweet sugarcane), the reeds are also used to build homes, boats and crafts. The islands are constructed from many layers of the *totora*, which are constantly replenished from the top as they rot from the bottom, so the ground is always soft and springy.

Some islands also have elaborately designed versions of traditional tightly bundled reed boats on hand and other whimsical reed creations, such as archways and even swing sets. Be prepared to pay for a boat ride (S10) or to take photographs. Intermarriage with the Aymara-speaking indigenous people has seen the demise of the pure-blooded Uros, who nowadays all speak Aymara. Always a small tribe, the

Miniature reed boat

RAFAL CICHAWA / GETTY IMAGES ©

ℹ Need to Know

Boat tours take you to the islands, 7km east of Puno.

✕ Take a Break

Food isn't sold on the boats or on Islas Uros, so bring snacks and water.

★ Top Tip

Handicrafts sold on the islands are an important livelihood for inhabitants, who sometimes see little tour money.

Uros began their unusual floating existence centuries ago in an effort to isolate themselves from the aggressive Collas and Incas.

The popularity of the islands has led to aggressive commercialization in some cases. The most traditional reed islands are located further from Puno through a maze of small channels, only visited by private boat. Islanders there continue to live in a relatively traditional fashion and prefer not to be photographed.

Homestays

An outstanding option is staying in the reed huts of Isla Khantati on a **homestay** (☏951-69-5121, 951-47-2355; uroskhantati@hotmail.com; per person full board S180) with boundless personality Cristina Suaña, an Uros

native whose entrepreneurship earned her international accolades. Over a number of years, her family have built a group of impeccable semitraditional huts (with solar power and outhouses) that occupy half the tiny island, along with shady decks, cats and the occasional flamingo. The rates include transfers from Puno, fresh and varied meals, fishing, some cultural explanations, and the pleasure of the company of the effervescent Cristina. The hyper-relaxed pace means a visit here is not ideal for those with little time on their hands.

Getting There & Away

Getting to the Uros is easy – there's no need to go with an organized tour, though you will miss out on the history lesson given by the guides. Ferries leave from the Uros port for Uros (return trip S10) at least once an hour from 6am to 4pm. The community-owned ferry service visits two islands, on a rotation basis. Ferries to Taquile and Amantaní can also drop you off in the Uros.

ARTIE PHOTOGRAPHY (ARTIE NG) / GETTY IMAGES ©

Chullpas

The ancient Colla people who once dominated the Lake Titicaca area buried their nobility in imposing chullpas (funerary towers), which can be seen scattered widely around the hilltops of the region.

The Colla people were a warlike, Aymara-speaking tribe, who later became the southeastern group of the Incas. Their *chullpas* housed the remains of complete family groups, along with plenty of food and belongings for their journey into the next world. The *chullpas'* only opening was a small hole facing east, just large enough for a person to crawl through, which would be sealed immediately after a burial. Nowadays, nothing remains of the burials, but the chullpas are well preserved.

Sillustani

Sitting on rolling hills on the Lago Umayo peninsula, the funerary towers of **Sillustani** (admission S10) stand out for miles against a desolate altiplano landscape.

The walls of the towers are made from massive coursed blocks reminiscent of

Great For...

☑ Don't Miss

Lago Umayo (partially encircling Sillustani), home to a wide variety of plants and Andean water birds.

Puma detail, Cutimbo

STEPHEN COLLECTOR / GETTY IMAGES ©

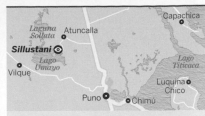

ⓘ Need to Know

Sillustani tours leave Puno at 2:30pm daily (from S30; taxi S80); Cutimbo tours cost from US$59.

★ Top Tip

A *turismo vivencia* (homestay) means you can help a host family with farming and visit lesser-known archaeological sites.

✕ Take a Break

Tours often include visiting local families and eating boiled potato dipped in *arcilla* (edible clay).

Inca stonework, but are considered to be even more complicated. Carved but unplaced blocks and a ramp used to raise them are among the site's points of interest, and you can also see the makeshift quarry. A few of the blocks are decorated, including a well-known carving of a lizard on one of the *chullpas* closest to the parking lot.

On a tour, the round-trip takes about 3½ hours and allows you about 1½ hours at the ruins. If you'd prefer more time at the site, hire a private taxi for S80 with one-hour waiting time. To save money, catch any bus to Juliaca and ask to be let off where the road splits (S3.50, 25 minutes). From there, occasional *combis* (S3, 20 minutes) go to the ruins.

Cutimbo

Just over 20km from Puno, the dramatic site of **Cutimbo** (admission S8) has an extraordinary position atop a table-topped volcanic hill surrounded by a fertile plain. Its modest number of well-preserved *chullpas,* built by the Colla, Lupaca and Inca cultures, come in both square and cylindrical shapes. You can still see the ramps used to build them. Look closely and you'll find several monkeys, pumas and snakes carved into the structures.

This remote place receives few visitors, which makes it both enticing and potentially dangerous for independent travelers, especially women. Go in a group and keep an eye out for muggers.

Combis en route to Laraqueri leave the cemetery by Parque Amista, 1km from the center of Puno (S3, one hour). You can't miss the signposted site, which is on the left-hand side of the road — just ask the driver where to get off. Otherwise, the pricier options from Puno are taking a taxi (about S30 return with a 30-minute wait) or a package tour.

Archway overlooking Lake Titicaca, Isla Taquile

NIVEK NESLO / GETTY IMAGES ©

Isla Taquile

In the strong island sunlight, the deep, red-colored soil of Taquile contrasts with the intense blue of the lake and the glistening backdrop of Bolivia's snowy Cordillera Real.

Inhabited for thousands of years, Isla Taquile is a tiny 7-sq-km island with a population of about 2200 people. Taquile's lovely scenery is reminiscent of the Mediterranean, with several hills that boast Inca terracing on their sides and small ruins on top.

Taquile's People

Quechua-speaking islanders are distinct from most of the surrounding Aymara-speaking island communities and maintain a strong sense of group identity. They rarely marry non-Taquile people.

Handicrafts

Taquile has a fascinating tradition of handicrafts, and the islanders' creations are made according to a system of deeply ingrained social customs. Men wear tightly woven woolen hats that resemble floppy

Great For...

☑ Don't Miss

Fiesta de San Diego – a celebration with dancing and music from July 25 until early August.

A woman spinning wool, Isla Taquile

❶ Need to Know

Ferries leave Puno's port for Taquile (35km east of Puno) from 6:45am.

✕ Take a Break

Restaurants all offer delicious *sopa de quinua* (quinoa soup) and lake trout; dishes from S20.

★ Top Tip

There are no roads or streetlights, so bring a flashlight for an overnight stay.

nightcaps, which they knit themselves – only men knit, learning from the age of eight. These hats are closely bound up with social symbolism: men wear red hats if they are married and red-and-white hats if they are single, and different colors can denote a man's current or past social position.

Taquile women weave thick, colorful waistbands for their husbands, which are worn with roughly spun white shirts and thick, calf-length black pants. Women wear eye-catching outfits comprising multi-layered skirts and delicately embroidered blouses. These fine garments are considered some of the most well-made traditional clothes in Peru, and can be bought in the cooperative store on the island's main plaza.

Visiting

Visitors are free to wander around, explore the ruins and enjoy the tranquility. The island is a lovely place to catch a sunset and gaze at the moon, which looks twice as bright in the crystalline air, rising over the breathtaking peaks of the Cordillera Real.

A stairway of more than 500 steps leads from the dock to the center of the island. The climb takes a breathless 20 minutes if you're acclimatized – more if you're not.

Make sure you already have lots of small bills in local currency, as change is limited and there's nowhere to exchange dollars. You may want to bring extra money to buy some of the exquisite crafts sold in the cooperative store.

The *hospedajes* (small, family-owned inns) on Taquile offer basic accommodations for around S20 a night. Meals are additional (S10 to S15 for breakfast, S20 for lunch or dinner). Options range from a room in a family house to small guesthouses. As the community rotates visitors to lodgings, there is little room for choosing.

Puno

With a regal plaza, concrete-block buildings and crumbling bricks that blend into the hills, Puno has its share of both grit and cheer. It serves as the jumping-off point for Lake Titicaca and is a convenient stop for those traveling between Cuzco and La Paz. But it may just capture your heart with its own rackety charm.

◉ SIGHTS

Catedral de Puno Church
(⊙8am-noon & 3-6pm) **FREE** Puno's baroque cathedral, on the western flank of the Plaza de Armas, was completed in 1757. The interior is more spartan than you'd expect from the well-sculpted facade, except for the silver-plated altar, which, following a 1964 visit by Pope Paul VI, has a Vatican flag to its right.

> *Puno may just capture your heart with its own rackety charm*

Catedral de Puno

Casa del Corregidor Historic Building
(☑051-35-1921; www.casadelcorregidor.pe; Deustua 576; ⊙9am-8pm Mon-Sat, 10am-7pm Sun) **FREE** An attraction in its own right, this 17th-century house is one of Puno's oldest residences. A former community center, it now houses a small fair-trade arts-and-crafts store and a cafe.

Museo Carlos Dreyer Museum
(Conde de Lemos 289; admission with English-speaking guide S15; ⊙9am-7pm Mon-Fri, to 1pm Sat) This museum houses a fascinating collection of Puno-related archaeological artifacts and art. Upstairs there are three mummies and a full-scale fiberglass *chullpa*.

It's around the corner from Casa del Corregidor.

Coca Museum Museum
(☑051-36-5087; Deza 301; admission S5; ⊙9am-1pm & 3-8pm) Tiny and quirky, this museum offers lots of interesting information – historical, medicinal, cultural – about the coca plant and its many uses. Presentation isn't that interesting, though: reams of text (in English only) are stuck to the wall and

GLOW IMAGES / GETTY IMAGES ©

interspersed with photographs and old Coca-Cola ads. The display of traditional costumes is what makes a visit worthwhile.

Though the relation between traditional dress and coca is unfathomable, the museum is a boon for making sense of the costumes worn in street parades.

Yavari   Historic Site
The oldest steamship on Lake Titicaca, the famed **Yavari** (☑051-36-9329; www. yavari.org; admission by donation; ☺8am-1pm & 3-5:30pm) has turned from British gunship to a museum and recommended bed and breakfast, with bunk-bed lodging and attentive service under the stewardship of its captain.

The *Yavari* is moored behind the Sonesta Posada Hotel del Inca, in what is probably the most tranquil spot in Puno, about 5km from the center. Its devoted crew happily gives guided tours and, with prior notice, enthusiasts may even be able to see the engine fired up.

⊕ TOURS

Edgar Adventures   Cultural Tour
(☑051-35-3444; www.edgaradventures.com; Lima 328) Longtime agency with positive community involvement.

All Ways Travel   Cultural Tour
(☑051-35-3979; www.titicacaperu.com; 2nd fl, Deustua 576) Offers both classic and 'non-tourist' tours.

Las Balsas Tours   Boat Tour
(☑051-36-4362; www.balsastours.com; Lima 419 No 213, 2nd fl) Offers classic tours on a daily basis.

Nayra Travel   Boat Tour
(☑051-36-4774; www.nayratravel.com; Lima 419 No 105) Local package-tour operator.

🛍 SHOPPING

Artesanías (handicrafts, from musical instruments and jewelry to scale models of reed islands), wool and alpaca sweaters,

Staying Healthy at Altitude

Ascend to nearly 4000m direct from the coast and you run a real risk of getting *soroche* (altitude sickness). Plan on spending some time in elevation stops such as Arequipa (2350m) or Cuzco (3326m) first to acclimatize, or take it very easy after arriving in Puno. Higher-end hotels (and even some buses) offer oxygen, but this is a temporary fix; your body still needs to acclimatize at its own pace.

High altitude makes for extreme weather conditions. Nights get especially cold, so check if your hotel provides heating. During the winter months of June to August (the tourist high season), temperatures can drop well below freezing. Meanwhile, days are very hot and sunburn is a common problem.

and other typical tourist goods are sold in every second shop in the town center and at the port entrance.

✖ EATING

La Casa del Corregidor   Cafe $
(drinks S4-9, snacks S8-21; 📶📩) La Casa del Corregidor is just off the plaza but feels like a world and era away. Vinyl records of Peru's yesteryear decorate the walls, while board games and clay teapots are ready to adorn the table. Try the good fresh infusions or alpaca BBQ sticks.

Loving Hut   Vegetarian $
(www.lovinghut.com; Choque Huanca 188; menú S12, mains S15-18; ☺9am-6pm Mon-Sat; 📩🐾) Filling vegetarian lunches with salad, gluten, soy-meat and brown-rice options in Asian and Peruvian styles. Try the quinoa burger or *anticuchos veganos* (vegan beef skewers). The warm unsweetened soy milk

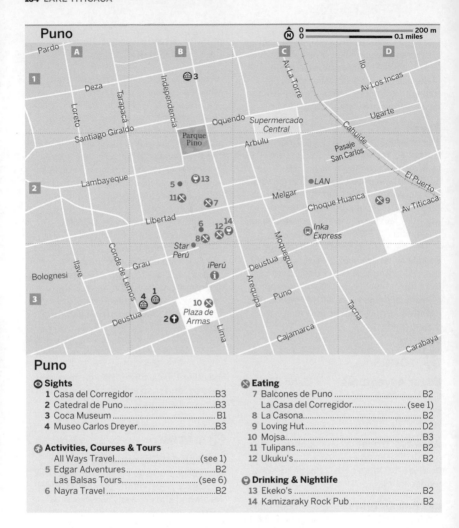

Puno

or *mate* (tea) on tap makes the *menú* (set meal) worth it alone.

Mojsa — Peruvian $$

(☏051-36-3182; Jr Lima 635; mains S22-30; ⊙noon-9.30pm) The go-to place for locals and travelers alike, Mojsa lives up to its name, Aymara for 'delicious.' It has a thoughtful range of Peruvian and international food, including innovative trout dish-es and a design-your-own-salad option. All meals start with fresh bread and a bowl of local olives. In the evening crisp brick-oven pizzas are on offer.

Balcones de Puno — Peruvian $$

(☏051-36-5300; Libertad 354; mains S15-35) Dinner-show venue with traditional local food. The nightly show (7:30pm to 9pm) stands out for its quality and sincerity – no

> *The courtyard patio is attractive for warm days*

panpipe butchering of 'El Cóndor Pasa' here. Save room for dessert, a major focus of dining here. Reserve ahead.

Tulipans   Pizzeria $$
(☏051-35-1796; Lima 394; mains S15-30; ⊙11am-10pm) Highly recommended for its yummy sandwiches, big plates of meat and piled-high vegetables, this cozy spot is warmed by the pizza oven in the corner. It also has a selection of South American wines. The courtyard patio is attractive for warm days – whenever those happen! Pizzas are only available at night. Tulipans is inside La Casona Parodi.

Ukuku's   Peruvian $$
(Grau 172, 2nd fl; mains S20-27, dinner menú S25; ⊙noon-10pm; 🎵🍴) Crowds of travelers and locals thaw out in this toasty restaurant, which dishes up good local and Andean food (try alpaca steak with baked apples, or the quinoa omelet), as well as pizza, pasta, Asian-style vegetarian fare and espresso drinks. The good-value dinner set menu includes a pisco.

La Casona   Peruvian $$
(☏051-35-1108; http://lacasona-restaurant.com; Lima 423, 2nd fl; mains S22-42) A solid choice for upscale *criollo* (spicy Peruvian fare with Spanish and African influences) and international food, even if portions are on the small side. Trout comes bathed in garlic or chili sauce. There's also pasta, salad and soup.

🍸 DRINKING & NIGHTLIFE

Ekeko's   Club
(Lima 355, 2nd fl; ⊙9pm-late) Travelers and locals alike gravitate to this tiny, ultra-violet dance floor above a restaurant, splashed with psychedelic murals. It moves to a thumping mixture of modern beats and old favorites, from salsa to techno trance, which can be heard several blocks away.

Kamizaraky Rock Pub   Pub
(Grau 158) With a classic-rock soundtrack, grungy cool bartenders and liquor-infused coffee drinks essential for staying warm during Puno's bone-chilling nights, it may be a hard place to leave.

ℹ️ INFORMATION

Puno's helpful and well-informed multi-lingual tourist office, **iPerú** (☏051-36-5088; Plaza de Armas, cnr Lima & Deustua; ⊙9am-6pm Mon-Sat, to 1pm Sun), also runs Indecopi, the tourist-protection agency, which registers complaints about travel agencies and hotels.

ℹ️ GETTING THERE & AWAY

AIR
The nearest airport is in Juliaca, about an hour away. Official airport taxis go to Puno (S80); hotels can book you a shuttle bus for around S15. Airlines with offices in Puno include **LAN** (☏051-36 7227; Tacna 299) and **Star Perú** (Jirón Lima 154).

BUS
The **terminal terrestre** (☏051-36-4737; Primero de Mayo 703), three blocks down Ricardo Palma from Av El Sol, houses Puno's long-distance bus companies.

Civa (☏051-365-882; www.civa.com.pe) Goes to Lima.

Cruz del Sur (☏in Lima 01-311-5050; www.cruzdelsur.com.pe) Has services to Arequipa.

Ormeño (☏051-36-8176; www.grupo-ormeno.com.pe; terminal terrestre) The safest company, with the newest, fastest buses.

Tour Perú (☏051-20-6088; www.tourperu.com.pe; Tacna 285) Goes to Cuzco and also crosses to La Paz, Bolivia, via Copacabana, daily at 7:30am.

The most enjoyable way to get to Cuzco is via **Inka Express** (☏051-36-5654; www.inkaexpress.com; Tacna 346); its luxury buses with panoramic

Fiestas & Folklore

The folkloric capital of Peru, Puno boasts as many as 300 traditional dances and celebrates numerous fiestas throughout the year. Although dances often occur during celebrations of Catholic feast days, many have their roots in pre-colonial celebrations usually tied in with the agricultural calendar. The dazzlingly ornate and imaginative costumes worn on these occasions are often worth more than an entire household's everyday clothes.

Accompanying music uses a host of instruments, from Spanish-influenced brass and string instruments to percussion and wind instruments that have changed little since Inca times. Keep an eye out for *flautas* (flutes): from simple bamboo pennywhistles called *quenas* to large blocks of hollowed out wood. The most esoteric is the *piruru,* which is traditionally carved from the wing bone of an Andean condor.

Seeing street fiestas can be planned, but it's often simply a matter of luck. Ask at the tourist office in Puno about any fiestas in the surrounding area while you're in town.

If you plan to visit during a festival, either make reservations in advance or show up a few days early, and expect to pay premium rates for lodgings.

Festival, Isla Taquile
ILLUIS VINAGRE - WORLD PHOTOGRAPHY / GETTY IMAGES ©

windows depart every morning at 8am. Buffet lunch is included, along with an English-speaking tour guide and oxygen. The trip takes about eight hours and costs S159.

TRAIN

The train ride from Puno to Cuzco retains a certain renown from the days – now long gone – when the road wasn't paved and the bus journey was a nightmare. The fancy Andean Explorer train, which includes a glass-walled observation car and complimentary lunch, costs US$289. This one's for train buffs, since it's only marginally more comfortable than the better buses, and the tracks run next to the road for much of the way, so the scenery, while wonderful, is comparable to a much cheaper bus ride.

Trains depart from Puno's **train station** (☑051-36-9179; www.perurail.com; Av La Torre 224; ⏱7am-noon & 3-6pm Mon-Fri, 7am-3pm Sat) at 8am, arriving at Cuzco around 6pm.

ⓘ GETTING AROUND

A short taxi ride anywhere in town (and as far as the transport terminals) costs S4.50.

Juliaca

The region's only commercial airport makes Juliaca, the largest city on the altiplano, an unavoidable transit hub. Daytime muggings and drunks on the street are not uncommon. Since Juliaca has little to offer travelers, it is advisable to visit nearby Lampa or move on to Puno.

If you are in a pinch, **Royal Inn Hotel** (☑051-32-1561; www.royalinnhoteles.com; San Román 158; s/d/tr incl breakfast S315/330/420) is an excellent upmarket choice. This towering hotel boasts recently revamped modern rooms with hot showers, heating and cable TV, plus one of Juliaca's best restaurants.

Hotels, restaurants, *casas de cambio* (foreign-exchange bureaus) and internet cafes abound along San Román, near Plaza Bolognesi. ATMs and banks are nearby on Nuñez.

Lampa

This charming little town, 36km northwest of Juliaca, is known as La Ciudad Rosada (the Pink City) for its dusty, pink-colored buildings. A significant commercial center in colonial days, it still shows a strong Spanish influence. It's an excellent place to kill a few hours before flying out of Juliaca, or to spend a quiet night.

◎ SIGHTS

Just out of town is a pretty colonial **bridge**, and about 4km west is **Cueva de los Toros**, a bull-shaped cave with prehistoric carvings of llamas and other animals. The cave is on the right-hand side of the road heading west. Its entrance is part of a large, distinctive rock formation. En route you'll see several *chullpas*, not unlike the ones at Sillustani and Cutimbo.

Iglesia de Santiago Apostol   Church

(Plaza de Armas; tour S10; ⊘9am-12:30pm & 2-4pm) Worth seeing and the pride of locals, this lime-mortar church includes fascinat-ing features such as a life-sized sculpture of the *Last Supper;* Santiago (St James) atop a real stuffed horse, returning from the dead to trample the Moors; creepy catacombs; secret tunnels; a domed tomb topped by a wonderful copy of Michelan-gelo's *Pietà*; and hundreds of skeletons arranged in a ghoulishly decorative, skull-and-crossbones pattern. It truly has to be seen to be believed. Excellent Spanish-speaking guides are on hand daily.

Lampa Municipalidad   Notable Building

(Lampa Town Hall; ⊘8am-6pm Mon-Fri) **FREE**
In the small square beside the church, the town hall is recognizable by its murals depicting Lampa's history – past, present and future. Inside there's a gorgeous court-yard, a replica of the *Pietà* and a museum honoring noted Lampa-born painter Víctor Humareda (1920–86).

Museo Kampac   Museum

(☑95-182-0085; cnr Ugarte & Ayacucho; suggested donation S5; ⊘8am-6pm Mon-Fri) Staff at the shop opposite this museum,

Pucará (p138)

two blocks west of the Plaza de Armas, will give you a Spanish-language guided tour of the museum's small but significant collection. It includes pre-Inca ceramics and monoliths, plus one mummy. They may also show you a unique vase inscribed with the sacred cosmology of the Incas.

❶ GETTING THERE & AWAY

If you have time to kill after checking in at Juliaca airport, get a taxi to drop you off in Lampa (S5).

Pucará

More than 60km northwest of Juliaca, the sleepy village of Pucará is famous for its celebrations of **La Virgen del Carmen** on July 16 and its earth-colored pottery – including the ceramic *toritos* (bulls) often seen perched on the roofs of Andean houses for good luck. Several local workshops are open to the public and offer classes where you can make your own ceramics.

◉ SIGHTS

Museo Lítico Pucará Museum
(Jirón Lima; admission S10; ⊙8:30am-5pm Tue-Sun) The Museo Lítico Pucará displays a surprisingly good selection of anthropomorphic monoliths from the town's pre-Inca site, **Kalasaya**. The ruins themselves sit above the town, a short way up Jirón Lima away from the main plaza. Just S10 gets you into both sites, though there's nobody to check your ticket at the ruin.

❸ COURSES

Maki Pucará Course
(📞951-79-0618) You can make your own earth-colored pottery – including ceramic toritos. The reader-recommended Maki Pucará is on the highway near the bus stop.

❶ GETTING THERE & AWAY

Buses to Juliaca (S3.50, one hour) run from 6am to 8pm from Jr 2 de Mayo.

From left: Isla Taquile (p130); Women sailing on reed boat; prow of a reed boat, Islas Uros (p126); Templo de la Fertilidad, Chucuito

South Shore Towns

These bucolic villages, noted for their colonial churches and beautiful views, offer a relatively untouristed peek at the region's traditional culture. If you can coordinate the transportation connections, you can visit a few south-shore villages in a day trip from Puno or continue along the road to Bolivia.

ℹ️ GETTING THERE & AWAY

For public transport to any south-shore town, go to Puno's *terminal zonál*. *Combis* leave when full. Direct transport to the towns closer to Puno is more frequent, but *combis* to most towns leave at least hourly – more often for closer destinations.

Colectivos for Pomata (S8, 1½ hours) are marked with signs for Yunguyo or Desaguadero.

For Luquina Chico (S4.50, 1½ hours) you can also take the ferry to or from Taquile and ask the driver to drop you off.

Ichu

Ten kilometers out of Puno, this rural community, spread across a gorgeous green valley, is home to a little-known ruin

with superb views. It's a great place for a hike.

Leave the Panamericana at Ichu's second exit (after the service station) and head inland past the house marked 'Villa Lago 1960.' Walk 2km, bearing left at the junction, aiming for the two small, terraced hills you can see in the left of the valley. After bearing left at a second junction (you'll pass the school if you miss it), the road takes you between the two hills. Turn left again and head straight up the first one. Fifteen minutes of stiff climbing brings you to the top, where you'll be rewarded with the remains of a multilayered temple complex, and breathtaking 360-degree views.

This can be done as an easy half-day trip from Puno. Take plenty of water and food as there's no store.

Chucuito

Quiet Chucuito's principal attraction is the outlandish **Templo de la Fertilidad** (Inca Uyu; admission S5; ☉8am-5pm). Its dusty grounds are scattered with large stone phalluses, some up to 1.2m in length. Local guides tell various entertaining stories

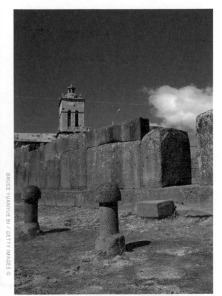

about the carvings, including tales of maidens sitting atop the stony joysticks to increase their fertility. Further uphill from the main road is the main plaza, which has two attractive colonial churches, **Santo Domingo** and **Nuestra Señora de la Asunción**.

You'll have to track down the elusive caretakers to get a glimpse inside.

Luquina Chico

This tiny community, 53km east of Puno on the Chucuito peninsula, is stunning. If you want to relax in a rural community, Luquina Chico also boasts the best standard of homestay accommodations of any community around the lake. The community is making economic strides thanks to tourism.

Sweeping views of Puno, Juliaca and all the islands of the lake can be taken in from the headland's heights or the fertile flats by the lake. In the wet season, a lagoon forms, which attracts migrating wetland birds.

Chullpitas (miniature burial towers) are scattered all around this part of the peninsula. They are said to house the bodies of *gentiles*, little people who lived here in ancient times, before the sun was born and sent them underground.

Homestays (from S20) offer full board (S70). Ask around about renting kayaks. Edgar Adventures (p133) can also get you here on a mountain bike, a somewhat grueling but extremely scenic ride along the peninsula.

Juli

Past Chucuito and the turnoff for Luquino Chico, the road curves southeast away from the lake and through the commercial center of **Ilave**, best known for its livestock market and a lively sense of community justice, manifested most famously with the lynching of the town mayor in 2004. Ilave is best avoided in times of civil strife. Sleepy, friendly Juli is a more tourist-friendly stop. It's called Peru's *pequeña Roma* (little Rome) on account of its four colonial churches from the 16th and 17th centuries, which are slowly being restored. Churches are most likely to be open on Sundays, though opening hours here should not be taken as gospel. It's worth hammering on the door if one seems closed.

Sunday is also the day of Juli's market, the region's largest. Wednesday is a secondary market day.

Dating from 1570, the adobe baroque church of **San Juan de Letrán** (admission S8; ☉8:30am-5pm Tue-Sun) contains richly framed *escuela cuzqueña* (Cuzco school) paintings that depict the lives of saints.

The imposing 1557 church of **Nuestra Señora de la Asunción** (admission S8; ☉8:30am-5pm Tue-Sun) has an expansive courtyard approach and an airy interior. The pulpit is covered in gold leaf.

Other churches nearby include **Santa Cruz**, which has lost half its roof and remains closed for the foreseeable future. The 1560 stone church of **San Pedro**, on the main plaza, is in the best condition, with carved ceilings and a marble baptismal font.

Pomata

Beyond Juli, the road continues southeast to Pomata, 105km from Puno. Just out of Pomata, the road forks. The main road continues southeast through Zepita to the unsavory border town of Desaguadero. The left fork hugs the shore of Lake Titicaca and leads to another, more pleasant border crossing at **Yunguyo**. If you're going this way, consider stopping off at the **Mirador Natural de Asiru Patjata** lookout, a few kilometers from Yunguyo. Here, a 5000m-long rock formation resembles a *culebra* (snake), whose head is a viewpoint looking over to Isla del Sol. The area around Pomata is known for its isolated villages and shamans.

The **Templo de Pomata Santiago Apóstolo** (admission S2) is totally out of proportion with the town, in terms of both size and splendor – dramatically located on top of a small hill. Founded in 1700, it is known for its windows made of translucent alabaster and its intricately carved baroque sandstone facade.

★ **Don't Miss**

In Pomata, look for the the puma carvings at Templo de Pomata Santiago Apóstolo; the town's name means 'Place of the Puma' in Aymara.

Clockwise from top: Juli; Archway, Isla Taquile (p130); Ceramic *toritos* (bulls)

Plaza de Armas (p156)

CUZCO

Cuzco at a Glance...

Cosmopolitan Inca capital, Cuzco (also Cusco, or Qosq'o in Quechua) today thrives with a measure of contradiction. Ornate cathedrals squat over Inca temples, massage hawkers ply the narrow cobblestone streets, a woman in traditional skirt and bowler offers bottled water to a pet llama, while the finest boutiques sell alpaca knits for small fortunes.

The city is now the undisputed archaeological capital of the Americas, as well as the continent's oldest continuously inhabited city. Few travelers to Peru will skip visiting this premier South American destination, also the gateway to Machu Picchu.

Cuzco in Two Days

Visit the city's many museums. **Museo Quijote** (p162) and the **Museo Histórico Regional** (p162) are highly recommended for fine art; **El Museo de Arte Popular** (p163) for folksy art; and the **Museo Inka** (p161) for pre-conquest Peruvian artifacts. On the second day, see relics left by the Incas and Spanish conquistadors at **Qorikancha** (p150) and **La Catedral** (p157).

Cuzco in Four Days

Start day three with a *jugo* (fruit juice) in **Mercado San Pedro** (p169). Then follow the **walking tour** (p154) up through arty San Blas to the impressive fortress of **Sacsaywamán** (p152). Day four can be spent on one of the many nearby hikes, or by popping back to San Blas to visit the **artisan workshops** (p169) and picking up some local textiles.

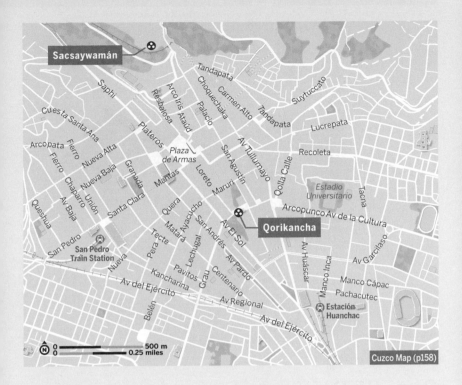

Arriving in Cuzco

Aeropuerto Internacional Alejandro Velazco Astete Official taxis from the airport to addresses near the city center cost S20 to S25. Plans are pending to build an airport in the Sacred Valley near Chinchero.

Terminal terrestre The bus terminal lies about 2km out of town toward the airport; a taxi is about S14.

Where to Stay

While restored colonial buildings with interior courtyards are charming, they can also echo resoundingly with noise from other guests or the street outside.

For more on where to stay, see p179.

Anticuchos (beef-heart skewers)

Cuzco's Cuisine

Cuzco's location, nearly dropping off the eastern edge of the Andes, gives it access to an unbelievable range of crops, from highland potatoes and quinoa to avocados and ají picante *(hot chili).*

Most popular local restaurants are outside the historic center and focus on lunch; few open for dinner. Don't expect to encounter any language other than Spanish in these places, but the food is worth the effort.

Cuzco Specialties

Steaming soups, fresh-grilled meats and an ice-cold *chela* (that's Peruvian slang for beer).

Look for the following foods in local restaurants, on the street and at festivals:

Anticucho Beef heart on a stick, punctuated by a potato, is the perfect evening street snack.

Caldo de gallina Healthy, hearty chicken soup is the local favorite to kick a hangover.

Great For...

☑ Don't Miss

Sampling *cuy* (guinea pig) – its rich flavors are a cross between rabbit and quail, and when correctly prepared it makes an exceptional feast.

Cuy

BY ELIKOVA, OKSANA / GETTY IMAGES ©

❶ Need to Know

Often not advertised, a lunchtime *menú* (set meal) includes soup, a main course, drink, and sometimes dessert.

✕ Take a Break

Pampa de Castillo, a street near Qori-kancha, is where local workers lunch on Cuzco classics.

★ Did You Know

In many indigenous interpretations of *The Last Supper,* Jesus and his disciples are eating a hearty feast of *cuy* (guinea pig).

Chicharrón Definitely more than the sum of its parts: deep-fried pork served with corn, mint leaves, fried potato and onion.

Choclo con queso Huge, pale cobs of corn served with a teeth-squeaking chunk of cheese in the Sacred Valley.

Cuy Guinea pig, raised on grains at home; the faint of heart can ask for it served as a filet (without the head and paws).

Lechón Suckling pig with plenty of crackling, served with tamales (corn cakes).

The Guinea Pig's Culinary Rise

Love it or loathe it, *cuy* is an Andean favorite that's been part of the local culinary repertoire since pre-Inca times. And before you dredge up childhood memories of cuddly mascots in protest, know that these rascally rodents were gracing Andean dinner plates long before anyone in the West considered them worthy pet material.

It's believed that *cuy* may have been domesticated as early as 7000 years ago in the mountains of southern Peru, where wild populations of *cuy* still roam today. Direct evidence from Chavín de Huántar shows that they were certainly cultivated across the Andes by 900 BC.

Cuy are practical animals to raise and have adapted well over the centuries to survive in environments ranging from the high Andean plains to the barren coastal deserts. You'll often see them scampering around Andean kitchens in true free-range style. *Cuy* are the ideal livestock alternative: they're high in protein, feed on kitchen scraps, breed profusely and require much less room and maintenance than traditional domesticated animals.

Inti Raymi

HUGHES HERVÁ© / GETTY IMAGES ©

Festivals & Events

Cuzco and the surrounding highlands celebrate many lively fiestas and holidays.

Great For...

☑ **Don't Miss**

Inti Raymi, the drawcard festival of Cuzco.

El Señor de los Temblores

Meaning 'the Lord of the Earthquakes,' this procession on the Monday before Easter dates to the earthquake of 1650.

Crucifix Vigil

On May 2 to 3, a Crucifix Vigil is held on all hillsides with crosses atop them.

Corpus Christi

Held on the ninth Thursday after Easter, Corpus Christi usually occurs in early June and features fantastic religious processions and celebrations in the cathedral.

Corpus Christi statues

GCOLES / GETTY IMAGES ©

pakarina (mythical place of sacred origin) of llamas and alpacas, and controls their health and fertility.

Q'oyoriti is a pilgrimage – the only way in is by trekking three or more hours up a cold mountain, arriving around dawn. The sight of a solid, endless line of people quietly wending their way up or down the track and disappearing around a bend in the mountain is unforgettable, as is Q'oyoriti's eerie, otherworldly feel.

Many *cuzqueños* (inhabitants of Cuzco) believe that if you attend Q'oyoriti three times, you'll get your heart's desire.

The Q'oyoriti Pilgrimage

Incredibly elaborate costumes, days of dancing, repetitive brass-band music, fireworks and sprinklings of holy water: welcome to one of Peru's less well-known, but most intense, festivals, Q'oyoriti (Star of the Snow).

Held at the foot of Ausangate the Tuesday before Corpus Christi, in late May or early June, this is a dizzy, delirious spectacle, yet no alcohol is involved or even allowed. Offenders are whipped by anonymous men dressed as *ukukus* (mountain spirits) with white masks that hide their features.

At 6384m, **Ausangate** is the Cuzco department's highest mountain and the most important *apu* (sacred deity) in the area. The subject of countless legends, it's the

Inti Raymi

Cuzco's most important festival, the 'Festival of the Sun' is held on June 24. It attracts tourists from all over Peru and the world, and the whole city celebrates in the streets. The festival culminates in a reenactment of the Inca winter-solstice festival at Sacsaywamán. Despite its commercialization, it's still worth seeing the street dances and parades, as well as the pageantry at Sacsaywamán.

Santuranticuy Artisan Crafts Fair

A crafts fair is held in Plaza de Armas on December 24 (Christmas Eve).

Qorikancha

If you visit only one site in Cuzco, make it these Inca ruins. Qorikancha was once the richest temple in the Inca empire; all that remains today is the masterful stonework.

Great For...

☑ Don't Miss

Paintings outside the courtyard depicting God's guard dogs (*dominicanus* in Latin) holding torches.

The temple was built in the mid-15th century during the reign of the 10th *inca* (king), Túpac Yupanqui. Today it belongs to the Dominicans and forms the base of the colonial church and convent of Santo Domingo. Its site is a bizarre combination of Inca and colonial architecture, topped with a roof of glass and metal.

In Inca times, Qorikancha (Quechua for 'Golden Courtyard') was literally covered with gold. The temple walls were lined with some 700 solid-gold sheets, each weighing about 2kg. There were life-sized gold and silver replicas of corn, which were ceremonially 'planted' in agricultural rituals. Also reported were solid-gold treasures such as altars, llamas and babies, as well as a replica of the sun,

Plaza de Armas · Ruinas · Recoleta · Av Tullumayo · Qolla Calle · Loreto · AV El Sol · Maruri · Plazoleta Santo Domingo · Arcopunco · Quera · San Andrés · San Andrés · ⊕ **Qorikancha** · Jardín Sagrado

ⓘ Need to Know

Plazoleta Santo Domingo; admission S10; ⊗8:30am-5:30pm Mon-Sat, 2-5pm Sun

✕ Take a Break

Head to Pampa de Castillo near Qorikancha, where local workers lunch on Cuzco classics.

★ Did You Know

The curved, perfectly fitted 6m-high wall (seen inside and outside) has withstood all the violent earthquakes that leveled Cuzco's colonial buildings.

ALESSANDRO_PINTO / GETTY IMAGES ©

which was lost. But within months of the arrival of the first conquistadors, this incredible wealth had all been looted and melted down.

Rituals

Various religious rites took place in the temple. It is said that the mummified bodies of several previous *incas* were kept here, brought out into the sunlight each day and offered food and drink, which was then ritually burnt. Qorikancha was also an observatory where high priests monitored celestial activities. Most of this is left to the imagination of the modern visitor, but the remaining stonework ranks with the finest Inca architecture in Peru.

Architecture

Once inside the site, the visitor enters a courtyard. The octagonal font in the middle was originally covered with 55kg of solid gold. Inca chambers lie to either side of the courtyard. The largest, to the right, were said to be temples to the moon and the stars, and were covered with sheets of solid silver. The walls are perfectly tapered upward and, with their niches and doorways, are excellent examples of Inca trapezoidal architecture. The fitting of the individual blocks is so precise that in some places you can't tell where one block ends and the next begins.

Opposite these chambers, on the other side of the courtyard, are smaller temples dedicated to thunder and the rainbow. Three holes have been carved through the walls of this section to the street outside, which scholars think were drains, either for sacrificial *chicha* (fermented corn beer), blood or, more mundanely, rainwater.

FRANS LEMMENS / ALAMY STOCK PHOTO ©

Sacsaywamán

This immense ruin of both religious and military significance is 2km from Cuzco. The long Quechua name means 'Satisfied Falcon,' though tourists will inevitably remember it by the mnemonic 'sexy woman.'

Sacsaywamán feels huge, but only about 20% of the original structure remains. Soon after the conquest, the Spaniards tore down many walls and used the blocks to build their own houses, leaving the largest and most impressive rocks, especially the main battlements.

Rebel Base

In 1536 the fort was the site of one of the most bitter battles of the Spanish conquest. More than two years after Pizarro's entry into Cuzco, the rebellious Manco Inca recaptured the lightly guarded Sacsaywamán and used it as a base to lay siege to the conquistadors in Cuzco. Manco was on the brink of defeating the Spaniards when a desperate last-ditch attack by 50 Spanish cavalry led by Juan Pizarro, Francisco's

Great For...

☑ **Don't Miss**

Arriving at dawn (though not alone, for safety) to have the site almost to yourself.

VOLANTHEVIST / GETTY IMAGES ©

Sacsaywamán

Tandapata
Saphi
Coricalle
Tecsecocha
Ese
Ataúd
Choquechaka
Palacio
Angelitos
Plazoleta
Meloc
Plaza
de Armas
Recoleta

ℹ Need to Know

The *boleto turístico* (tourist card; adult/
student under 26 with ISIC card S130/70)
used for entry is valid for 10 days and
covers 16 other sites.

✕ Take a Break

Bring snacks and water.

★ Top Tip

Take a taxi tour (S70) to Sacsaywamán that also includes the ancient
Q'enko, Pukapukara and Tambom-
achay sites.

these 22 zigzagged walls as the teeth of the
puma. The walls also formed an extremely
effective defensive mechanism that forced
attackers to expose their flanks.

brother, succeeded in retaking Sacsaywamán and putting an end to the rebellion.
Manco Inca survived and retreated to the
fortress of Ollantaytambo, but most of
his forces were killed. Thousands of dead
littered the site after the Incas' defeat, at-
tracting swarms of carrion-eating Andean
condors. The tragedy was memorialized by
the inclusion of eight condors in Cuzco's
coat of arms.

Zigzag Fortifications

The site is composed of three different
areas, the most striking being the magnificent three-tiered zigzag fortifications. One
stone, incredibly, weighs more than 300
tons. It was the ninth *inca,* Pachacutec,
who envisioned Cuzco in the shape of a
puma, with Sacsaywamán as the head, and

Five Thousand Warriors

Opposite is the hill called **Rodadero**, with
retaining walls, polished rocks and a finely
carved series of stone benches known
as the **Inca's Throne**. Three towers once
stood above these walls. Only the foundations remain, but the 22m diameter of the
largest, Muyuc Marca, gives an indication
of how big they must have been. With its
perfectly fitted stone conduits, this tower
was probably used as a huge water tank
for the garrison. Other buildings within the
ramparts provided food and shelter for an
estimated 5000 warriors. Most of these
structures were torn down by the Spaniards and later inhabitants of Cuzco.

Central Cuzco Walking Tour

At every turn, Cuzco's architecture exhibits the collision of the city's Inca and colonial past. There are refreshments everywhere, and small supermarkets near Plaza de Armas.

Start Plaza de Armas
Distance 4km
Duration 3 hours

2 As you pass through **Plaza Regocijo**, there is a beautiful building on your left, once a hotel that now houses restaurants and chic boutiques.

3 Calle Garcilaso is named for the Inca chronicler Garcilaso de la Vega, whose childhood home now houses the **Museo Histórico Regional** (p162).

4 On Sundays, Quechua-speaking country folk meet in **Plaza San Francisco**. Drop in to the **Iglesia San Francisco** (p162) and its **museum**.

5 If it's open, peek inside the **church and convent of Santa Clara**. The mirrors were used in colonial times to entice curious indigenous people into the church.

Take a Break... Mercado San Pedro (p169) Order a juice from one of the many stalls.

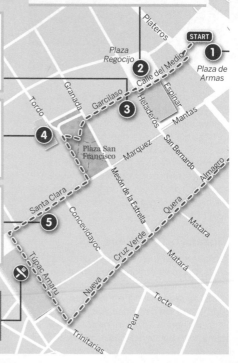

10 Last, forge uphill to **Sacsaywamán** (p152).

Classic Photo of Plaza San Blas

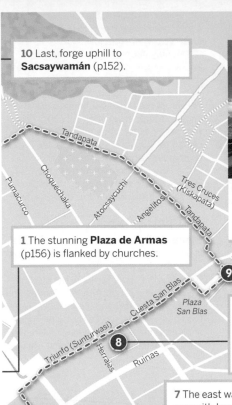

9 From **Plaza San Blas**, Cuzco's bohemian HQ, head along **Tandapata** for the classic cobblestone experience.

1 The stunning **Plaza de Armas** (p156) is flanked by churches.

8 The **Museo de Arte Religioso** (p161) is housed in the former palace of the sixth *inca* (king), Roca. Its wall on Hatunrumiyoc, is home to the **12-sided stone**.

7 The east wall of **Loreto**, a walkway with Inca walls on both sides, is one of the best and oldest in Cuzco, belonging to the Acllahuasi (House of the Chosen Women). Post conquest, it became part of the **Iglesia y Monasterio de Santa Catalina** (p162).

6 The **Palacio de Justicia** is a big white building where llamas mow the back garden.

N
0 ____ 200 m
0 ____ 0.1 miles

⊙ SIGHTS

While the city is sprawling, areas of interest to visitors are generally within walking distance, with some steep hills in between.

The alley heading away from the northwest side of Plaza de Armas is Procuradores (Tax Collectors), nicknamed 'Gringo Alley' for its tourist restaurants, tour agents and other services. Watch out for predatory touts. Beside the hulking cathedral on Plaza de Armas, narrow Calle Triunfo leads steeply uphill toward Plaza San Blas, the heart of Cuzco's eclectic, artistic *barrio* (neighborhood).

A resurgence of indigenous pride means many streets have been signposted with new Quechua names, although they are still commonly referred to by their Spanish names. The most prominent example is Calle Triunfo, which is signposted as Sunturwasi.

At tourist sites, freelance guides speak some English or other foreign languages. For more extensive tours at major sites, such as Qorikancha or the cathedral, always agree to a fair price in advance.

Otherwise, a respectable minimum tip for a short tour is S5 per person in a small group, and a little more for individuals.

Opening hours are erratic and can change for any reason – from Catholic feast days to the caretaker slipping off for a beer with his mates. A good time to visit Cuzco's well-preserved colonial churches is in the early morning (from 6am to 8am), when they are open for Mass. Officially, they are closed to tourists at these times, but if you go in quietly and respectfully as a member of the congregation, you can see the church as it should be seen. Flash photography is not allowed inside churches or museums.

⊙ Central Cuzco

Plaza de Armas   Plaza

In Inca times, the plaza, called Huacaypata or Aucaypata, was the heart of the capital. Today it's the nerve center of the modern city. Two flags usually fly here – the red-and-white Peruvian flag and the rainbow-colored flag of Tahuantinsuyo. Easily mistaken for an international gay-pride banner, it represents the four quarters of the Inca empire.

Plaza de Armas

Colonial arcades surround the plaza, which in ancient times was twice as large, also encompassing the area now called the Plaza Regocijo. On the plaza's northeastern side is the imposing cathedral, fronted by a large flight of stairs and flanked by the churches of Jesús María and El Triunfo. On the southeastern side is the strikingly ornate church of La Compañía de Jesús. The quiet pedestrian alleyway of Loreto, which has Inca walls, is a historic means of access to the plaza.

It's worth visiting the plaza at least twice – by day and by night – as it takes on a strikingly different look after dark, all lit up.

La Catedral
Church

(Plaza de Armas; admission S25; ⏱10am-5:45pm)
A squatter on the site of Viracocha Inca's palace, the cathedral was built using blocks pilfered from the nearby Inca site of Sacsaywamán. Its construction started in 1559 and took almost a century. It is joined by **Iglesia del Triunfo** (1536) to its right and **Iglesia de Jesús María** (1733) to the left.

El Triunfo, Cuzco's oldest church, houses a vault containing the remains of the famous Inca chronicler Garcilaso de la Vega, who was born in Cuzco in 1539 and died in Córdoba, Spain, in 1616. His remains were returned in 1978 by King Juan Carlos of Spain.

The cathedral is one of the city's greatest repositories of colonial art, especially for works from the *escuela cuzqueña* (Cuzco school), noted for its decorative combination of 17th-century European devotional painting styles with the color palette and iconography of indigenous Andean artists. A classic example is the frequent portrayal of the Virgin Mary wearing a mountain-shaped skirt with a river running around its hem, identifying her with Pachamama (Mother Earth).

One of the most famous paintings of the *escuela cuzqueña* is *The Last Supper* by Quechua artist Marcos Zapata. Found in the northeast corner of the cathedral, it depicts one of the most solemn occasions in the Christian faith, but graces it with a small feast of Andean ceremonial food;

🔭 Stargazing with the Ancients

The Incas were the only culture in the world to define constellations of darkness as well as light. Astronomy wasn't taken lightly: some of Cuzco's main streets are designed to align with the stars at certain times of the year. Understanding their interest is a nifty way to learn more about the Inca worldview.

Pencil in a visit to the **Cuzco Planetarium** (📞974-782-692; www.planetarium cusco.com; Carretera Sacsayhuamán, Km 2; per person with transport S50) before you head out trekking and watching the night sky on your own – think of how clever you'll feel pointing out the Black Llama to your fellow hikers. Reservations are essential, and the price includes transfer from Plaza Regocijo.

Andean night-sky
POPO / A.COLLECTIONRF / GETTY IMAGES ©

look for the plump and juicy-looking roast *cuy* stealing the show with its feet held plaintively in the air.

Also look for the oldest-surviving painting in Cuzco, showing the entire city during the great earthquake of 1650. The inhabitants can be seen parading around the plaza with a crucifix, praying for the earthquake to stop, which it miraculously did. This precious crucifix, called **El Señor de los Temblores** (The Lord of the Earthquakes), can still be seen in the alcove to the right of the door leading into El Triunfo. Every year on Holy Monday, the Señor is taken out on parade and devotees throw

Cuzco

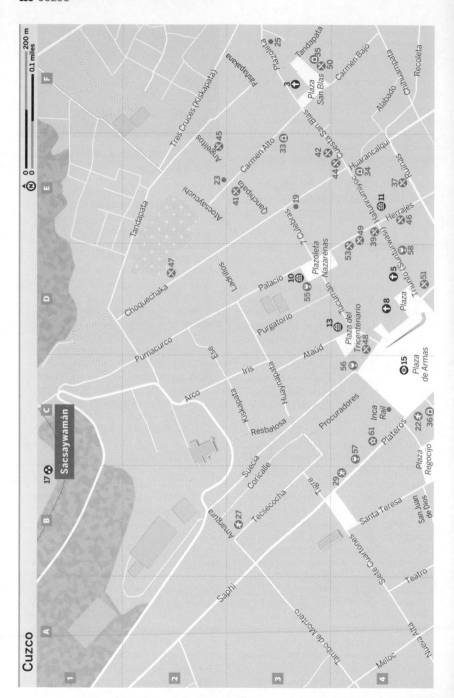

0 200 m
0 0.1 miles

A **B** **C** **D** **E** **F**

1 **2** **3** **4**

Sacsaywamán

17

47

25
Plazoleta
Tandapata
35
50
Plaza
San Blas
3
Carmen Bajo
Recoleta
Alabado
Chihuampata
Tres Cruces (Kiskapata)
Pantipatana
Tandapata
Angelitos
45
Carmen Alto
33
42
Cuesta San Blas
Huarancalqui
34
Ruinas
37
23
Qanchipata
Atocsaycuchi
41
19
Hatunrumiyoc
11
Herrajes
46
7 Culebras
Choquechaka
Plazoleta
Nazarenas
53
49
39
Triunfo (Sunturwasi)
58
Ladrillos
Palacio
10
55
Tucumán
5
51
Purgatorio
13
Plaza del
Tricentenario
48
8
Plaza
Pumacurco
Ese
Ataúd
56
15
Plaza
de Armas
Iris
Hatunhuaylla
Arco
Kiskapata
Procuradores
61
Inca
Rail
22
36
Resbalosa
57
Plateros
Suecia
Coricalle
Tigre
29
Plaza
Regocijo
27
Amargura
Tecsecocha
Santa Teresa
San Juan
de Dios
Saphi
Siete Cuartones
Teatro
Tambo de Montero
Nueva Alta
Meloc

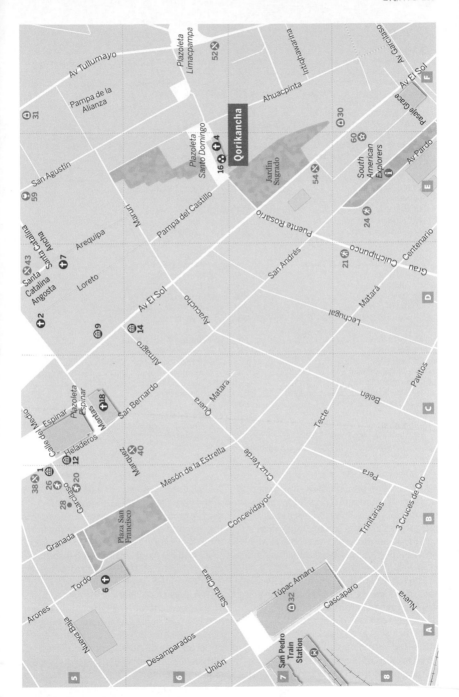

Cuzco

ñucchu flowers at him – these resemble droplets of blood and represent the wounds of crucifixion. The flowers leave a sticky residue that collects smoke from votive candles lit beneath the statue: this is why he's now black. Legend has it that under his skirt, he's lily white.

The sacristy of the cathedral is covered with paintings of Cuzco's bishops, starting with Vicente de Valverde, the friar who accompanied Pizarro during the conquest. The crucifixion at the back of the sacristy is attributed to the Flemish painter Anthony van Dyck, though some guides claim it to be the work of the 17th-century Spaniard

Alonso Cano. The original wooden altar is at the very back of the cathedral, behind the present silver altar, and opposite both is the magnificently carved choir, dating from the 17th century. There are also many glitzy silver and gold side chapels with elaborate platforms and altars that contrast with the austerity of the cathedral's stonework.

The huge main doors of the cathedral are open to genuine worshippers between 6am and 10am. Religious festivals are a superb time to see the cathedral. During the feast of Corpus Christi, for example, it is filled with pedestals supporting larger-than-life statues of saints, surrounded by thousands of candles and bands of musicians honoring them with mournful Andean tunes.

Iglesia de La Compañía de Jesús   Church

(Plaza de Armas; admission S15; ⊙9-11:30am & 1-5:30pm) Built upon the palace of Huayna Cápac, the last Inca to rule an undivided, unconquered empire, the church was built by the Jesuits in 1571 and reconstructed after the 1650 earthquake. Two large canvases near the main door show early marriages in Cuzco in wonderful period detail. Local student guides are available to show you around the church, as well as the grand view from the choir on the 2nd floor, reached via rickety steps. Tips are gratefully accepted.

The Jesuits planned to make it the most magnificent of Cuzco's churches. The archbishop of Cuzco, however, complained that its splendor should not rival that of the cathedral, and the squabble grew to a point where Pope Paul III was called upon to arbitrate. His decision was in favor of the cathedral, but by the time word had reached Cuzco, La Compañía de Jesús was just about finished, complete with an incredible baroque facade and Peru's biggest altar, all crowned by a soaring dome.

Museo Inka   Museum

(☏084-23-7380; Tucumán near Ataúd; admission S10; ⊙8am-6pm Mon-Fri, 9am-4pm Sat) The charmingly modest Museo Inka, a steep block northeast of the Plaza de Armas, is the best museum in town for those interested in the Incas. The restored interior is jam packed with a fine collection of metalwork and gold, jewelry, pottery, textiles, mummies, models and the world's largest collection of *queros* (ceremonial Inca wooden drinking vessels). There's excellent interpretive information in Spanish, and English-speaking guides are usually available for a small fee.

The museum building, which rests on Inca foundations, is also known as the Admiral's House, after the first owner, Admiral Francisco Aldrete Maldonado. It was badly damaged in the 1650 earthquake and rebuilt by Pedro Peralta de los Ríos, the count

of Laguna, whose crest is above the porch. Further damage from the 1950 earthquake has now been fully repaired, restoring the building to its position among Cuzco's finest colonial houses. Look for the massive stairway guarded by sculptures of mythical creatures, and the corner window column that from the inside looks like a statue of a bearded man but from the outside appears to be a naked woman. The ceilings are ornate, and the windows give good views straight out across the Plaza de Armas.

Downstairs in the sunny courtyard, highland Andean weavers demonstrate their craft and sell traditional textiles directly to the public.

Museo de Arte Religioso   Museum

(cnr Hatunrumiyoc & Herrajes; admission S10; ⊙8-11am & 3-6pm Mon-Sat) Originally the palace of Inca Roca, the foundations of this museum were converted into a grand colonial residence and later became the archbishop's palace. The beautiful mansion is now home to a religious-art collection notable for the accuracy of its period detail, and especially its insight into the interaction of indigenous peoples with the Spanish conquistadors.

There are also some impressive ceilings and colonial-style tile work that's not original, having been replaced during the 1940s.

Templo y Convento de La Merced   Church

(☏084-23-1821; Mantas 121; admission S10; ⊙8am-noon & 2-5pm Mon-Sat, cloister 8-11am) Cuzco's third-most-important colonial church, La Merced was destroyed in the 1650 earthquake, but was quickly rebuilt. To the left of the church, at the back of a small courtyard, is the entrance to the monastery and museum. Paintings based on the life of San Pedro Nolasco, who founded the order of La Merced in Barcelona in 1218, hang on the walls of the beautiful colonial cloister.

The chapel on the far side of the cloister contains the tombs of two of the most famous conquistadors: Diego de Almagro and Gonzalo Pizarro (brother of Francisco). Also on the far side of the cloister is a small religious museum that houses vestments rumored to have belonged to conquistador and friar Vicente de Valverde. The museum's most famous possession is a priceless solid-gold monstrance, 1.2m high and covered with rubies, emeralds and no fewer than 1500 diamonds and 600 pearls. Ask to see it if the display room is locked.

Iglesia San Francisco   Church
(Plaza San Francisco; museum admission S5; ⊙6:30-8am & 5:30-8pm Mon-Sat, 6:30am-noon & 6:30-8pm Sun, museum 9am-noon & 3-5pm Mon-Fri, 9am-noon Sat) More austere than many of Cuzco's other churches, Iglesia San Francisco dates from the 16th and 17th centuries and is one of the few that didn't need to be completely reconstructed after the 1650 earthquake. It has a large collection of colonial religious paintings and a beautifully carved cedar choir.

The attached **museum** houses supposedly the largest painting in South America, which measures 9m by 12m and shows the family tree of St Francis of Assisi, the founder of the order. Also of macabre interest are the two crypts, which are not totally underground. Inside are human bones, some of which have been carefully arranged in designs meant to remind visitors of the transitory nature of life.

Iglesia y Monasterio de Santa Catalina   Church
(Arequipa s/n; admission S8; ⊙8:30am-5:30pm Mon-Sat) This convent houses many colonial paintings of the *escuela cuzqueña*, as well as an impressive collection of vestments and other intricate embroidery. The baroque side chapel features dramatic friezes, and many life-sized (and sometimes startling) models of nuns praying, sewing and going about their lives. The convent also houses 13 real, live contemplative nuns.

Museo de Arte Precolombino   Museum
(☑084-23-3210; http://map.museolarco.org; Plazoleta Nazarenas 231; admission S20; ⊙9am-10pm) Inside a Spanish colonial mansion with an Inca ceremonial courtyard, this

dramatically curated pre-Columbian art museum showcases a stunningly varied, if selectively small, collection of archaeological artifacts previously buried in the vast storerooms of Lima's Museo Larco. Dating from between 1250 BC and AD 1532, the artifacts show off the artistic and cultural achievements of many of Peru's ancient cultures, with exhibits labeled in Spanish, English and French.

Highlights include the Nazca and Moche galleries of multicolored ceramics, *queros* and dazzling displays of jewelry made with intricate gold- and silver-work.

Museo Quijote   Museum
(www.museoelquijote.com; Galería Banco la Nacion, Calle Almagro s/n; ⊙9am-6pm Mom-Fri, to 1pm Sun) FREE In a new location housed inside a bank, this privately owned museum of contemporary art houses a diverse, thoughtful collection of painting and sculpture ranging from the folksy to the macabre. There's good interpretive information about 20th-century Peruvian art history, some of it translated into English.

Museo Histórico Regional   Museum
(Calle Garcilaso at Heladeros; adult/student under 26 with ISIC card S130/70; ⊙8am-5pm Tue-Sun) This eclectic museum is housed in the colonial Casa Garcilaso de la Vega, the house of the Inca-Spanish chronicler who now lies buried in the cathedral. The chronologically arranged collection begins with arrowheads from the Preceramic Period and continues with ceramics and jewelry of the Wari, Pukara and Inca cultures. Admission is with the *boleto turístico* tourist card only, which is valid for 10 days and covers 16 other sites.

There is also a Nazca mummy, a few Inca weavings, some small gold ornaments and a strangely sinister scale model of the Plaza de Armas. A big, helpful chart in the courtyard outlines the timeline and characters of the *escuela cuzqueña*.

Choco Museo   Museum
(Garcilaso 210; www.chocomuseo.com; ⊙10:30am-6:30pm) FREE While the museum is only mildly interesting, the best part of

this French-owned enterprise are the organic **chocolate-making workshops** (S70 per person). You can also come for fondue or a fresh cup of fair-trade hot cocoa. It's multilingual and kid-friendly.

◎ San Blas

Known as the artists' neighborhood, San Blas is nestled on a steep hillside next to the center. With classic architecture, signature blue doors and narrow passageways without cars, the area has become a hip attraction full of restaurants, watering holes and shops.

Iglesia de San Blas   Church

(Plaza San Blas; admission S10; ⓧ10am-6pm Mon-Sat, 2-6pm Sun) This simple adobe church is comparatively small, but you can't help but be awed by the baroque, gold-leaf principal altar. The exquisitely carved pulpit, made from a single tree trunk, has been called the finest example of colonial wood carving in the Americas.

Legend claims that its creator was an indigenous man who miraculously recovered from a deadly disease and subsequently dedicated his life to carving the pulpit for this church. Supposedly, his skull is nestled in the topmost part of the carving. In reality, no one is certain of the identity of either the skull or the woodcarver.

◎ Avenida El Sol & Downhill

Museo de Arte Popular   Museum

(Basement, Av El Sol 103; adult/student under 26 with ISIC card S130/70; ⓧ9am-6pm Mon-Sat, 8am-1pm Sun) Winning entries in Cuzco's annual Popular Art Competition are displayed in this engaging museum. This is where the artisans and artists of San Blas showcase their talents in styles ranging from high art to cheeky, offering a fascinating, humorous take on ordinary life amid the pomp and circumstance of a once-grandiose culture. Admission is with the *boleto turístico* tourist card only, which is valid for 10 days and covers 16 other sites.

Small-scale ceramic models depict drunken debauchery in the *picantería* (local restaurant), torture in the dentist's chair, carnage in the butcher shop, and even a

Statue at Plaza de Armas (p156), with the bell tower of Iglesia San Franciso in the background

MARKO STAVRIC PHOTOGRAPHY / GETTY IMAGES ©

Salkantay Trek

caesarean section. There's also a display of photographs, many by renowned local photographer Martín Chambi, of Cuzco from the 1900s to the 1950s, including striking images of the aftermath of the 1950 earthquake in familiar streets.

Iglesia de Santo Domingo Church
FREE The church of Santo Domingo is next door to Qorikancha. Less baroque and ornate than many of Cuzco's churches, it is notable for its charming paintings of archangels depicted as Andean children in jeans and T-shirts. Opening hours are erratic.

ACTIVITIES

Scores of outdoor outfitters in Cuzco offer trekking, rafting and mountain-biking adventures, as well as mountaineering, horseback riding and paragliding. Price wars can lead to bad feelings among locals, with underpaid guides and overcrowded vehicles. The cheaper tours are liable to be the most crowded, multilingual affairs. Due to tax exemptions for new agencies, cheaper outfits also regularly change names and offices, so ask other foreign tourists for the most recent recommendations.

No company can ever be 100% recommended, but those we list are reputable outfits that have received mostly positive feedback from readers.

For some pampering or a post-trekking splurge, visit the luxurious **Samana Spa** (☎084-23-3721; www.samana-spa.com; Tecsecocha 536; ☉10am-7pm Mon-Sat).

Hiking

The department of Cuzco is a hiker's paradise. Ecosystems range from rainforest to high alpine, and trekkers may come upon isolated villages and ruins lost in the undergrowth. Of course, most come to hike the famed Inca Trail to Machu Picchu. Be aware that it's not the only 'Inca trail.' What savvy tourism officials and tour operators have christened the Inca Trail is just one of dozens of footpaths that the Incas built to reach Machu Picchu, out of thousands that crisscrossed the Inca empire.

ED NORTON / GETTY IMAGES ©

One longer, more spectacular trek than the Inca Trail is the **Salkantay Trek**, a scenic, but demanding, five-to-seven-day hike that ranges from jungle to alpine terrain, peaking at 4700m. It's possible to do independently or with a guide.

Closer to Cuzco, imaginative operators have developed multiday Sacred Valley trekking itineraries that go well off the beaten track to little-visited villages and ruins.

Other recommended treks include **Lares** and **Ausangate** and, for archaeological sites, **Choquequirau** and **Vilcabamba**.

The best time to go trekking in the Andes or the Amazon is during the colder dry season between May and September. Make reservations for treks during high seasons several months in advance, and up to a year in advance for the Inca Trail. In the wettest months of January to March, trails have a tendency to turn into muddy slogs, and views disappear under a blanket of clouds. Note that the Inca Trail is completely closed during the month of February for its annual cleanup.

As altitudes vary widely, it is essential to properly acclimatize before undertaking any trek. Take water-purification tablets or a purification system from home. Once you're trekking, there is usually nowhere to buy food, and the small villages where treks begin have very limited supplies, so shop in advance in Cuzco. If you're on a guided trek, take a stash of cash for tipping the guide and the *arrieros* (mule drivers). About US$12 per day per trekker is the minimum decent tip to a guide; a similar amount to divide between *arrieros* is appropriate.

Apu's Peru   Hiking

(☑084-23-3691; www.apus-peru.com; Cuichipunco 366) A recommended outfitter for the Inca Trail, also offering conventional tours. Responsible and popular with travelers.

X-Treme Tourbulencia   Hiking

(☑084-22-4362; www.x-tremetourbulencia.com; Plateros 364) A recommended Cuzco-based tour operator offering multisport access

to Machu Picchu via Santa Teresa and the Inca Jungle Trail. Multilingual guides.

Eco Trek Peru   Hiking

(☑084-24-7286; www.ecotrekperu.com) A trekking specialist.

Peru Treks   Hiking

(☑084-22-2722; www.perutreks.com; Av Pardo 540) Offers hiking tours to Machu Picchu.

🟢 Rafting

Rafting isn't regulated in Peru – literally anyone can start a rafting company. Rafting companies that take advance bookings online are generally more safety conscious (and more expensive) than those just operating out of storefronts in Cuzco.

Despite the sewage, the Ollantaytambo to Chilca (class II to III) section of Río Urubamba through the Sacred Valley is surprisingly popular, offering 1½ hours of gentle rafting with only two rapids of note.

There are a variety of cleaner sections closer to Cuzco. Pampa to Huambutio (class I to II) is beautiful, ideal for small children (three years and over) as an introduction to rafting.

Río Santa Teresa offers spectacular rafting in the gorge between the towns of Santa Teresa and Santa María, and downstream as far as Quillabamba.

Run from May to November, the Río Apurímac offers three- to 10-day trips through deep gorges and protected rainforest. Apurímac features exhilarating rapids (classes IV and V) and wild, remote scenery with deep gorges.

An even wilder expedition, the 10- to 12-day trip along the demanding Río Tambopata can only be run from May to October.

Amazonas Explorer   Rafting

(☑084-25-2846; www.amazonas-explorer.com; Av Collasuyu 910 Miravalle) A professional international operator with top-quality equipment and guides, offering rafting trips on the Ríos Apurimac and Tambopata.

Sacred Vision For Sale

Shamanic ceremonies may be native to the Amazon, but they have become a hot commodity in Cuzco and the Sacred Valley. The psychedelic properties of the San Pedro and *ayahuasca* plants have earned them fame and piqued public curiosity. In Cuzco, San Pedro is offered alongside massages by street hawkers, and *ayahuasca* ceremonies are advertised in hostels. Of course, travelers can decide what is right and wrong for them, but it's important to note that these are not recreational drugs and can be highly toxic in the wrong hands. A real shaman knows the long list of dos and don'ts for practitioners, and may screen participants. Ceremonies can require multiple days for preparation, fasting and extended rituals.

It is hard not to be skeptical about a store-bought spiritual experience, and many locals believe that it's a mockery to turn these sacred ceremonies into moneymakers. Still, participating in a 'guided ceremony' can be a lot safer than scarfing down a powerful narcotic by yourself, as long as you trust the practitioners (in some cases, female guests have been attacked while under the influence). If you are thinking of going ahead, it's advisable to look carefully into the ceremonies and ask previous participants about their experience before signing up.

Preparing *ayahuasca*

Apumayo
Rafting

(☎084-24-6018; www.apumayo.com; Jirón Ricardo Palma Ñ-11, Urb Santa Monica) A professional outfitter that takes advance international bookings for Río Tambopata trips. Also equipped to take travelers with disabilities.

River Explorers
Rafting

(☎084-26-0926; www.riverexplorers.com; Urb Kennedy A, B-15) This popular outfitter runs all sorts of sections, including trips of up to six days on Río Apurímac.

Mayuc
Rafting

(☎084-24-2824; www.mayuc.com; Portal Confiturías 211) This monster operator, very popular with bargain hunters, dwarfs the competition.

🟢 Mountain Biking

Mountain-biking tours are a growing industry in Cuzco, and the local terrain is superb. Rental bikes are poor quality, and it is most common to find *rígida* (single suspension) models, which can make for bone-chattering downhills. If you're a serious mountain biker, consider bringing your own bike from home. Selling it in Cuzco is eminently viable.

If you're an experienced rider, some awesome rides are quickly and easily accessible by public transport or bike operators.

Many longer trips are possible, but a professionally qualified guide and a support vehicle are necessary. The partly paved road down from Abra Málaga to Santa María, though not at all technical, is a must for any cyclist. It is part of the Inca Jungle Trail, offered by many Cuzco operators.

Amazonas Explorer
Mountain Biking

(☎084-25-2846; www.amazonas-explorer.com; Av Collasuyu 910, Miravalle) Offers excellent two- to 10-day mountain-biking adventures; great for families, with kids' bikes available.

Gravity Peru
Mountain Biking

(☎084-22-8032; www.gravityperu.com; Santa Catalina Ancha 398) Allied with well-known Gravity Bolivia, this professionally run

Mountain biking above Cuzco

operator is the only one offering double-suspension bikes for day trips. Its 'Back door Machu Picchu' tour (via adventure options and biking) has become a hugely popular alternative to accessing the ruins. Highly recommended.

Party Bike Adventure Tour
(☑084-24-0399; www.partybiketravel.com; Carmen Alto 246) Traveler recommended, with downhills, tours to the Sacred Valley and through Cuzco.

COURSES

Marcelo Batata
Cooking Class Cooking
(www.cuzcodining.com; Calle Palacio 135; S240; ⊙2pm) If you've fallen for Peruvian cooking, this four-hour course is a worthwhile foray. A fully stocked market pantry demystifies some of the exotic flavors of the region and the kitchen setup is comfortable. Includes appetizers, a pisco tasting and a main course. In English, Spanish or Portuguese. Accommodates vegetarians.

☞ TOURS

Cuzco has hundreds of ever-changing registered travel agencies, so ask other travelers for recommendations.

Standard tours often travel in large groups and can be rushed. Classic options include a half-day tour of the city and/or nearby ruins, a half-day trip to the Sunday markets at Pisac or Chinchero and a full-day tour of the Sacred Valley (eg Pisac, Ollantaytambo and Chinchero).

Agents also offer expensive Machu Picchu tours that include transport, admission tickets to the archaeological site, an English-speaking guide and lunch. Since you only get to spend a few hours at the ruins, it's more enjoyable (not to mention much cheaper) to DIY and hire a guide at Machu Picchu.

If you are short on time to see the sights outside Cuzco, consider taking a taxi tour. From Cuzco, a tour of the Sacred Valley (possibly including Pisac, Ollantaytambo, Chinchero, Maras and Moray) runs around S180 (for the whole car); to the Southern

From left: Juice stalls at Mercado San Pedro; River crossing on the Salkantay Trek (p165); market in Cuzco

Valley (with options to Tipón, Pikillacta and Raqcchi) costs around S270.

One reliable option is **Virgin Estrella Taxi Tours** (974-955-374, 973-195-551) in Cuzco.

Chaski Ventura   Cultural

(084-23-3952; www.chaskiventura.com; Manco Cápac 517) Pioneer of alternative and community tourism, with quality itineraries and guides, also involved in community development. Offers package trips to the jungle, overnights in Sacred Valley communities and Machu Picchu. French, English and Spanish spoken.

Antipode   Adventure

(970-440-448; www.antipode-travel.com; Choquechaca 229) An attentive, French-run outfit offering classic tours, treks and shorter local adventure outings.

Fertur   Tour

(084-22-1304; www.fertur-travel.com; Calle Simon Bolivar F23) Local office of long-established, very reliable agency for flights and all conventional tours. Highly recom-

mended by readers. The office is located near the bus terminal.

InkaNatura   Tour

(984-691-838, 084-23-1138, 084-25-5255; www.inkanatura.com; Ricardo Palma J1 Urb Santa Mónica & Plateros 361) InkaNatura is a highly respected international agency and co-owner of the Manu Wildlife Center. The operators can combine a visit here with trips to other parts of the southern Peruvian rainforest, including Pampas del Heath near Puerto Maldonado, where it also has a lodge (the Heath Wildlife Center).

Journey Experience   Adventure

(JOEX; 084-24-5642; www.joextravel.com; Av Tupac Amaru V-2-A, Progreso) A recommended outfitter for hiking and cultural activities.

Milla Turismo   Tour

(084-23-1710; www.millaturismo.com; Av Pardo 800) Reputable conventional tour operator with travel-agency services and recommended private tours with knowledgeable drivers.

OLIVIERO OLIVIERI / ROBERTHARDING / GETTY IMAGES ©

Turismo Caith
Cultural

(☏084-23-3595; www.caith.org; Centro Yana-panakusun, Urb Ucchullo Alto, N4, Pasaje Santo Toribio) 🖢 Leader in community tourism as well as standard single and multiday trips. Participants can help with educational projects.

Respons
Cultural

(Responsible Travel Peru; ☏084-23-3903; www.responsibletravelperu.com; Suyt'u Qhatu 777-B) High-end sustainable tour operator working with community development in the Sacred Valley. Offers a tour of a weaving community near Pisac and chocolate and coffee tours on the Inca Jungle Trail. Available in English, Spanish and French.

SAS Travel
Tour

(☏084-24-9194; www.sastravelperu.com; Calle Garcilaso 270) A direct operator with local owners. Offers high-end package tours to Machu Picchu, Inca Trail treks, jungle travel and Cuzco tours. While there are complaints that this outfitter charges more than the competition, traveler satisfaction is generally high.

🔒 SHOPPING

San Blas – the plaza itself, Cuesta San Blas, Carmen Alto, and Tandapata cast of the plaza – offers Cuzco's best shopping. It's the artisan quarter, packed with local workshops and showrooms.

Mercado San Pedro
Market

(Plazoleta San Pedro) Cuzco's central market is a must-see. Pig heads for *caldo* (soup), frogs (to enhance sexual performance), vats of fruit juice, roast *lechón* (suckling pig) and tamales are just a few of the foods on offer. Around the edges are typical clothes, spells, incense and other random products to keep you entertained for hours.

Taller Olave
Arts, Crafts

(☏084-23-1835; Plaza San Blas 651) Taller Olave sells reproductions of colonial sculptures and precolonial ceramics.

Taller Mendivil
Arts, Crafts

(☏084-23-3247; cnr Hatunrumiyoc & Choquechaca) One of several outlets of a well-known artisan shop selling religious figures and ornate mirrors.

Taller and Museo
Mérida   Arts, Crafts
(22-1714; Carmen Alto 133) Taller and Museo
Mérida offers striking earthenware statues
that straddle the border between craft
and art.

Center for Traditional
Textiles of Cuzco   Handicrafts
(Av El Sol 603A; ⊘7:30am-8:30pm) This
nonprofit organization, founded in 1996,
promotes the survival of traditional weaving. You may be able to catch a shop-floor
demonstration illustrating different weaving techniques in all their finger-twisting
complexity. Products for sale are high end.

For those who love textiles, there's a
wonderful on-site museum (free).

Inkakunaq Ruwaynin   Handicrafts
(084-26-0942; www.tejidosandinos.com; inside
CBC, Tullumayo 274; ⊘9am-7pm) This weaving
cooperative with quality goods is run by 12
mountain communities from Cuzco and
Apurimac; it's at the far end of the inner
courtyard. There's also an online catalog.

Tatoo   Clothing
(☑084-25-4211; Calle del Medio 130; ⊘9am-
9:30pm) Tatoo has brand-name outdoor
clothing and technical gear at high prices.

⊗ EATING

For self-caterers, small, overpriced grocery
shops are located near Plaza de Armas,
including **Gato's Market** (Santa Catalina
Ancha 377; ⊘9am-11pm) and **Market** (Mantas
119; ⊘8am-11pm). For a more serious stock-
up, head to supermarket **Mega** (cnr Matará &
Ayacucho; ⊘10am-8pm Mon-Sat, to 6pm Sun).

⊗ Central Cuzco

El Hada   Ice Cream $
(Qanchipata 596; ice creams from S10; ⊘8am-
7pm) Served in fresh-made cones with a
hint of vanilla or lemon peel, these exotic
ice creams are ecstasy. Flavors like Indone-
sian cinnamon, bitter chocolate or roasted
apples do not disappoint. Cap it off with an
espress – Café Bisetti, Peru's best roaster,
is offered.

Plaza San Blas

Aldea Yanapay
Cafe $

(☏084-25-5134; Ruinas 415, 2nd fl; lunch buffet S10, mains from S22; ⊗9am-11:30pm; 🖋) The stuffed animals, board games and decor perfectly evoke the circus you dreamed of running away with as a child. Aldea Yanapay is pitched at families but will appeal to anyone with a taste for the quixotic. Food includes burritos, falafel and tasty little fried things to pick at, and a great-value vegetarian lunch buffet.

Profits go to projects helping abandoned children. Highly recommended.

El Ayllu
Cafe $

(Marquez 263; mains S7-16; ⊗6:30am-10pm Mon-Sat, to 1pm Sun) Longtime staff chat up clients and serve traditional pastries like *lengua de suegra* ('mother-in-law's tongue', a sweet pastry confection) and pork sandwiches. Traditional breakfasts are worth trying and coffee is roasted the traditional local way – with orange, sugar and onion peels.

Valeriana
Bakery $

(☏084-50-6941; Av del Sol 576; mains S2-14; ⊗7am-10pm Mon-Sat, 8am-9pm Sun; 🛜) Facing the sacred garden, this ambient bakery sells truffled cupcakes, whole-wheat sandwiches and good veggie empanadas served on patterned china. There are also coffee drinks and refreshing juices blended with medicinal herbs. A fine stop to charge your batteries.

Cicciolina
International $$

(☏084-23-9510; Triunfo 393, 2nd fl; mains S35-55; ⊗8am-late) On the 2nd floor of a lofty colonial courtyard mansion, Cicciolina has long been among Cuzco's best restaurants. The eclectic, sophisticated food is divine, starting with house-marinated olives, and continuing with crisp polenta squares with cured rabbit, huge green salads, charred octopus and satisfying mains like squid-ink pasta, beet ravioli and tender lamb. Impeccable service and warmly lit seating.

🗨 The Lucky Toad

Ever wondered what the locals do to relax instead of whiling away the hours over a game of darts or pool in the local bar? Well, next time you're in a *picantería* (local restaurant) or *quinta* (house serving typical Andean food), look out for a strange metal *sapo* (frog or toad) mounted on a large box and surrounded by various holes and slots. Men will often spend the whole afternoon drinking *chicha* (fermented corn beer) and beer while competing at this old test of skill in which players toss metal disks as close to the toad as possible. Top points are scored for landing one smack in the mouth. Legend has it that the game, known as *juego de sapo*, originated with Inca royals, who used to toss gold coins into Lake Titicaca in the hopes of attracting a *sapo* believed to possess magical healing powers and to have the ability to grant wishes.

Juego de sapo box
ALFONSO DE TOMAS / SHUTTERSTOCK ©

La Bodega 138
Pizzeria $$

(☏084-26-0272; Herrajes 138; mains S23-35; ⊗6:30-11pm Mon-Sat) Sometimes you are homesick for good atmosphere, uncomplicated menus and craft beer. In comes La Bodega, a fantastic laid-back enterprise run by a family in what used to be their home. Thin crust pizzas are fired up in the adobe oven, organic salads are fresh and abundant and the prices are reasonable. A true find. Cash only.

The Navel of the Earth

According to legend, in the 12th century, the first *inca* (king), Manco Cápac, was ordered by the ancestral sun god Inti to find the spot where he could plunge a golden rod into the ground until it disappeared. At this spot – deemed the navel of the earth (*qosq'o* in the Quechua language) – he founded Cuzco, the city that would become the thriving capital of the Americas' greatest empire.

Marcelo Batata — Peruvian $$

(Calle Palacio 121; mains S23-43; ⊙2-11pm) A sure bet for delectable Andean cuisine with a twist. Marcelo Batata innovates with traditional foods to show them at their best – like the humble *tarwi* pea, which makes a mean hummus. The chicken soup with *hierba Luisa* (a local herb), is exquisite, alongside satisfying beet *quinotto* (like risotto), tender *anticuchos* and twice-baked Andean potatoes that offer crispy-creamy goodness.

A daring array of cocktails is best savored on the rooftop deck – the city views make it the best outdoor venue in Cuzco.

Green's Organic — Cafe $$

(☑084-24-3399; Santa Catalina Angosta 235, 2nd fl; mains S28-46; ⊙11am-10pm; 🛜🍴) 🌱 With all-organic food and a bright farmhouse feel, Green's Organic oozes health. Inventive salads with options like roasted fennel, goat cheese, beets and spring greens are a welcome change of pace and the heartier fare includes pastas and alpaca dishes. Come early (or late) as it fills up fast and service is notably slow.

Limo — Peruvian $$

(☑084-24-068; Portal de Carnes 236, 2nd fl; mains S20-60; ⊙11am-11pm Mon-Sat) Tart pisco sours perfectly complement Limo's Peruvian-Asian seafood creations. For starters, native potatoes and sauces are a fun change from the traditional bread basket. *Tiraditos* (raw fish in a fragrant sauce) simply melt on the tongue. Other hits are the creamy *causas* (potato dish) and *sudadito* (a mix of greens, corn and seared scallops). Elegant ambiance and attentive service.

Trujillo Restaurant — Peruvian $$

(☑084-233-465; Av Tullumayo 542; mains S17-37; ⊙9am-8pm Mon-Sat, to 5pm Sun) Run by a northern Peruvian family, this simple, spotless dining hall by Qorikancha nails northern classics such *seco de cabrito* (goat stewed in beer and cilantro) and a variety of ceviches served with jars of *chicha morada* (a nonalcoholic purple maize drink). The *aji de gallina* (a creamy chicken stew served with rice and potatoes) is the best in all of Cuzco. It's near Plaza Limacpampa.

Uchu Peruvian Steakhouse — Peruvian $$

(☑084-24-6598; Calle Palacio 135; mains S28-59; ⊙12:30-11pm) With a cozy, cavernous ambience of low-lit adobe, dark tables and bright turquoise walls, this chic eatery has a simple menu of meat (steak, alpaca or chicken) and fish cooked on hot volcanic stones at your table, served with delicious sauces. Starters are great – like the gingery ceviche with fish shipped fresh daily. Staff is knowledgeable and quick, a real treat.

Papachos — Burgers $$

(www.papachos.com; Portal de Belen 115; mains S29-39; ⊙noon-midnight) You could do worse than satisfying your fast-food craving at a Gaston Acurio outlet. Papachos does big, beautiful burgers topped with goodies both exotic and comforting. There are veggie options, wings doused in Amazonian pepper sauce and fish and chips.

Chicha — Novo Andino $$$

(☑084-24-0520; Regocijo 261, 2nd fl; mains S34-65) A Gastón Acurio venture serving up haute versions of Cuzco classics in an open kitchen. Its riff on *anticuchos* is a delectable barbecued octopus with crisp herbed pota-to wedges. Other contenders include *rocoto relleno* (stuffed peppers), the wonton-style *sopa de gallina* (chicken soup) and *chairo* (beef soup) served in a clay pot. The *chicha morada* is beyond fresh.

⊗ San Blas

Jack's Café   Cafe $
(☑084-25-4606; Choquechaca 509; mains S12-26; ☺7:30am-11:30pm) A line often snakes out the door at this consistently good Western-style eatery with Aussie roots. With fresh juices blended with mint or ginger, strong coffee and eggs heaped with smoked salmon or roasted tomatoes, it's easy to get out of bed. Also has nice cafe food, soups and good service.

Juanito's   Sandwiches $
(Angelitos 638; sandwiches S12-24; ☺11am-10pm Mon-Sat) With the griddle hopping, this sandwich shop churns out satisfying made-to-order numbers with a variety of sauces.

Vegetarians get big fried-egg sandwiches, and combos like chicken and walnuts prove tasty.

Meeting Place   Cafe $
(☑084-24-0465; Plazoleta San Blas; mains S15-21; ☺8:30am-4pm Mon-Sat; 🛜) This British-Peruvian owned cafe nails gringo breakfast. Start with organic coffee or nice loose-leaf teas, and move on to oversized waffles and egg combinations. The thick milkshakes have their devotees. Swift, friendly service and a good book exchange.

Granja Heidi   Cafe $$
(☑084-23-8383; Cuesta San Blas 525, 2nd fl; mains S10-46; ☺11:30am-9:30pm Mon-Sat) A cozy Alpine cafe serving healthy fare that's consistently good, some of it provided from the small farm of the German owner. In addition to wonderful Peruvian fare (*rocoto relleno* is served vegetarian, with stuffed chili and peanuts), there are crepes and huge bowls of soups and salads. Save room for dessert.

Rooftops overlooking the Plaza de Armas (p156)

ILUS VINAGRE WORLD PHOTO / GETTY IMAGES ©

Cuzco women dressed in traditional clothing

La Quinta Eulalia   Peruvian $$

(☏084-22-4951; Choquechaca 384; mains S25-54; ⊙9am-7pm Tue-Sun) This Cuzco classic has been in business for over half a century and its courtyard patio is a score on a sunny day. The chalkboard menu features the tenderest roast lamb, alpaca and traditional sides like the phenomenal *rocotto relleno* (spicy peppers stuffed with beef, peas and carrots topped with dribbling cheese). It is one of the best places to order *cuy*.

🍷 DRINKING & NIGHTLIFE

Museo del Pisco   Bar

(☏084-26-2709; museodelpisco.org; Santa Catalina Ancha 398; ⊙11am-1am) When you've had your fill of colonial religious art, investigate this pisco museum, where the wonders of the national drink are extolled, exalted and – of course – sampled. Opened by an enthusiastic expat, this museum-bar is Pisco 101, combined with a tapas lounge. Grab a spot early for show-stopping live music (9pm to 11pm nightly).

Ambitions go far beyond the standard pisco sour to original cocktails like *valicha* (pisco with jungle fruit *kion*, spearmint and sour apple). Tapas, such as alpaca miniburgers on sesame buns and *tiradito* (a Japanese-influenced version of ceviche) marinated in cumin-chili, sate your hunger. Look for special tastings and master-distiller classes announced on the Facebook page.

Fallen Angel   Cocktail Bar

(☏084-25-8184; Plazoleta Nazarenas 221; ⊙6pm-late) This ultrafunky lounge redefines kitsch with glitter balls, fake fur and even bathtub-cum-aquarium tables complete with live goldfish. It isn't cheap, but the decor really is worth seeing and the occasional theme parties held here are legendary.

Memoria   Bar

(☏084-24-4111; Plateros 354; ⊙8pm-late) A wonderful, elegant bar with attentive bartenders and drinks that merit seconds. Check its Facebook site for events like live jazz, acoustic and techno music.

Inka Team Club

(Portal de Carnes 298; ⊗8pm-late) Though it may change names, this place usually has the most up-to-the-minute electronic-music collection, with trance, house and hip-hop mixed in with mainstream. There are chill-out sofas upstairs but this isn't the place for chat. A good mix of locals and tourists hang out here. Happy hour is 9pm to midnight.

Muse Lounge

(☑984-23-1717, 084-25-3631; Triunfo 338, 2nd fl; 🛜) Known as a good place to start your night out, this restaurant-lounge, a longtime Cuzco hangout, has very cool staff and live music in the evenings. Food includes good vegetarian options.

⭐ ENTERTAINMENT

Ukuku's Live Music

(☑084-24-2951; Plateros 316; ⊗8pm-late) The most consistently popular nightspot in town, Ukuku's plays a winning combination of crowd-pleasers – Latin and Western rock, reggae and *reggaetón* (a blend of Puerto Rican *bomba,* dancehall and hip-hop), salsa, hip-hop etc – and often hosts live bands. Usually full to bursting after midnight with as many Peruvians as foreign tourists, it's good, sweaty, dance-a-thon fun. Happy hour is 8pm to 10:30pm.

Centro Qosqo de Arte Nativo Performing Arts

(☑084-22-7901; www.boletoturisticocusco.net/arte-nativo.html; Av El Sol 604; adult/student under 26 with ISIC card S130/70) Has live nightly performances of Andean music and dance at 6:45pm. Admission is with the *boleto turístico* tourist card only, which is valid for 10 days and covers 16 other sights and venues.

INFORMATION

DANGERS & ANNOYANCES

Bags may be stolen from the backs of chairs in public places. Walk around with a minimum of cash and belongings. If you keep your bag in your lap and watch out for pickpockets in crowded streets, transport terminals and markets, you are highly unlikely to be a victim of crime in Cuzco.

Use only official taxis, especially at night. (Look for the company's lit telephone number on top of the car.) Lock your doors from the inside, and never allow the driver to admit a second passenger. Readers have reported overcharging with *ticos* (taxi rickshaws).

Avoid walking by yourself late at night or very early in the morning. Revelers returning late from bars or setting off for the Inca Trail before sunrise are particularly vulnerable to 'choke and grab' attacks.

Drink spiking has been reported. Women especially should keep an eye on their glass and not accept drinks from strangers.

Take care not to overexert yourself during your first few days if you've flown in from lower elevations. You may find yourself quickly becoming winded while traipsing up and down Cuzco's narrow streets.

EMERGENCY

Policía de Turismo (☑084-23-5123; Plaza Túpac Amaru s/n; ⊗24hr) If you have something stolen, you'll need to come here for an official police report for insurance claims.

INTERNET ACCESS

Internet cafes are found on almost every street corner. Many hotels and cafes offer free wi-fi.

LAUNDRY

Lavanderías (laundries) will wash, dry and fold your clothes from around S4 per kilo. They're everywhere, but cluster just off the Plaza de Armas on Suecia, Procuradores and Plateros, and on Carmen Bajo in San Blas. The further you get from the Plaza de Armas, the cheaper they get.

LEFT LUGGAGE

If you're going trekking or on an overnight excursion, any hostel will store your bags for free. Always get a receipt and lock the bags. The bags should have identifying tags showing your name and the drop-off and expected pickup dates.

For soft-sided bags, we recommend placing them inside a larger plastic bag and sealing

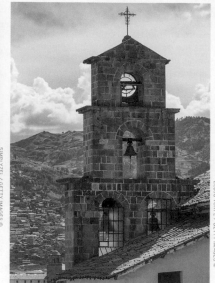

From left: Dolls at a market stall; bell tower of Iglesia de San Blas (p163); Inti Raymi festival (p149)

them shut with tape. Then sign your name across the seal, so that you can tell if your bag has been opened while you were away.

Keep all valuables (eg passport, credit cards, money) on your person. Trekkers are required to carry their passport with them on the Inca Trail.

MONEY

ATMs abound in and around the Plaza de Armas, and are also available at the airport, Huanchaq train station and the bus terminal. All accept Visa, most accept MasterCard. There are several big bank branches on Av El Sol; go inside for cash advances above daily ATM limits. *Casas de cambio* (foreign-exchange bureaus) give better exchange rates than banks, and are scattered around the main plazas and especially along Av El Sol. Money changers can be found outside banks, but rip-offs are common.

ⓘ GETTING THERE & AWAY

AIR

Cuzco's **Aeropuerto Internacional Alejandro Velasco Astete** (CUZ; ☎084-22-2611) receives national and international flights. Most arrivals come in the morning since afternoon conditions make landings and takeoffs more difficult. If you have a tight connection, it's best to reserve the earliest flight available, as later ones are more likely to be delayed or canceled.

There are daily flights to Lima, Juliaca, Puerto Maldonado and Arequipa. Check in at least two hours ahead as overbooking errors are commonplace. During rainy season, flights to Puerto Maldonado are often seriously delayed.

BUS

All international services depart from the **terminal terrestre** (☎084-22-4471; Vía de Evitamiento 429), about 2km out of town toward the airport. Take a taxi (S14) or walk via Av El Sol. Buses for more unusual destinations leave from elsewhere, so check carefully in advance.

To Bolivia, **Transportes Internacional Litoral** (☎084-23-1155; www.litoral-miramar.com), **Tour Peru** (☎084-23-6463; www.tourperu.com.pe) and **Transzela** (☎084-23-8223; www.transzela.com.pe) offer daily services to Copacabana (S60 to S80, 10 hours) and, along with **Transporte Salvador** (☎084-23-3680), to La Paz via Desaguadero (S80 to S120, 12 hours).

HUGHES HERVÉ/HEMIS.FR / GETTY IMAGES ©

Ormeño (☏084-24-1426) travels to most South American capitals.

Ormeño and **Cruz del Sur** (☏084-74-0444; www.cruzdelsur.com.pe) have the safest and most comfortable buses across the board. Of the cheaper companies, Tour Peru and **Wari Palomino** (☏084-22-2694) have the best buses.

The most enjoyable way to get to Puno is via **Inka Express** (☏084-24-7887; www.inkaexpress.com; Av 28 de Julio 211) or **Turismo Mer** (☏084-24-5171; www.turismomer.com; El Óvalo, Av LaPaz A3), which run luxury buses every morning. The service includes lunch and an English-speaking tour guide, who talks about the four sites that are briefly visited along the way.

Departures to Arequipa cluster around 6am to 7am and 7pm to 9:30pm. Ormeño offers a deluxe service at 9am.

Buses to Quillabamba via Santa María leave from Calle Antonio Lorena, offering air-conditioned, speedy comfort in modern minivans. Departures at 8am, 10am, 1pm and 8pm. Change at Santa María to get to Santa Teresa. From Cuzco, only **Turismo Cusco Imperial** (☏940-223-356; Terminal Santiago) goes to Santa Teresa (S25, six hours), three times daily.

Transportes Siwar (☏993-407-105; Av Tito Condemayta 1613) and other companies have buses to Ocongate and Tinqui (S10, three hours), the start of the Ausangante trek, leaving from behind the Coliseo Cerrado every half hour.

Several buses and minivans depart daily to Paucartambo (S9 to S12, three hours) from Paradero Control in distrito de San Jerónimo – a taxi will know where to drop you off.

Travel times are approximate and apply only if road conditions are good. Long delays are likely during the rainy season, particularly to Puerto Maldonado or Lima via Abancay. This road is now paved, but landslides can block the road in the rainy season.

CAR & MOTORCYCLE

Given all the headaches and potential hazards of driving yourself around, consider hiring a taxi for the day – it's cheaper than renting a car. If you must, you'll find a couple of car-rental agencies in the bottom block of Av El Sol.

Motorcycle rentals are offered by a couple of agencies in the first block of Saphi heading away from Plaza de Armas.

Salkantay Trek (p165)

TRAIN

Cuzco has two train stations. **Estación Huanchac** (📞084-58-1414; ⏰7am-5pm Mon-Fri, to midnight Sat & Sun), near the end of Av El Sol, serves Juliaca and Puno on Lake Titicaca. **Estación Poroy**, east of town, serves Ollantaytambo and Machu Picchu. The two stations are unconnected, so it's impossible to travel directly from Puno to Machu Picchu. (Downtown Estación San Pedro is used only for local trains, which foreigners cannot board.)

You can take a taxi to Poroy (S30) or the station in Ollantaytambo (S80) from Cuzco.

You can buy tickets at Huanchac station, and there are ATMs in the station, but the easiest way is directly through the train companies.

From January through March there is no train service between Cuzco and Aguas Calientes (for Machu Picchu) because of frequent landslides on the route. Instead, there's a bus from Estacion Huanchac to Ollantaytambo where you can board a train there for the remainder of the trip.

🛈 GETTING AROUND

TO/FROM THE AIRPORT

The airport is about 6km south of the city center. A taxi to or from the city center to the airport costs S20. An official radio taxi from within the airport costs S25. With advance reservations, many hotels offer free pickup.

TAXI

There are no meters in taxis, but there are set rates. At the time of writing, trips within the city center cost S5, and to destinations further afield, such as El Molino, were S8. Check with your hotel whether this is still correct. Official taxis, identified by a lit company telephone number on the roof, are safer than taxis flagged down on the street.

Unofficial 'pirate' taxis, which only have a taxi sticker in the window, have been complicit in crimes.

AloCusco (📞084-22-2222) is a reliable company to call.

Where to Stay

Peak accommodations season is between June and August, especially during the 10 days before Inti Raymi on June 24 and during Fiestas Patrias (Independence Days) on July 28 and 29. Book in advance for these dates.

Neighborhood	Atmosphere
Central Cuzco	Though Plaza de Armas is the most central area, premium rates are charged for the location.
West & Northwest of the Plaza de Armas	Many of the side streets that climb northwest away from the plaza toward Sacsaywamán (especially Tigre, Tecsecocha, Suecia, Kiskapata, Resbalosa and 7 Culebras) are bursting with cheap crash pads.
	There are also many options west of the Plaza de Armas around Plaza Regocijo, in the commercial area toward the Mercado Central, and downhill from the center in the streets northeast of Av El Sol.
San Blas	Hilly San Blas has the best views and is deservedly popular.
Avenida El Sol & Downhill	Similar to central Cuzco, accommodations along Av El Sol tend to be bland, expensive and set up for tour groups.

THE SACRED VALLEY

The Sacred Valley at a Glance...

Tucked under the tawny skirts of formidable foothills, the beautiful Río Urubamba Valley, known as El Valle Sagrado (The Sacred Valley), is about 15km north of Cuzco as the condor flies, via a narrow road of hairpin turns. Long the home of attractive colonial towns and isolated weaving villages, in recent years it has become a destination in its own right.

Star attractions are the markets and the lofty Inca citadels of Pisac and Ollantaytambo, but the valley is also packed with other Inca sites. Trekking routes are deservedly gaining in popularity. Adrenaline activities range from rafting to rock climbing.

The Sacred Valley in Two Days

Head to the stunning **Pisac Ruins** (p184) with lofty views of plunging gorges. Follow a series of hiking trails around the area, allowing several hours to go at your own pace. On day two, see what was left behind by the Incas at the lofty fortress and temple at the **Ollantaytambo Ruins** (p186).

The Sacred Valley in Four Days

On day three, visit **Chinchero** (p188), typifying an Andean village by combining Inca ruins with a colonial church. On day four, **visit rural communities** (p191) and learn to cook local Andean dishes, trek to highland lakes, and hear about local natural medicine and artisan traditions.

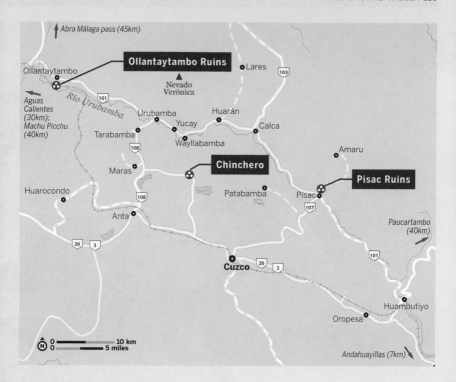

Arriving in the Sacred Valley

Bus Urubamba is the valley's principal transportation hub. The bus terminal is about 1km west of town.

Minivan or taxi The most comfortable option to Pisac, the entry point to the valley.

Train Two companies run between Ollantaytambo and Aguas Calientes. The station is less than 1km southwest of the village center.

Where to Stay

Foreign-run mystical and spiritual retreats on the outskirts of Pisac offer packages with shamanic ceremonies; some are vastly more commercial than others.

Ollantaytambo hosts lots of budget and midrange accommodations in the streets east of the Plaza de Armas.

OLIVER J DAVIS PHOTOGRAPHY / GETTY IMAGES ©

Pisac Ruins

A truly awesome site with relatively few tourists, this hilltop Inca citadel lies high above the village on a triangular plateau with a plunging gorge on either side.

Great For...

☑ Don't Miss

Judging for yourself whether the terraces resemble the wings of a bird. Pisac gets its name from 'Pisaca', which is the Quecha word for 'partridge'.

Terracing

The most impressive feature is the agricultural terracing, which sweeps around the south and east flanks of the mountain in huge and graceful curves, almost entirely unbroken by steps (which require greater maintenance and promote erosion). Instead, the terracing is joined by diagonal flights of stairs made of flagstones set into the terrace walls. Above the terraces are cliff-hugging footpaths, watched over by caracara falcons and well defended by massive stone doorways, steep stairs and a short tunnel carved out of the rock.

Water channels

ⓘ Need to Know

Admission with **boleto turístico card** (adult/student under 26 with ISIC card S130/70; ☺dawn–dusk)

✕ Take a Break

Vendors sell drinks and snacks at the top.

★ Top Tip

Note that organized tours, while often informative, are more rushed than private tours.

Temples

This dominating site guards not only the Urubamba Valley below, but also a pass leading into the jungle to the northeast. Topping the terraces is the site's ceremonial center, with an *intihuatana* (literally 'hitching post of the sun'; an Inca astronomical tool), several working water channels, and some painstakingly neat masonry in the well-preserved temples.

A path leads up the hillside to a series of ceremonial baths and around to the military area. Looking across the Kitamayo Gorge from the back of the site, you'll also see hundreds of holes honeycombing the cliff wall. These are Inca tombs that were plundered by *huaqueros* (grave robbers), and are now completely off-limits to tourists.

Hiking

Allow several hours to explore. To walk from town, a steep but spectacular 4km trail starts above the west side of the church. It's a two-hour climb a 1½-hour return. Worthwhile, but grueling, it's good training for the Inca Trail! A more leisurely option is to take a taxi up and walk back; hire a taxi from near the bridge into town.

For those taking the footpath, there are many crisscrossing trails, but if you aim toward the terracing, you won't get lost. To the west, or the left of the hill as you climb up on the footpath, is the Río Kitamayo Gorge; to the east, or right, is the Río Chongo Valley. It's busiest when tour groups flood in mid-morning on Sunday, Tuesday and Thursday.

Ollantaytambo Ruins

Both fortress and temple, these spectacular Inca ruins rise above Ollantaytambo, making a splendid half-day trip.

Great For...

☑ Don't Miss

Hiring a local guide to demonstrate how to turn on the faucet of the royal baths.

Inca Victory

The huge, steep terraces that guard Ollantaytambo's spectacular Inca ruins mark one of the few places where the Spanish conquistadors lost a major battle.

The rebellious Manco Inca had retreated to this fortress after his defeat at Sacsaywamán. In 1536 Hernando Pizarro, Francisco's younger half-brother, led a force of 70 cavalrymen to Ollantaytambo, supported by large numbers of indigenous and Spanish foot soldiers, in an attempt to capture Manco Inca.

The conquistadors, showered with arrows, spears and boulders from atop the steep terracing, were unable to climb to the fortress. In a brilliant move, Manco Inca flooded the plain below the fortress through previously prepared channels.

KELLY CHENG TRAVEL PHOTOGRAPHY / GETTY IMAGES ©

❶ Need to Know

Admission with **boleto turístico card** (adult/student under 26 with ISIC card S130/70; ☉7am-5pm)

✖ Take a Break

There are bars and local restaurants just around the corner from the ruins.

★ Top Tip

The *boleto turístico* tourist card, used for admission, is valid for 10 days and for 16 other sites across the region.

With Spaniards' horses bogged down in the water, Pizarro ordered a hasty retreat, chased down by thousands of Manco Inca's victorious soldiers.

Yet the Inca victory would be short lived. Spanish forces soon returned with a quadrupled cavalry force and Manco fled to his jungle stronghold in Vilcabamba.

Construction

Though Ollantaytambo was a highly effective fortress, it also served as a temple. A finely worked ceremonial center is at the top of the terracing. Some extremely well-built walls were under construction at the time of the conquest and have never been completed.

The stone was quarried from the mountainside 6km away, high above the opposite bank of the Río Urubamba. Transporting the huge stone blocks to the site was a stupendous feat. The Incas' crafty technique to move massive blocks across the river meant carting the blocks to the riverside then diverting the entire river channel around them.

Hiking & Views

The 6km hike to the Inca quarry on the opposite side of the river is a good walk from Ollantaytambo. The trail starts from the Inca bridge by the entrance to the village. It takes a few hours to reach the site, passing several abandoned blocks known as *piedras cansadas* (tired stones).

Looking back toward Ollantaytambo, you can see the enigmatic optical illusion of a pyramid in the fields and walls in front of the fortress. A few scholars believe this marks the legendary place where the original Incas first emerged from the earth.

Iglesia Colonial de Chinchero

Chinchero

Known to the Incas as the birthplace of the rainbow, this typical Andean village combines Inca ruins with a colonial church, some wonderful mountain views and a colorful Sunday market.

Great For...

☑ Don't Miss

Centro de Textiles Tradicionales on Manzares, the best artisan workshop in town.

On a high plain with sweeping views to snow-laden peaks, Chinchero's setting is starkly beautiful. As it is very high, it's unwise to spend the night until you're somewhat acclimated. Entry to the historic precinct, where the ruins, the church and the museum are all found, is by the *boleto turístico* (adult/student under 26 with ISIC card S130/70), valid for 10 days.

Ruinas Inca

The most extensive ruins here consist of terracing. If you start walking away from the village through the terraces on the right-hand side of the valley, you'll also find various rocks carved into seats and staircases.

Weaving, Chinchero

BARTOSZ HADYNIAK / GETTY IMAGES ©

ⓘ Need to Know

Combis (minibuses) and *colectivos* (shared transportation) traveling between Cuzco and Urubamba stop on the corner of the highway and Calle Manco Capac II.

✕ Take a Break

Other than the restaurants attached to accommodations (open to nonguests), there are few eating options in town.

★ Top Tip

Chinchero is the best value, most authentic place to buy woven goods in the region. Each weaving cooperative has its own specialty design.

Iglesia Colonial de Chinchero

Among the most beautiful churches in the valley, the **Iglesia Colonial de Chinchero** (entry with boleto turístico; ⊗8am-5:30pm) is built on Inca foundations. The interior, decked out in merry floral and religious designs, is well worth seeing.

Museo del Sitio

A small archaeological museum opposite the church, the **Museo del Sitio** (☑084-22-3245; adult/student under 26 with ISIC card S70/35; ⊗9am-5pm Tue-Sun) ✆ houses a collection heavy on broken pots. Admission is via the partial *boleto turístico* tourist ticket (valid for 2 days and for nearby ruins).

Mercado de Chinchero

The Chinchero market, held on Tuesday, Thursday and especially Sunday, is less touristy than its counterpart in Pisac and well worth a special trip. On Sunday, traditionally dressed locals descend from the hills for the produce market, where the ancient practice of *trueco* (bartering) still takes place; this is a rare opportunity to observe genuine bartering.

Pisac

It's not hard to succumb to the charms of sunny Pisac, a bustling and fast-growing colonial village at the base of a spectacular Inca fortress perched on a mountain spur. It's a magnet for both spiritual seekers and mainstream travelers, with ruins, a fabulous market and weaving villages nearby that should not be missed. Located just 33km northeast of Cuzco by a paved road, it's the most convenient starting point to the Sacred Valley.

◎ SIGHTS

Mercado de Artesania   Market
Pisac is known far and wide for its market, by far the biggest and most touristy in the region. Official market days are Tuesday,

> *the fabulous market and weaving villages nearby should not be missed*

Thursday and Sunday, when tourist buses descend on the town in droves. However, the market has taken over Pisac to such an extent that it fills the Plaza de Armas and surrounding streets every day; visit on Monday, Wednesday, Friday or Saturday if you want to avoid the worst of the crowds.

Horno Colonial
San Francisco   Landmark
(Mariscal Castilla s/n; snacks S2.50; ◷6am-6pm)
Huge clay ovens for baking empanadas and other goodies and *castillos de cuyes* (miniature castles inhabited by guinea pigs) are found in many nooks and crannies, particularly on Mariscál Castilla. But this is the town's most authentic – a colonial oven dating back to 1830.

La Capilla   Church
In recent times, the Instituto Nacional de Cultura (INC), in a characteristically controversial move, demolished the church in the main square in order to reconstruct it in colonial style. Masses, which have moved to a nearby chapel, are worth visiting. On

Market stall, Mercado de Artesania

TIM DRAPER / GETTY IMAGES ©

Sunday, a Quechua-language mass is held at 11am.

Traditionally dressed locals descend from the hills to attend, including men in traditional highland dress blowing horns, and *varayocs* (local authorities) with silver staffs of office.

🏃 ACTIVITIES

Club Royal Inka   Swimming

(admission S10; ☺8am-4pm) Ideal for families, this private recreation area is a fabulous place to while away an afternoon. A day pass allows access to an Olympic-sized indoor pool that's decked with fountains, grassy areas and an ornamental duck pond. There's also a restaurant, sauna, a trout pond and facilities for barbecues, billiards, table tennis, volleyball, tennis and *sapo* (see The Lucky Toad on p171). It's about 1.5km out of town.

🔒 SHOPPING

Horno Típico de
Santa Lucia   Handicrafts

(Manuel Prado s/n) Horno Típico de Santa Lucia unites huge clay ovens with *castillos de cuyes* of these with an *artesanía* (crafts) shop. If, for some strange reason, you only have five minutes in Pisac, spend it here – you'll get a pretty good feel for the place.

🍴 EATING

Ulrike's Café   Cafe $$

(☎084-20-3195; Manuel Prado s/s; veggie/meat menú S22/25, mains from S15-33; ☺9am-9pm; 🛜🍴) This sunny cafe serves consistently tasty food, with a great vegetarian *menú* (set menu), plus homemade pasta and melt-in-the-mouth cheesecake and a fluffy carrot cake that is legendary. There's a book exchange, DVDs and special events. English, French and German are spoken.

Community Tourism in the Sacred Valley

In recent times, rural communities of the valley have become far more accessible to visitors. While usually hospitable to passersby, they feature little infrastructure for travelers, so it's best to organize a visit in advance. For a guided trip to visit traditional communities, check out Journey Experience (www.thejoex.com), Chaski Ventura (www.chaskiventura.com) or Respons (www.respons.org), or contact the following:

La Tierra de los Yachaqs (☎971-502-223; www.yachaqs.com) A rural tourism network. Guests visit Andean communities, trek to highland lakes and learn about natural medicine and artisan traditions.

Parque de la Papa (☎084-24-5021; www.parquedelapapa.org; Pisac) Day treks and cooking workshops are some of the offerings of this new nonprofit that promotes potato diversity and communal farming.

Mullu   Fusion $$

(☎084-20-3073; www.mullu.pe; San Francisco s/n, 2nd fl; mains S14-32; ☺9am-9pm) The balcony may be the best spot to watch market-day interactions in the plaza below. Chill and welcoming, its menu is fusion (think Thai meets Amazonian and flirts with highland Peruvian). Traditional lamb is tender to falling-off-the-bone, soups and blended juices also satisfy.

Restaurante
Cuchara de Palo   International $$

(☎084-20-3062; Plaza de Armas; mains S15-38; ☺7:30-9:30am & noon-8pm) Inside Pisac Inn, this fine-dining restaurant offers organic salads and original dishes like pumpkin ravioli drizzled with corn and cream. Service can be slow but it has great ambience, with candlelit courtyard tables.

 Señor de Choquechilca

Occurring during Pentecost in late May or early June, Ollantaytambo (p194) commemorates the local miracle of the Christ of Choquechilca, when a wooden cross appeared by the Incan bridge. It's celebrated with music, dancing and colorful processions.

Pentecost celebrations, Ollantaytambo
PANORAMIC IMAGES / GETTY IMAGES ©

ⓘ GETTING THERE & AWAY

Buses to Urubamba (S3, one hour) leave frequently from the downtown bridge between 6am and 8pm. Minibuses to Cuzco (S5, one hour) leave from Calle Amazonas when full. Many travel agencies in Cuzco also operate tour buses to Pisac, especially on market days.

Urubamba

A busy and unadorned urban center, Urubamba is a transport hub surround-ed by bucolic foothills and snowy peaks. The advantages of its lower altitude and relative proximity to Machu Picchu make it popular with both high-end hotels and package tours. While there is little of historical interest, nice countryside and great weather make it a convenient base from which to explore the extraordinary salt flats of Salinas and the terracing of Moray.

⊙ SIGHTS

Salinas   Terrace
(admission S5) This is one of the most spectacular sights in the area: thousands of salt pans that have been used for salt extraction since Inca times. A hot spring at the top of the valley discharges a small stream of heavily salt-laden water, which is then diverted into these mountainside pans and evaporated to produce salt for cattle licks. It may sound pedestrian, but the visuals are beautiful and surreal.

It's about a 500m uphill hike. A rough dirt road that can be navigated by taxi enters Salinas from above, giving spectacular views. Tour groups visit via this route most days. A taxi from Urubamba to visit Salinas and nearby Moray costs around S80.

✦ ACTIVITIES

Many outdoor activities that are organized from Cuzco take place near here, including horseback riding, rock climbing, mountain biking, paragliding and hot-air balloon trips.

Cusco for You   Horseback Riding
(☏084-79-5301, 987-841-000; www.cuscofor you.com; Carretera a Salineras de Maras; day trip US$170) Highly recommended for horseback-riding and trekking trips from one to eight days long. Horseback riding day trips go to Moray and Salinas and other regional destinations. Ask about special rates for families and groups.

Sacred Wheels   Cycling
(☏954-700-844; www.sacredwheels.com) Even the casual rider can enjoy these mountain-bike tours that visit the valley and urban Urubamba.

🔒 SHOPPING

Seminario Cerámicas   Ceramics
(☏084-20-1002; www.ceramicaseminario.com; Berriozabal 405; ⊙8am-7pm) The internation-ally known local potter Pablo Seminario creates original work with a preconquest influence. His workshop – actually a small

factory – is open to the public and offers a well-organized tour through the entire ceramics process.

⊗ EATING

Huacatay
Peruvian **$$**

(☏084-20-1790; Arica 620; mains S32-50; ⊙1-9:30pm Mon-Sat) In a little house tucked down a narrow side street, Huacatay makes a lovely night out. Though not every dish is a hit, the tender alpaca steak, served in a port-reduction sauce with creamy quinoa risotto and topped with a spiral potato chip, is the very stuff memories are made of. Staff aim to please and there's warm ambience.

Tres Keros Restaurant Grill & Bar
Novo Andino **$$**

(☏084-20-1701; cnr hwy & Señor de Torrechayoc; mains from S26; ⊙lunch & dinner) Garrulous chef Ricardo Behar dishes up tasty gourmet fare, smokes his own trout and imports steak from Argentina. Food is taken seriously here, and enjoyed accordingly. It's 500m west of town.

❶ INFORMATION

Banco de la Nación (Mariscal Castilla s/n) changes US dollars. There are ATMs at the *grifo* (gas station) on the corner of the highway and the main street, Mariscal Castilla, and along the highway to its east.

❶ GETTING THERE & AWAY

The bus terminal is about 1km west of town on the highway. Buses leave every 15 minutes for Cuzco via Pisac or Chinchero. Buses and *colectivos* (shared transportation) to Ollantaytambo leave frequently.

❶ GETTING AROUND

Since Urubamba is quite spread out, the mode of transport of choice are *mototaxis* (three-wheeled motorcycle rickshaw taxis). The Plaza de Armas is five blocks east and four blocks north of the terminal, bounded by Calle Comercio and Jirón Grau.

Salinas salt pans

NIGEL PAVITT / GETTY IMAGES ©

White-bellied hummingbird, Ollantaytambo

Ollantaytambo

Dominated by two massive Inca ruins, the quaint village of Ollantaytambo (known to locals and visitors alike as Ollanta) is the best surviving example of Inca city planning, with narrow cobblestone streets that have been continuously inhabited since the 13th century. After the hordes passing through on their way to Machu Picchu die down around late morning, Ollanta is a lovely place to be. It's perfect for wandering the mazy, narrow byways, past stone buildings and babbling irrigation channels, pretending you've stepped back in time. It also offers access to excellent hiking and biking.

⊕ ACTIVITIES

Serious birders should definitely get ahold of *Birds of the High Andes* by Jon Fjeldså and Niels Krabbe. One of the best Sacred Valley birding trips is from Ollantaytambo to Santa Teresa or Quillabamba, over Abra Málaga. This provides a fine cross section of habitats from 4600m to below 1000m. A good local field guide is *The Birds of Machu Picchu* by Barry Walker.

Ollantaytambo also offers access to excellent hiking and biking.

Sota Adventure   Adventure Sports
(☑984-455-841; www.sotaadventure.com) Sota Adventure comes highly recommended by readers, particularly for horseback riding. The family-run business also offers mountain biking and multiday hikes.

Ortiz Adventures Tours   Mountain Biking
(☑084-46-6735, 992-532-448; josemanuel_jjm@hotmail.com) Mountain-biking tours to Moray and Maras, Pumamarca, and other destinations more apt for advanced riders.

⊗ EATING

Tutti Amore   Ice Cream $
(Av Ferrocarril s/n; ice cream S5; ⊙8:30am-7pm) Andres from Rosario, Argentina, serves up homemade gelato-style ice cream, including some exotic jungle-fruit flavors worth a try. It's halfway down the hill to the train station.

El Albergue Restaurante International $$

(☑084-20-4014; Estación de Tren; mains S22-41; ☺5:30am-10am, noon-3pm & 6-9pm) ☝ This whistle-stop cafe serves elegant dinners of well-priced, classic Peruvian fare. It's inviting, with an open kitchen bordered by fruit bowls, and candles adorning linen-topped tables. Start with the *causas* (potato dish) or organic greens from the garden. Lamb medallions with *chimichurri* (herb sauce) are a standout, as well as the mole-pepper steak with spice from the tree outside.

It also serves local artisan beer. Those less hungry can order homemade pasta in half-portions. For train passengers, it may be worth stopping by the patio option Café Mayu for an espresso or homemade *aguantamayo* cheesecake.

Hearts Café Cafe $$

(☑084-20-4078; cnr Ventiderio & Av Ferrocarril; mains S10-28; ☺7am-9pm; ☑) Serving healthy and hearty food, beer and wine and fabulous coffee, Hearts is a longtime local presence, with some organic produce and box lunches for excursions. Breakfasts like huevos rancheros (fried eggs with beans served on a tortilla) target the gringo palate perfectly, and the corner spot with outdoor tables was made for people-watching.

DRINKING & NIGHTLIFE

Ganso Bar

(☑984-30-8499; Waqta s/n; ☺2pm-late) Treehouse meets circus meets *Batman*! The decor in tiny, friendly Ganso is enough to drive anyone to drink. A firefighter's pole and swing seats are the icing on the cake.

ⓘ INFORMATION

There are a couple of internet cafes and ATMs in and around Plaza de Armas. There are no banks, but several places change money.

ⓘ GETTING THERE & AWAY

Frequent *combis* (minibuses) and *colectivos* shuttle between Urubamba and Ollantaytambo.

Explore More Ollantaytambo

Charmed by Ollanta? There's plenty to do if you want to extend your stay:

Pinkulluna Ruins Explore this spectacular site, with great views of town. Take the entry on Calle Lari; the trail is very steep, so hike carefully and wear boots with good traction.

Intipunku (p204) Take a one-hour hike to the 'Sun Gate,' which was once was a controlled gateway to Machu Picchu.

Pumamarca Hike or mountain bike to this nearly forgotten Inca ruin, a half-day trip. Local hotels can provide directions.

Pinkulluna ruins
NICOLAMARGARET / GETTY IMAGES ©

To Cuzco, it's easiest to change in Urubamba, though occasional departures leave direct from the Ollantaytambo train station to Cuzco's Puente Grau.

A train between Ollantaytambo and Aguas Calientes (two hours) is offered by two companies, **Inca Rail** (☑084-43-6732; www.incarail. com; Av Ferrocarril s/n) and **Peru Rail** (www. perurail.com; Av Ferrocarril s/n; ☺5am-9pm).

ⓘ GETTING AROUND

Ollantaytambo Travel (☑084-62-4263, 984-537-329; www.ollantaytambotravel.com) is a reliable taxi service with responsible drivers available for taxi tours throughout the Sacred Valley and private airport transfers (S110 for three passengers).

MACHU PICCHU

Machu Picchu at a Glance...

For many visitors to Peru and even South America, a visit to the Inca city of Machu Picchu is the long-anticipated high point of their trip. In a spectacular location, it's the best-known archaeological site on the continent.

This awe-inspiring ancient city was never revealed to the conquering Spaniards and was virtually forgotten until the early part of the 20th century. Now, in the high season from late May until early September, 2500 people arrive daily. Despite this great tourist influx, the site manages to retain an air of grandeur and mystery, and is a must for all visitors to Peru.

Machu Picchu in Two Days

Machu Picchu is huge, so it's best to spend at least two days, using Aguas Calientes as a base camp to allow ample time to explore the ruins. Staying in town also allows you to get up early and beat the midday crowds at Machu Picchu. If you are also climbing **Wayna Picchu** (p205) or **Cerro Machu Picchu** (p206), you may need even more time.

Machu Picchu in Four Days

Alternatively, put aside at least four days to hike the **Inca Trail** (p210), with time to return and recover from the strenuous trek. The ancient trail was laid by the Incas, from the Sacred Valley to Machu Picchu. You will push yourself up and down across mountains, past rivers and lakes, and feel proud to reach Machu Picchu on day four.

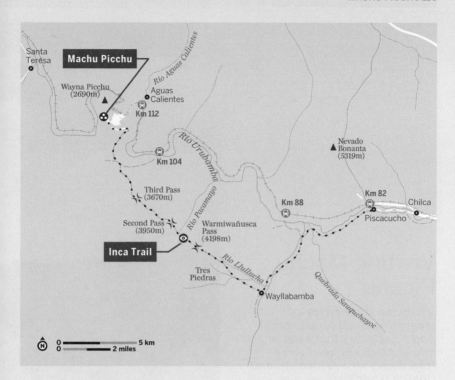

Arriving in Machu Picchu

Unless taking a trek on the Inca Trail, Aguas Calientes is the entry point to Machu Picchu. Cuzco is the launching point to Aguas Calientes.

Bus From Aguas Calientes, the only option up to Machu Picchu is a 20-minute bus ride.

Air The nearest airport is in Cuzco, which only serves Bolivia or domestic flights. Entry to Peru is always via Lima.

Where to Stay

Lodgings in Aguas Calientes are consistently overpriced – probably costing two-thirds more than counterparts in less exclusive locations. Yet spending the night offers one distinct advantage: early access to Machu Picchu, which turns out to be a pretty good reason to stay.

Visiting Machu Picchu

A sublime stone citadel. A staggering cloud-forest perch. And a backstory that's out of a movie. Machu Picchu is an extraordinary Inca settlement and Unesco World Heritage site.

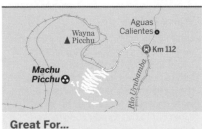

Great For...

ⓘ Need to Know

www.machupicchu.gob.pe; adult/student S128/65; ⊘6am-4pm

★ **Top Tip**

Try to visit outside peak times (between 10am and 2pm); June through August are the busiest months.

Unless you arrive via the Inca Trail, you'll officially enter the ruins through a ticket gate on the south side of Machu Picchu. About 100m of footpath brings you to the mazelike main entrance of Machu Picchu proper, where the ruins lie stretched out before you, roughly divided into two areas separated by a series of plazas.

Entrance tickets often sell out: buy them in advance in Cuzco. Guests can only enter until 4pm, though those inside are not expelled until 5pm. Check for changes in online purchasing: it is possible to use debit cards, but only for adult entry (to the ruins, Wayna Picchu and Cerro Machu Picchu). Student and child admission cannot be purchased online. The site is limited to 2500 visitors daily, with 400 paid spots

for hiking Wayna Picchu and Cerro Machu Picchu. While the government has tried enforcing set, limited hours for each visit, at present entrance remains more loosely controlled.

Local guides (per person S150, in groups of six to 10 S30) are readily available for hire at the entrance. Their expertise varies; look for one wearing an official guide ID from DIRCETUR.

Note that the names of individual ruins speculate their use – in reality, much is unknown. To get a visual fix of the whole site and to snap the classic postcard photograph, climb the zigzagging staircase on the left immediately after entering the complex, which leads to the Hut of the Caretake of the Funeraray Rock.

View from the Hut of the Caretaker of the Funerary Rock

Inside the Complex

Hut of the Caretaker of the Funerary Rock

The Hut of the Caretaker of the Funerary Rock offers an excellent viewpoint to take in the whole site. It's one of a few buildings that has been restored with a thatched roof, making it a good shelter in the case of rain. The Inca Trail enters the city just below this hut. The carved rock behind the hut may have been used to mummify the nobility, hence the hut's name.

☑ Don't Miss

Museo de Sitio Manuel Chávez Ballón (p216), by Puente Ruinas at the base of the climb to Machu Picchu.

EARLEIASON / GETTY IMAGES ©

Ceremonial Baths

If you head straight into the ruins from the main entry gate, you pass through extensive terracing to a beautiful series of 16 connected ceremonial baths that cascade across the ruins, accompanied by a flight of stairs.

Temple of the Sun

Just above and to the left of the ceremonial baths is Machu Picchu's only round building, a curved and tapering tower of exceptional stonework.

Royal Tomb

Below the Temple of the Sun, this almost-hidden, natural rock cave was carefully carved by Inca stonemasons. Its use is highly debated; though known as the Royal Tomb, no mummies were actually ever found here.

Sacred Plaza

Climbing the stairs above the ceremonial baths, there is a flat area of jumbled rocks, once used as a quarry. Turn right at the top of the stairs and walk across the quarry on a short path leading to the four-sided Sacred Plaza. The far side contains a small viewing platform with a curved wall, which offers a view of the snowy Cordillera Vilcabamba in the far distance and the Río Urubamba below.

Temple of the Three Windows

Important buildings flank the remaining three sides of the Sacred Plaza. The Temple of the Three Windows features huge trapezoidal windows that give the building its name.

Principal Temple

The 'temple' derives its name from the massive solidity and perfection of its construction. The damage to the rear right corner is the result of the ground settling

---

✖ Take a Break

Bring drinking water. Bringing food is not officially allowed.

below this corner rather than any inherent weakness in the masonry itself.

House of the High Priest

Little is known about these mysterious ruins, located opposite the Principal Temple.

Sacristy

Behind and connected to the Principal Temple lies this famous small building. It has many well-carved niches, perhaps used for the storage of ceremonial objects, as well as a carved stone bench. The Sacristy is especially known for the two rocks flanking its entrance; each is said to contain 32 angles, but it's easy to come up with a different number whenever you count them.

Intihuatana

This Quechua word loosely translates as the 'Hitching Post of the Sun' and refers to the carved rock pillar, often mistakenly called a sundial, at the top of the Intihuatana hill. The Inca astronomers were able to predict the solstices using the angles of this pillar. Thus, they were able to claim control over the return of the lengthening summer days. Its exact use remains unclear, but its elegant simplicity and high craftwork make it a highlight.

Central Plaza

The plaza separates the ceremonial sector from the residential and industrial areas.

Prison Group

At the lower end of this area is the Prison Group, a labyrinthine complex of cells, niches and passageways, positioned both under and above the ground.

Temple of the Condor

This 'temple' is named for a carving of the head of a condor with rock outcrops as outstretched wings. It is considered the centerpiece of the Prison Group.

Intipunku

(⊙checkpoint closes around 3pm) The Inca Trail ends after its final descent from the notch in the horizon called Intipunku (Sun Gate). Looking at the hill behind you as you enter the ruins, you can see both the trail and Intipunku. This hill, called Machu Picchu (old peak), gives the site its name.

Access here from Machu Picchu ruins may be restricted. It takes about an hour to reach Intipunku. If you can spare at least a half-day for the round-trip, it may be possible to continue as far as Wiñay Wayna. Expect to pay S15 or more as an unofficial reduced-charge admission fee to the Inca Trail, and be sure to return before 3pm, which is when the checkpoint typically closes.

Temple of the Sun (p203)

Inca Drawbridge

A scenic but level walk from the Hut of the Caretaker of the Funerary Rock takes you right past the top of the terraces and out along a narrow, cliff-clinging trail to the Inca drawbridge. In under a half-hour's walk, the trail gives you a good look at cloud-forest vegetation and an entirely different view of Machu Picchu. This walk is recommended, though you'll have to be content with photographing the bridge from a distance, as someone crossed the bridge some years ago and tragically fell to their death.

Wayna Picchu

Wayna Picchu is the small, steep mountain at the back of the ruins. Wayna Picchu is normally translated as 'Young Peak,' but the word *picchu,* with the correct glottal pro-nunciation, refers to the wad in the cheek of a coca-leaf chewer. Access to Wayna Picchu is limited to 400 people per day: the first 200 in line are let in at 7am, and another 200 at 10am. A ticket (S24), which includes a visit to the Moon Temple, may only be obtained when you purchase your Machu Picchu entrance ticket. These spots sell out a week in advance in low season

ⓘ Need to Know

Walking sticks or backpacks over 20L are not allowed into the ruins. There are baggage-check offices outside the entrance gate (S5 per item; 6am–4pm).

📖 Read All About It

For really in-depth explorations, take along a copy of *Exploring Cuzco* by Peter Frost.

RAFAL CICHAWA / GETTY IMAGES ©

and a month in advance in high season, so plan accordingly.

At first glance, it would appear that Wayna Picchu is a challenging climb but, although the ascent is steep, it's not technically difficult. However, it is not recommended if you suffer from vertigo. Hikers must sign in and out at a registration booth located beyond the central plaza between two thatched buildings. The 45- to 90-minute scramble up a steep footpath takes you through a short section of Inca tunnel.

Take care in wet weather as the steps get dangerously slippery. The trail is easy to follow, but involves steep sections, a ladder and an overhanging cave, where you have to bend over to get by. Part way up Wayna Picchu, a marked path plunges down to your left, continuing down the rear of Wayna Picchu to the small **Temple of the Moon**. From the temple, another cleared path leads up behind the ruin and steeply onward up the back side of Wayna Picchu.

The descent takes about an hour, and the ascent back to the main Wayna Picchu trail longer. The spectacular trail drops and climbs steeply as it hugs the sides of Wayna Picchu before plunging into the cloud forest. Suddenly, you reach a cleared area where the small, very well-made ruins are found.

Cerro Machu Picchu (S24) is a very good alternative if you miss out on Wayna Picchu tickets.

Machu Picchu

The Mystery of Machu Picchu

Machu Picchu is not mentioned in any of the chronicles of the Spanish conquistadors. Nobody apart from local Quechua people knew of Machu Picchu's existence until American historian Hiram Bingham was guided to it by locals in 1911.

Despite scores of more recent studies, knowledge of Machu Picchu remains sketchy. Even today archaeologists are forced to rely heavily on speculation and educated guesswork as to its function. Some believe the citadel was founded in the waning years of the last Incas as an attempt to preserve Inca culture or rekindle their predominance, while others think that it may have already become an uninhabited, forgotten city at the time of the conquest.

A more recent theory suggests that the site was a royal retreat or the country palace of Pachacutec, abandoned at the time of the Spanish invasion. The site's director believes that it was a city, a political, religious and administrative center. Its location, and the fact that at least eight access routes have been discovered, suggests that it was a trade nexus between Amazonia and the highlands.

It seems clear from the exceptionally high quality of the stonework and the abundance of ornamental work that Machu Picchu was once vitally important as a ceremonial center. Indeed, to some extent, it still is: Alejandro Toledo, the country's first indigenous Andean president, impressively staged his inauguration here in 2001.

Read Up on the Ruins

If you are wondering what it's like to hike the Inca Trail, or its lesser-known alternatives, pick up Mark Adams' *Turn Right at Machu Picchu* (2010). Not a hero's tale, the humorous travelogue is a first-person account of one adventure editor bumbling out into the wild. On the way, it provides an entertaining layman's look at Inca history and the striving explorations of Hiram Bingham.

BLACKDOVFX / GETTY IMAGES ©

★ Top Tip

There are no signposts here – it's not a museum – so read up or hire a guide.

☑ Don't Miss

Hiking an hour to Intipunku (p204) for a different angle overlooking Machu Picchu. It's also a popular spot to witness the sun rise.

Machu Picchu

This great 15th-century Inca citadel sits at 2430m on a narrow ridgetop above the Río Urubamba. Traditionally considered a political, religious and administrative center, new theories suggest that it was a royal estate designed by Pachacutec, the Inca ruler whose military conquests transformed the empire. Trails linked it to the Inca capital of Cuzco and important sites in the jungle. As invading Spaniards never discovered it, experts still dispute when the site was abandoned and why.

At its peak, Machu Picchu was thought to have some 500 inhabitants. An engineering marvel, its famous Inca walls have polished stone fitted to stone, with no mortar in between. The citadel took thousands of laborers 50 years to build – today its cost of construction would exceed a billion US dollars.

Making it habitable required leveling the site, channeling water from high mountain streams through stone canals and building vertical retaining walls that became agricultural terraces for corn, potatoes and coca. The drainage system also helped combat heavy rains (diverting them for irrigation), while east-facing rooftops and farming terraces took advantage of maximum sun exposure.

The site is a magnet to mystics, adventurers and students of history alike. While its function remains hotly debated, the essential grandeur of Machu Picchu is indisputable.

TOP TIPS

» **Visit** before mid-morning crowds

» **Allow** at least three hours to visit

» **Wear** walking shoes and a hat

» **Bring** drinking water

» **Gain** perspective walking the lead-in trails

Intihuatana

'Hitching Post of the Sun', this exquisitely carved rock was likely used by Inca astronomers to predict solstices. It's a rare survivor since invading Spaniards destroyed *intihuatanas* throughout the kingdom to eradicate pagan blasphemy.

Western Agricultural Terraces

Sacred Plaza

To Hut of the Caretaker of the Funerary Rock

Temple of the Three Windows

Enjoy the commanding views of the plaza below through the huge trapezoidal windows framed by three-ton lintels. Rare in Inca architecture, the presence of three windows may indicate special significance.

Wayna Picchu

This 2720m peak with ladders, caves and a small temple can be climbed in a 45- to 90-minute scramble. Take care, the steep steps are slippery when wet. Purchase a coveted permit ahead with admission.

POWEROFFOREVER/GETTY IMAGES ©

Central Plaza

This sprawling green area with grazing llamas separates the ceremonial sector of Machu Picchu from the more mundane residential and industrial sectors.

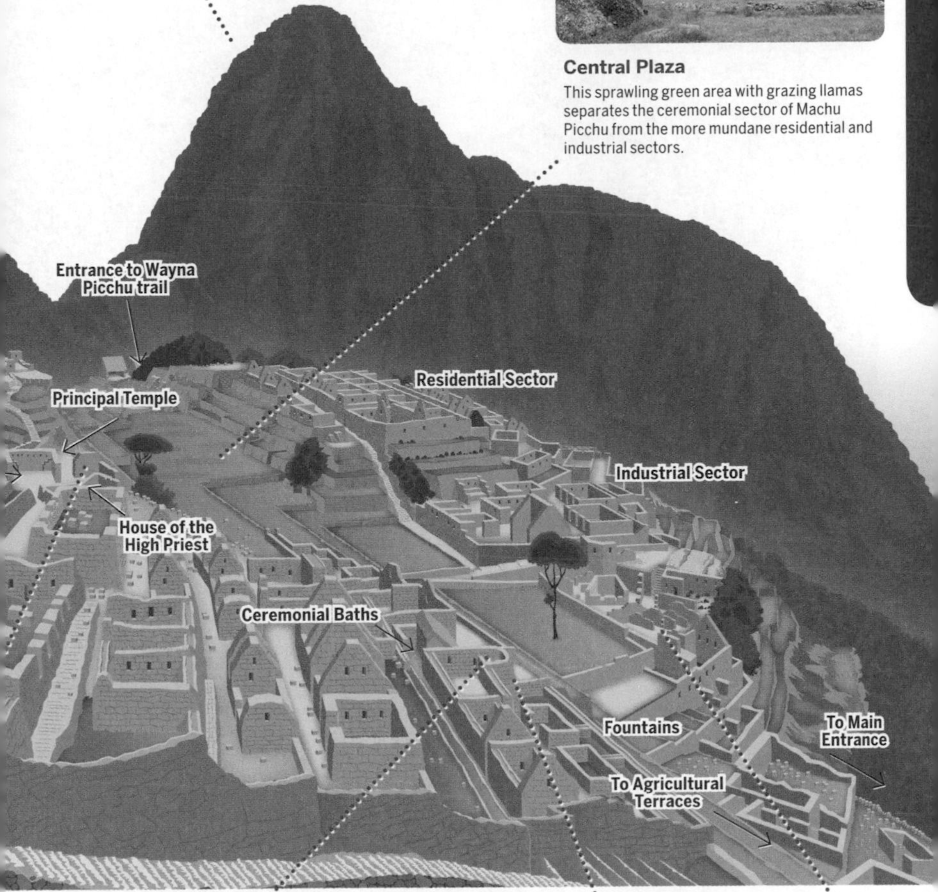

Entrance to Wayna Picchu trail

Principal Temple

Residential Sector

Industrial Sector

House of the High Priest

Ceremonial Baths

Fountains

To Main Entrance

To Agricultural Terraces

Temple of the Sun

This off-limits rounded tower is best viewed from above. Featuring the site's finest stone-work, an altar and trapezoidal windows, it may have been used for astronomical purposes.

GLOWIMAGES/GETTY IMAGES ©

Royal Tomb

Speculated to have special ceremonial significance, a natural rock cave sits below the Temple of the Sun. Though off-limits, visitors can view its step-like altar and sacred niches from the entrance.

GEORGE HOLTON/GETTY IMAGES ©

Temple of the Condor

Check out the condor head carving with rock outcrops that resemble outstretched wings. Behind, an off-limits cavity reaches a tiny underground cell that may only be entered by bending double.

The Inca Trail

The views of snowy mountain peaks, distant rivers and cloud forests are stupendous – and walking from one cliff-hugging pre-Columbian ruin to the next is a mystical and unforgettable experience.

Great For...

☑ Don't Miss

Hot springs in the towns along the way, which will help weary hiking legs to recover.

The most famous hike in South America, the four-day Inca Trail is walked by thousands every year. Although the total distance is only about 39km (24 miles), the ancient trail laid by the Incas from the Sacred Valley to Machu Picchu winds its way up and down and around the mountains, snaking over three high Andean passes en route, which have collectively led to the route being dubbed 'the Inca Trial.'

Booking Your Trip

It is important to book your trip at least six months in advance for dates between May and August. Outside these months, you may get a permit with a few weeks' notice, but it's very hard to predict. Only licensed operators can get permits, but you can check general availability at www.camino-inca.com.

❶ Need to Know

Most trekking agencies run buses to the start of the trail, also known as Piscacucho or Km 82.

✕ Take a Break

Most tours include meals and snacks. Bring a refillable water bottle.

★ Top Tip

The Inca Trail is best visited in the dry season, April to October, and is closed in February.

Consider booking a five-day trip to lessen the pace and enjoy more wildlife and ruins. Other positives include less-crowded campsites and being able to stay at the most scenic one – Phuyupatamarka (3600m) – on the third evening.

Make sure you have international travel insurance that covers adventure activities.

Regulations & Fees

The Inca Trail is the only trek in the Cuzco area that cannot be walked independently – you must go with a licensed operator. Prices range from US$550 to US$1465 and above.

Only 500 people each day (including guides and porters) are allowed to start the trail. You must go through an approved Inca Trail operator. Permits are issued to them on a first-come, first-served basis. You will need to provide your passport number to

get a permit, and carry the passport with you to show at checkpoints along the trail. Be aware that if you get a new passport but had applied with your old, it may present a problem.

Permits are nontransferrable: name changes are not allowed.

Choosing an Operator

While it may be tempting to quickly book your trek and move onto the next item on your To Do list, it's a good idea to examine the options carefully before sending that deposit. If price is your bottom line, keep in mind that agencies charging less than US$500 may cut corners by paying their guides and porters lower wages. Other issues are substandard gear (ie leaky tents) and dull or lackadaisical guiding.

Yet paying more may not mean getting more, especially since international operators take their cut and hire local Peruvian agencies. Talk with a few agencies to get a sense of their quality of service. You might ask if the guide speaks English (fluently or just a little), request a list of what is included and inquire about group size and the kind of transportation used. Ensure that your tour includes a tent, food, a cook, one-day admission to the ruins and the return train fare.

Porters who carry group gear – tents, food etc – are also included. You'll be expected to carry your own personal gear, including sleeping bag. If you are not an experienced backpacker, it may be a good idea to hire a porter to carry your personal gear; this usually costs around US$50 per day for about 10kg.

Part of the fun is meeting travelers from other parts of the world in your trekking group. Keep in mind that individual paces vary and the group dynamic requires some compromise.

If you prefer more exclusive services, it's possible to organize private trips with an independent licensed guide (US$1250 to US$2000 per person). This can be expensive but for groups of six or more it may in fact be cheaper than the standard group treks. Prices vary considerably, so shop around.

For a list of agencies and guides based in Cuzco, see p164.

The Two-Day Inca Trail

This 10km version of the Inca Trail gives a fairly good indication of what the longer trail is like. It's a real workout, and passes through some of the best scenery and most impressive ruins and terracing of the longer trail.

It's a steep three- or four-hour climb from Km 104 to Wiñay Wayna, then another two hours or so on fairly flat terrain to Machu Picchu. You may be on the trail a couple

Wiñay Wayna (p215)

of hours longer, just to enjoy the views and explore. We advise taking the earliest train possible from Cuzco or Ollantaytambo.

The two-day trail means overnighting in Aguas Calientes, and visiting Machu Picchu the next day, so it's really only one day of walking. The average price is US$400 to US$535.

What to Expect

Even if you are not carrying a full backpack, trekking the Inca Trail requires a good level of fitness. In addition to regularly exercis-

> ### ★ Top Tip
> On the trail, get your next day's water hot in a well-sealed bottle; you can use it as a sleeping bag warmer and it will be cool to drink by the time you're hiking.

MORTEN ELM / GETTY IMAGES ©

ing, you can get ready with hikes and long walks in the weeks before your trip (also a good time to test out your gear). Boots should be already worn in by the time you go. On the trail, you may have to deal with issues such as heat and altitude. Just don't rush it; keep a reasonable pace and you should do fine.

Day One

After crossing the Río Urubamba (2600m) and taking care of registration formalities, you'll climb gently alongside the river to the trail's first archaeological site, **Llactapata** (Town on Top of the Terraces), before heading south down a side valley of the Río Cusichaca. (If you start from Km 88, turn west after crossing the river to see the little-visited site of **Q'ente**, about 1km away, then return east to Llactapata on the main trail.)

The trail leads 7km south to the hamlet of **Wayllabamba** (Grassy Plain; 3000m), near which many tour groups will camp for the first night. You can buy bottled drinks and high-calorie snacks here, and take a breather to look over your shoulder for views of the snowcapped **Nevado Verónica** (5750m).

Day Two

Wayllabamba is situated near the fork of Ríos Llullucha and Cusichaca. The trail crosses the Río Llullucha, then climbs steeply up along the river. This area is known as **Tres Piedras** (Three White Stones; 3300m), though these boulders are no longer visible. From here it is a long, very steep 3km climb through humid woodlands.

The trail eventually emerges on the high, bare mountainside of **Llulluchupampa** (3750m), where water is available and the flats are dotted with campsites, which get

> ### ☑ Don't Forget
> Take cash (in Peruvian soles) for tipping; an adequate amount is S100 for a porter and S200 for a cook.

very cold at night. This is as far as you can reasonably expect to get on your first day, though many groups will actually spend their second night here.

From Llulluchupampa, a good path up the left-hand side of the valley climbs for a two- to three-hour ascent to the pass of **Warmiwañusca**, also colorfully known as 'Dead Woman's Pass.' At 4200m above sea level, this is the highest point of the trek, and leaves many a seasoned hiker gasping. From Warmiwañusca, you can see the Río Pacamayo (Río Escondido) far below, as well as the ruin of Runkurakay halfway up the next hill, above the river.

The trail continues down a long and knee-jarringly steep descent to the river, where there are large campsites at **Paq'amayo**. At an altitude of about 3600m, the trail crosses the river over a small

footbridge and climbs toward **Runkurakay**; at 3750m this round ruin has superb views. It's about an hour's walk away.

Day Three

Above Runkurakay, the trail climbs to a false summit before continuing past two small lakes to the top of the second pass at 3950m, which has views of the snow-laden Cordillera Vilcabamba. You'll notice a change in ecology as you descend from this pass – you're now on the eastern, Amazon slope of the Andes and things immediately get greener. The trail descends to the ruin of **Sayaqmarka**, a tightly constructed complex perched on a small mountain spur, which offers incredible views. The trail continues downward and crosses an upper tributary of the Río Aobamba (Wavy Plain).

Nevado Verónica (p213)

The trail then leads on across an Inca causeway and up a gentle climb through some beautiful cloud forest and an **Inca tunnel** carved from the rock. This is a relatively flat section and you'll soon arrive at the third pass at almost 3600m, which has grand views of the Río Urubamba Valley, and campsites where some groups spend their final night, with the advantage of watching the sun set over a truly spectacular view, but with the disadvantage of having to leave at 3am in the race to reach the Sun Gate in time for sunrise. If you are camping here, be careful in the early morning as the steep incline makes the following steps slippery.

PETER ADAMS / GETTY IMAGES ©

> ★ **Top Tip**
>
> As a courtesy, don't occupy the dining tent until late if it's where the porters sleep.

Just below the pass is the beautiful and well-restored ruin of **Phuyupatamarka** (City Above the Clouds), about 3570m above sea level. The site contains six beautiful ceremonial baths with water running through them. From Phuyupatamarka, the trail makes a dizzying dive into the cloud forest below, following an incredibly well-engineered flight of many hundreds of Inca steps (it's nerve-racking in the early hours – use a headlamp). After two or three hours, the trail eventually zigzags its way down to a collapsed red-roofed white building that marks the final night's campsite.

A 500m trail behind the old, out of use, pub leads to the exquisite little Inca site of **Wiñay Wayna**, which is variously translated as 'Forever Young,' 'To Plant the Earth Young' and 'Growing Young' (as opposed to 'growing old'). Peter Frost writes that the Quechua name refers to an orchid (*Epidendrum secundum*) that blooms here year-round. The semitropical campsite at Wiñay Wayna boasts one of the most stunning views on the whole trail, especially at sunrise. For better or worse, the famous pub located here is now deteriorated and no longer functioning. A rough trail leads from this site to another spectacular terraced ruin, called **Intipata**, best visited on the day you arrive at Wiñay Wayna (consider coordinating it with your guide if you are interested).

Day Four

From the Wiñay Wayna guard post, the trail winds without much change in elevation through the cliff-hanging cloud forest for about two hours to reach **Intipunku** (Sun Gate) – the penultimate site on the trail, where it's tradition to enjoy your first glimpse of majestic Machu Picchu while waiting for the sun to rise over the surrounding mountains.

The final triumphant descent takes almost an hour. Trekkers generally arrive long before the morning trainloads of tourists, and can enjoy the exhausted exhilaration of reaching their goal without having to push past enormous groups of visitors.

Aguas Callentes

Also known as Machu Picchu Pueblo, this town lies in a deep gorge below the ruins. A virtual island, it's cut off from all roads and enclosed by stone cliffs, towering cloud forest and two rushing rivers. Despite its gorgeous location, Aguas Calientes has the feel of a gold-rush town, with a large itinerant population, slack services that count on one-time customers and an architectural tradition of rebar and unfinished cement. With merchants pushing the hard sell, it's hard not to feel overwhelmed. Your best bet is to go without expectations.

◉ SIGHTS

Museo de Sitio Manuel Chávez Ballón   Museum

(admission S22; ◷9am-5pm) This museum has superb information in Spanish and English on the archaeological excava-tions of Machu Picchu and Inca building methods. Stop here before or after the ruins to get a sense of context (and to enjoy the air-conditioning and soothing music if you're walking back from the ruins after hours in the sun).

There's a small botanical garden with orchids outside, down a cool-if-nerve-testing set of Inca stairs. It's by Puente Ruinas, at the base of the footpath to Machu Picchu.

Las Termas   Hot Springs

(admission S10; ◷5am-8:30pm) Weary trekkers soak away their aches and pains in the town's hot springs, 10 minutes' walk up Pachacutec from the train tracks. These tiny, natural thermal springs, from which Aguas Calientes derives its name, are nice enough but far from the best in the area, and get scummy by late morning.

Towels can be rented cheaply outside the entrance.

Porters on the Inca Trail

WYSHE / GETTY IMAGES ©

⊕ ACTIVITIES

Putucusi Hiking

At the time of writing this steep hike was closed for serious maintenance. The toothy mini-mountain sits directly opposite Machu Picchu.

Follow the railway tracks about 250m west of town and you'll see a set of stairs; this is the start of a well-marked trail. Parts of the walk are up ladders, which get slippery in the wet season, but the view across to Machu Picchu is worth the trek. Allow three hours.

⊗ EATING

Touts standing in the street will try to herd you into their restaurant, but take your time making a selection. Standards are not very high in most restaurants – if you go to one that hasn't been recommended, snoop around to check the hygiene first. Since refrigeration can be a problem, it's best to order vegetarian if you're eating in low-end establishments.

La Boulangerie de Paris Bakery $

(☑084-79-7798; Jr Sinchi Roca s/n; snacks S3-10; ⊙5am-9pm; ⊛) We don't know how this French bakery got here, we're just thankful. This small cafe sells *pain au chocolat* (croissants stuffed with chocolate), fresh croissants, espresso drinks and desserts, with a few gluten-free items. You can also order boxed lunches.

Indio Feliz French $$

(☑084-21-1090; Lloque Yupanqui 4; mains S34-48; ⊙11am-10pm) Hospitality is the strong suit of French cook Patrik at this multi-award-winning restaurant, but the food does not disappoint. Start with *sopa criolla* (a potent and flavorful broth, served with hot bread, homemade butter and optional chilis). There are also nods to traditional French cooking – like Provençal tomatoes, crispy-perfect garlic potatoes and a melt-in-your-mouth apple tart.

The candlelit decor shows the imagination of a long-lost castaway with imitation

> *We don't know how this French bakery got here, we're just thankful*

Gauguin panels, carved figurehead damsels, colonial benches and vintage objects. The *menú* (set meal; S69) is an extremely good value for a decadent dinner. Indio Feliz has good wheelchair access and was in the process of adding an upstairs bar and terrace when we visited, which provides another reason not to leave here.

Tree House Fusion $$

(☑084-21-1101; Huanacaure s/n; S38-52; ⊙4:30am-10pm) The rustic ambience of Tree House provides a cozy setting for its inviting fusion menu served alongside South American wines, craft beers and cocktails. Dishes such as chicken soup with wontons and ginger, red quinoa risotto and crispy trout are lovingly prepared. For dessert, lip-smacking fruit crumble. It has raw and vegan options. Reserve ahead. It's part of the Rupa Wasi hotel.

Café Inkaterra Peruvian $$$

(☑084-21-1122; Machu Picchu Pueblo Hotel; menú lunch/dinner S54/90; ⊙11am-9pm; ☑) Upstream from the train station, this tucked-away riverside restaurant is housed in elongated thatched rooms with views of water tumbling over the boulders. There's only a set menu (starter, main dish and dessert), with gluten-free and vegetarian options. The perfectly executed *lomo salta-do* (strips of beef stir-fried with tomatoes, potatoes and chili) features a flavorful sauce and crisp red onions.

⊙ INFORMATION

BCP (Av Imperio de los Incas s/n) If this bank runs out of money (weekends are busiest), there are four others in town, including one on Av Imperio de los Incas.

Centro Cultural (Machu Picchu Tickets; ☑084-81-1196; Av Pachacutec; ⊙5:30am-8:30pm)

This new cultural center is the only spot in town selling Machu Picchu entrance tickets.

iPerú (📞084-21-1104; cuadra 1, Pachacutec; 🕑9am-1pm & 2-6pm Mon-Sat, to 1pm Sun) A helpful information center for everything Machu Picchu.

❶ GETTING THERE & AROUND

There are only three options to get to Aguas Calientes, and hence to Machu Picchu: trek it, catch the train via Cuzco and the Sacred Valley, or travel by road and train via Santa Teresa.

TRAIN

Buy a return ticket to avoid getting stranded in Aguas Calientes – outbound trains sell out much quicker than their inbound counterparts. All train companies have ticket offices in the train station, but you can check their websites for up-to-date schedule, and ticket purchases.

To C_____ ours), PeruRail (www.peru _____ to Poroy, from where taxis _____ nother 20 minutes away.

_____y's Ollantaytambo (two _____eru Rail and Inca Rail (www. incarail.com) provide service.

To Santa Teresa (45 minutes), Peru Rail travels at 8:53am, 2:55pm and 9:50pm daily, with other departures for residents only. Tickets (US$26) can only be bought from Aguas Calientes train station on the day of departure, but trains actually leave from the west end of town, outside the police station. You can also do this route as a guided multisport tour.

BUS

There is no road access to Aguas Calientes. The only buses go up the hill to Machu Picchu (round-trip S72, 25 minutes) from 5:30am to 3:30pm; buses return until 5:45pm.

Clockwise from left: Stone walkway on the Inca Trail (p210); Aguas Calientes train; Aguas Calientes (p216); Statue of Pachacutec, Aguas Calientes

TRUJILLO

Trujillo at a Glance...

Stand in the right spot and the glamorously colonial streets of old Trujillo look like they've barely changed in hundreds of years. Well, there are more honking taxis now — but the city, with its polychrome buildings and profusion of colonial-era churches, still puts on a dashing show.

Most people come here to visit the remarkable pre-Incan archaeological sites nearby, spending just a short time wandering the compact city center. The behemoth Chimú capital of Chan Chan, on the outskirts of town, was the largest pre-Columbian city in the Americas, making it the top attraction in the region. Other Chimú sites bake in the surrounding desert, among them the immense and impressive Moche-period Huacas del Sol y de la Luna (Temples of the Sun and Moon).

Trujillo in Two Days

Spend the first morning exploring **Chan Chan** (p224), the Chimú capital, including the **Museo de Sitio Chan Chan** (p225). Continue on to laid-back beachside **Huanchaco** (p231). On the second morning, visit the colonial mansion **Casa Ganoza Chopitea** (p226) and Plaza de Armas. Then head to the fascinating **Huacas del Sol y de la Luna** (p227).

Trujillo in Three Days

A third day gets you more time with the *casonas* (stately homes) in Trujillo, its Plaza de Armas, elegant colonial streets and the ancient Moche artefacts at **Museo de Arqueología** (p227), then spend the rest of the day leisurely visiting one of the best-preserved Chimú temples at **Huaca Arco Iris** (p229).

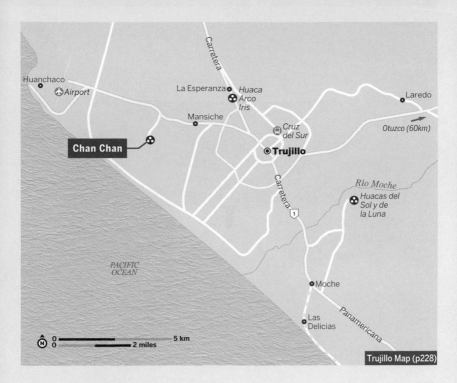

Trujillo Map (p228)

Arriving in Trujillo

Aeropuerto de Trujillo The airport is 10km northwest of town.

Bus Most buses arrive at the north end of town at España and Amazonas or, if coming from the south, at terminals on the Panamericana Sur.

Where to Stay

In Trujillo, the most comfortable and convenient location is anywhere within two blocks of Plaza de Armas, especially north near Calle Pizarro. Note that many budget and midrange hotels can be noisy if you get the streetside rooms.

Beach bums may consider staying in the laid-back surfer village of Huanchaco, just 20 minutes up the road.

Chan Chan

Built around AD 1300 and covering 36 sq km, Chan Chan is the largest pre-Columbian city in the Americas and the largest adobe city in the world.

Great For...

☑ Don't Miss

The sea-related friezes in the Audience Rooms.

At the height of the Chimú empire, Chan Chan housed an estimated 60,000 inhabitants and contained a vast wealth of gold, silver and ceramics (which the Spanish quickly looted).

The capital consisted of 10 walled citadels, also called royal compounds. Each contained a royal burial mound filled with vast quantities of funerary offerings, including dozens of sacrificed young women and chambers full of ceramics, weavings and jewelry. Over time, devastating El Niño floods and heavy rainfall have severely eroded the mud walls of the city – you'll need an active imagination to fill in the details. Today the most impressive aspect of the site is its sheer size.

Note that Chan Chan is best visited with a guide from Trujillo or on-site, as signage

Wooden statue in front of carved adobe wall

ALEX ROBINSON / GETTY IMAGES ©

Mansiche

Chan
Chan

Carretera

Trujillo

Carretera

ℹ️ Need to Know

Admission incl musem S10, guide per person S15, minimum 3 people; ⏰9am-4pm, museum closed Mon

🍴 Take a Break

The only food sold nearby are the snacks near the ticket booth.

★ Top Tip

Chan Chan is on the road between Trujillo and Huanchaco, making it easy to visit the ruins and beach in one day.

---

is extremely limited. Much of the site is covered with tentlike structures to protect it from erosion.

Tschudi Complex

The area known as the Tschudi Complex – also called the Palacio Nik-An – is the only area within the site that is open to visitors. The complex's centerpiece is a massive restored **Ceremonial Courtyard**, with 4m-thick interior walls that are decorated with recreated geometric designs. Ground-level designs closest to the door, representing three or four sea otters, are the only originals left. Nearby, an outside wall – one of the best restored in the complex – displays friezes of fish and seabirds.

Other elements in the complex include the set of labyrinthine **Audience Rooms**, filled with friezes of birds, fish and waves, as well as a well that once supplied the daily water needs of the royal compound. Also on view is a **Mausoleum**, where a king was buried with human sacrifices, as well as the fascinating **Assembly Room**, a large rectangular room with 24 seats set into niches in the walls. Its acoustic properties are such that speakers sitting in any one of the niches can be clearly heard all over the room.

Museum

The site museum contains exhibits explaining Chan Chan and the Chimú culture. It is a short walk away on the main road, about 500m before the Chan Chan turnoff. The museum has a few signs in Spanish and English, but a guide is still useful. A sound-and-light show plays in Spanish every 30 minutes. The aerial photos and maps showing the huge extension of Chan Chan are fascinating, as tourists can only visit a tiny portion of the site.

Trujillo

◉ SIGHTS

Plaza de Armas   Square

Trujillo's spacious and spit-shined main square, surely the cleanest in the Americas and definitely one of the prettiest, hosts a colorful assembly of preserved colonial buildings and an impressive statue dedicated to work, the arts and liberty. Elegant mansions abound, including **Hotel Libertador** (Independencia 485). To the northeast, the plaza is fronted by **Basilica Menor Catedral** (admission to museum S4; ⏲church 10-11am, museum 9am-1pm & 4-7pm Mon-Fri, 9am-noon Sat), which dates back to 1647 and contains a museum of religious and colonial art.

At 9am on Sundays there is a **flag-raising ceremony** on the Plaza de Armas, complete, on special occasions, with a parade, *caballos de paso* (pacing horses) and performances of the *marinera* (a typical coastal Peruvian dance involving much romantic waving of handkerchiefs).

Casa Ganoza Chopitea   Notable Building

(Independencia 630) Northeast of the cathedral, this c 1735 mansion, also known as Casa de los Léones, is considered to be the best-preserved mansion of the colonial period in Trujillo. The details are stunning, from the elaborate gateway at the entrance to 300-year-old frescoes, Oregon-pine pillars and rustic ceilings inside, some tied together with sheepskin.

Casa de Urquiaga   Historic Building

(Pizarro 446; ⏲9:15am-3:15pm Mon-Fri, 10am-1pm Sat) FREE Owned and maintained by Banco Central de la Reserva del Perú since 1972, this beautiful colonial mansion's history dates to 1604, though the original house was completely destroyed in the earthquake of 1619. Rebuilt and dramatically preserved since, it now houses exquisite period furniture, including a striking writer's desk once used by Simón Bolívar, who organized much of his final campaign to liberate Peru from the Spanish empire from Trujillo in 1824.

Trujillo street

HUGHES HERVE / HEMIS.FR / GETTY IMAGES ©

Palacio Iturregui Notable Building

(Pizarro 688; ⊘9am-5pm) This bright yellow 19th-century mansion is unmistakable and impossible to ignore unless you're color blind. Built in neoclassical style, it has beautiful window gratings, 36 slender interior columns and gold moldings on the ceilings. General Juan Manuel Iturregui lived here after he famously proclaimed independence.

Museo de Arqueología Museum

(Junín 682; admission S5; ⊘9am-5pm Mon-Sat, to 1pm Sun) This well-curated museum features a rundown of Peruvian history from 12,000 BC to the present day, with an emphasis on Moche, Chimu and Inca civilizations as well as the lesser-known Cupisnique and Salinar cultures. But it's also worth popping in for the house itself, a restored 17th-century mansion known as La Casa Risco, which features striking cedar pillars and gorgeous painted courtyard walls.

Casa de la Emancipación Notable Building

(Pizarro 610) Now the Banco Continental, this building features a mishmash of colonial and Republican styles and is best known as the site where Trujillo's independence from colonial rule was formally declared on December 29, 1820. Check out the unique cubic Cajabamba marble stone flooring; there are also galleries dedicated to revolving art exhibitions, Peruvian poet César Vallejo and period furniture. It hosts live-music events as well – look for posters around town on your visit.

Museo Cassinelli Museum

(N de Piérola 607; admission S7; ⊘9am-1pm & 3-6pm Mon-Sat) This private archaeological collection housed in the basement of a Repsol gas station (the one on the west side of the intersection, not the east side) is fascinating, with some 2000 ceramic pieces on display (curated from a collection owned by Italian immigrants) that certainly don't belong under a gritty gas station.

 North & West of Plaza de Armas

There are several interesting churches near the Plaza de Armas that are not open for visitation but well worth viewing from the outside on a walking tour of the city: Iglesia de la Compañía, now part of the Universidad Nacional de Trujillo; Iglesia de Santa Ana; Iglesia de Santo Domingo; and Iglesia de Santa Clara.

Basilica Menor Catedral
DIEGO GRANDI / SHUTTERSTOCK ©

Huacas del Sol y de la Luna Ruin

(www.huacasdemoche.pe; site admission S10, museum S5; ⊘9am-4pm) The Temples of the Sun and the Moon are more than 700 years older than Chan Chan and are attributed to the Moche period. They are on the south bank of the Río Moche, about 10km southeast of Trujillo. The entrance price includes a guide. The Huaca del Sol is not currently open to visitation as research continues on the site.

Huaca del Sol is the largest single pre-Columbian structure in Peru, although about a third of it has been washed away. The structure was built with an estimated 140 million adobe bricks, many of them marked with symbols representing the workers who made them.

At one time the pyramid consisted of several different levels connected by steep flights of stairs, huge ramps and walls sloping at 77 degrees. The last 1500 years have wrought their inevitable damage, and today the pyramid looks like a giant pile of

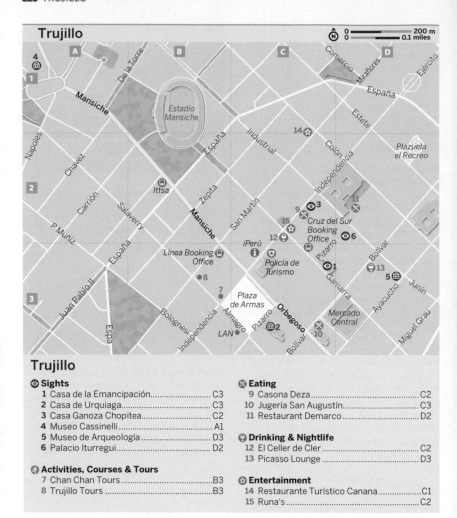

Trujillo

crude bricks partially covered with sand. The few graves within the structure suggest it may have been a huge ceremonial site. Certainly, its size alone makes the pyramid an awesome sight.

Size isn't everything, however. The smaller but more interesting **Huaca de la Luna** is about 500m away across the open desert. This structure is riddled with rooms that contain ceramics, precious

metals and some of the beautiful polychrome friezes for which the Moche were famous. The *huaca* (tomb or grave) was built over six centuries to AD 600, with six succeeding generations expanding on it and completely covering the previous structure.

Archaeologists are currently onion-skinning selected parts of the *huaca* and have discovered that there are friezes of stylized figures on every level, some of which have been perfectly preserved by the later levels built around them. It's well worth a visit; you'll see newly excavated friezes every year, and the excellent **Museo Huacas de Moche** (admission S3; ⊘9am-4:30pm) is a long-time-coming permanent home for numerous objects excavated from the site. There's a research center and theater as well. A taxi here costs about S15.

Huaca Arco Iris   Ruin
(Rainbow Temple; with Chan Chan ticket admission free) Also known locally as Huaca del Dragón, Huaca Arco Iris is in the suburb of La Esperanza, about 4km northwest of Trujillo. Dating from the 12th century, it is one of the best preserved of the Chimú temples – simply because it was buried under sand until the 1960s. Its location was known to a handful of archaeologists and *huaqueros* (grave robbers), but excavation did not begin until 1963. Unfortunately, the 1983 El Niño caused damage to the friezes.

 TOURS

There are dozens of tour agencies in Trujillo. Entrance fees are *not* included in the listed tour prices. Most full-day tours cost around S65, including transport and guide. If you prefer a private guide, ask at iPerú (p230) for a list of certified guides and contact details.

Trujillo Tours   Cultural
(⌨044-23-3091; www.trujillotours.com; Almagro 301; ⊘7:30am-1pm & 4-8pm) This friendly operation has three- to four-hour tours to Chan Chan, Huanchaco, Huacas del Sol y de la Luna, as well as city tours. Tours are available in English, French, Portuguese and German.

Chan Chan Tours   Cultural
(⌨044-24-3016; chanchantourstrujillo@hotmail.com; Independencia 431; ⊘8am-1pm & 3-8pm) Right on Plaza de Armas, this established agency organizes trips to Chan Chan and

Moche Huacas Sol y de la Luna, as well as trips further afield. The guides speak some English.

 EATING

The 700 cuadra of Pizarro is where Trujillo's power brokers hang out and families converge, and they're kept well fed by a row of trendy yet reasonably priced cafes and restaurants. Some of the best eateries in Trujillo are found a short taxi ride outside the town center.

Jugería San Augustín   Juice, Snacks $
(Bolívar 526; sandwiches S6-8; ⊘8:30am-1pm & 4-8pm Mon-Sat, 9am-1pm Sun) You can spot this place by the near-constant lines snaking around the corner in summer as locals queue for the drool-inducing juices (S2–5). But don't leave it at that. The chicken and *lechón* (suckling pig) sandwiches, slathered with all the fixings, are what you'll be telling friends back home about on a postcard.

Mar Picante   Peruvian $$
(www.marpicante.com; Húsares de Junín 412; mains S18-30; ⊘10am-5pm) If you come to Trujillo without sampling this bamboo-lined seafood palace's *ceviche mixto* ordered with a side of something spicy, you haven't lived life on the edge. You'll get raw fish, crab, scallops and onions, marinated as usual in lime juice, piled on top of yucca and sweet potato with a side of toasted corn *(canchas)* and corn on the cob.

This is the north coast's best ceviche! Service is swift and friendly as well, no small feat considering it's always packed. Take a taxi (S3.50) or leg it southwest on Larco from the center. Húsares de Junín splits off to the southeast 200m south of España.

Casona Deza   Peruvian $$
(Independencia 630; mains S22-35; ☎) ✿ Expect excellent espresso, house-made desserts and tasty pizzas and sandwiches, often sourced organically, at this spacious, atmospheric cafe that occupies one of

the city's most fiercely preserved colonial homes.

The Casa Ganoza Chopitea mansion (c 1735) was resurrected via auction by a local team of brothers passionate about Trujillo. Whether you're here for coffee, wine, sustenance or architectural oohing and aahing, it's an addictive spot.

Restaurant Demarco   Peruvian $$

(☑044-23-4251; Pizarro 725; mains S10-45; ☺7:30am-11pm; 🛜) An elegant choice with veteran cummerbund-bound waiters who fawn over you like in the '40s, this tableclothed classic offers a long list of sophisticated meat and seafood dishes along with good-value lunch specials (S14.50) and pizzas.

It has mouthwatering *chupe de camarones*, a seafood stew of jumbo shrimp simmering in a buttery broth with hints of garlic, cumin and oregano, and the desserts are excellent, from classic tiramisu to milehigh *tres leches* (a spongy cake made with evaporated milk).

El Celler de Cler   Peruvian $$

(cnr Gamarra & Independencia; mains S24-48; ☺6pm-1am) This atmospheric spot is the only place in Trujillo to enjoy dinner (coupled with an amazing cocktail) on a 2nd-floor balcony; the wraparound number dates to the early 1800s. The food is upscale, featuring pasta and grills, and delicious. Antiques fuel the decor, from a '50s-era American cash register to an extraordinary industrial revolution pulley lamp from the UK.

🍷 DRINKING & NIGHTLIFE

Picasso Lounge   Bar

(Bolivar 762) This shotgun-style cafe and bar approaches Trujillo's trendiness tipping point and is a great place to check out some contemporary local art. Exhibitions change every two months. When the bartender is on (Thursday to Saturday from 8pm), there's a well-rounded cocktail list with some creative pisco concoctions.

✪ ENTERTAINMENT

Restaurante Turístico Canana   Live Music

(☑044-23-2503; San Martín 791; cover S20; ☺from 11pm Thu-Sat) Although this place serves good Peruvian coastal food, late Thursday to Saturday is the time to go. Local musicians and dancers perform, starting at around 11pm, and you just might find yourself joining in. Better start drinking now.

Runa's   Live Music

(Independencia 610; cover S15) This cool colonial bar has an outside patio and live music on weekends. The airy feel is a nice break from the cacophonous discos nearby. The cover charge generally includes a drink.

ℹ INFORMATION

iPerú (☑044-29-4561; www.peru.travel; Independencia 467, oficina 106; ☺9am-6pm Mon-Sat, to 2pm Sun) Provides tourist information and a list of certified guides and travel agencies.

Policía de Turismo (☑044-29-1770; Independencia 572) Shockingly helpful. Tourist police wear white shirts around town and some deputies speak English, Italian and/or French.

ℹ GETTING THERE & AWAY

AIR

The airport is 10km northwest of town. Both **LAN** (☑044-22-1469; www.lan.com; Pizarro 340) and **Avianca** (☑0-800-1-8222; www.avianca. com; Real Plaza, César Vallejo Oeste 1345) have multiple daily flights to/from Lima.

BUS

Buses fill up, so book in advance. Several companies that go to southern destinations have terminals on the Panamericana Sur, the southern extension of Moche, and Ejército; check where your bus actually leaves from when buying a ticket.

There's an enclave of bus companies around España and Amazonas offering Lima-bound night buses (eight hours).

If you want to travel to Huaraz by day, you'll need to go to Chimbote and catch a bus from there. For more frequent buses to Cajamarca and the northern Highlands, head to Chiclayo.

Cruz del Sur (📞0801-11111; www.cruzdelsur. com.pe; Amazonas 437) One of the biggest and most comfortable companies. Travels to Lima and Guayaquil. It also has a **booking office** (Gamarra 439; h9am-9pm Mon-Sat) in the centre.

Ittsa (📞044-25-1415; www.ittsabus.com; Mansiche 143) Has Piura as well as 11 Lima-bound departures.

Línea (📞044-29-7000; www.linea.pe) The **booking office** (📞044-24-5181; cnr San Martín & Obregoso; 🕗8am-9pm Mon-Sat) is conveniently located in the historical center, although all buses leave from the **terminal** (📞044-29-9666; Panamerica Sur 2855), a taxi ride away. Goes to Lima, Piura, Cajamarca, Chiclayo, Chimbote and Huaraz.

Móvil Tours (📞01-716-8000; www.moviltours. com.pe; Panamerica Sur 3955) Specializes in very comfortable long-haul tourist services to Lima, Huaraz, Caraz, Chachapoyas and Tarapoto.

ⓘ GETTING AROUND

A taxi from the airport to the city center costs S15.

For sightseeing, taxis charge about S20 (in town) to S25 (out of town) per hour.

Huanchaco

This once-tranquil fishing hamlet, 12km outside Trujillo, woke up one morning to find itself a brightly highlighted paragraph on Peru's Gringo Trail. The village's fame came in large part from the long, narrow reed boats you'll see lining the Malecón. The slow pace of life attracts a certain type of beach bum and the town has managed to retain much of its villagey appeal. Today, Huanchaco is happy to dish up a long menu of accommodations and dining options to tourists, and great waves for budding surfers. Come summertime, legions of local and foreign tourists descend on its lapping shores, and this fast-growing resort town makes a great alternative base for exploring the ruins surrounding Trujillo.

Caballitos de tortora fishing boats (p233)

CHRISTIAN VINCES / SHUTTERSTOCK ©

Surfers, Huanchaco

Huanchaco offers great waves for budding surfers

✪ Activities

You can rent surfing gear (S30 per day for a wet suit and surfboard) from several places along the main drag. Lessons cost about S50 for an hour-and-a-half to two-hour session.

✖ Eating

Not surprisingly, Huanchaco has oodles of seafood restaurants, especially near the *caballitos de tortora* (narrow reed boats) stacked at the north end of the beach.

Otra Cosa Vegetarian $
(Larco 921; dishes S6-13; ⊘from 8am; 🛜🖉)
🖋 This Dutch-Peruvian beachside pad is Huanchaco's requisite traveler's hub, serving up yummy vegetarian victuals like falafel, crepes, Spanish tortillas, Dutch apple pie and tasty curry-laced burritos

(one of which is *almost* a breakfast burrito). Coffee is organic as well. The restaurant has a great record for giving back to the community.

Restaurant Big Ben Peruvian $$
(🖉044-46-1378; www.bigbenhuanchaco.com; Larco 836; mains S17-40; ⊘11:30am-5:30pm; 🛜) This sophisticated seafooder at the far north end of town specializes in lunchtime ceviches (S39 to S46) and is the best in town for top-notch seafood. Though ceviche is the main draw, the menu is also heavy on fresh fish, *sudados* (seafood stews) and prawn dishes, all of which go down even better on the 3rd-floor patio with ocean views.

Restaurante Mococho Peruvian, Seafood $$
(www.facebook.com/RestauranteMococho; Bolognesi 535; menú S45; ⊘1-3pm, closed Mon) This tiny place sits secluded in a walled garden where the legend of chef Don Victor is carried on by his widow and

son, Wen. It's not cheap, but it's fresh and excellent, despite the Halls served as an after-meal mint.

Local fishers knock on the door here every morning shouting, 'Hey Chinese! The catch of the day is ...' and Wen, the only Chinese-Peruvian restaurateur in town, serves up just two dishes with whatever's fresh that day: a ceviche appetizer and a steamed whole fish (filets for solo diners) in a sharply colored, wildly flavorful *criollo* (spicy Peruvian fare with Spanish and African influences) sauce.

🍷 DRINKING & NIGHTLIFE

Entertainment is of the reggae and beer variety. On weekends, *trujillanos* (residents of Trujillo) descend on the town and things are a little more lively.

Jungle Bar Bily Bar
(Larco 420; cocktails S12-18; ⊘closed Mon; 🛜)
Travelers gravitate to this quasi-Polynesian-themed bar due to location (across from the pier), good music (U2, R.E.M.) and a popular S15 ceviche, among other good-value seafood. Happy hour (6pm to 10pm) nets a 50% discount on selected cocktails.

ℹ️ INFORMATION

Next to the municipalidad (town hall) are three ATMs that accept MasterCard and Visa cards.

ℹ️ GETTING THERE & AWAY

Some bus companies (Línea and TRC Express) keep a ticket office in Huanchaco, but buses depart from Trujillo. *Combis* (minibuses) to Huanchaco frequently leave from Trujillo (S1.50). To return, just wait on the beachfront road for the bus as it returns from the north end. A taxi to or from Trujillo should cost S12.

💬 Caballitos de Totora

Huanchaco's defining characteristic is that a small number of local fishermen are still using the very same narrow reed boats depicted on 2000-year-old Moche pottery. The fishers paddle and surf these neatly crafted boats like seafaring cowboys, with their legs dangling on either side – which explains the nickname given to these elegantly curving steeds, *caballitos de tortora* (little horses). The inhabitants of Huanchaco are among the few remaining people on the coast who remember how to construct and use the boats, each one only lasting a few months before becoming waterlogged. The fishermen paddle out as far as a mile, but can only bring in limited catches because of the size of their vessels (which now also integrate styrofoam for bouyancy).

The days of Huanchaco's reed boat fisher is likely numbered. Recent reports say that erosion and other environmental factors are affecting the beds where the fishers plant and harvest the reeds, and many youngsters are opting to become surf instructors, professionals or commercial fishers rather than following their ancestors' traditional livelihoods.

Fisher preparing *caballito de tortora*, Huanchaco
CHRISTIAN VINCES / SHUTTERSTOCK ©

THE CORDILLERAS

The Cordilleras at a Glance...

Ground zero for outdoor-adventure worship in Peru, the Cordilleras are one of the preeminent hiking, trekking and backpacking spots in South America. Some of Peru's most majestic vistas are here: from glaciated white peaks razoring their way through expansive lime-green valleys to scores of pristine jade lakes, ice caves and torrid springs.

Huaraz is a hotbed of hiking inspiration. New adventurers mix it up with experienced climbers to share their recent thrills and show off their snaps. Arrive here first to fill up on good food and plan your next adventure in the Cordilleras.

The Cordilleras in Three Days

On day one, hang in **Huaraz** (p246) to plan your trek and acclimatize to the altitude. Get your bearings from the nearby viewpoint at **Mirador de Retaqeñua** (p247), then make your way out to the ruins of **Monumento Nacional Wilkahuaín** (p246), with a replica of the Chavín temple. Devote the second and third days to an overnight trek to **Laguna 69** (p239) and seeing the beautiful lakes there.

The Cordilleras in Five Days

A fourth day allows time to take a tour on the six-hour return trip out to the Unesco-recognized ruins of **Chavín de Huántar** (p242). On the fifth day, take a one-day hike to the emerald-green lake of **Laguna Churup** (p239).

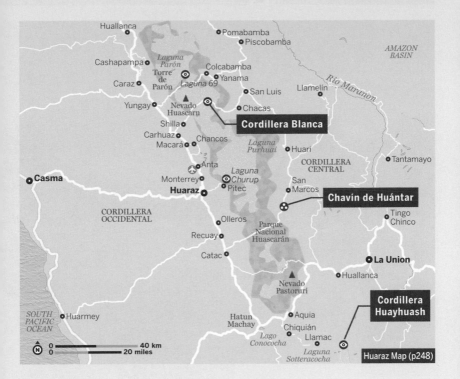

Huaraz Map (p248)

Arriving in the Cordilleras

Comandante FAP Germán Arias Graziani Airport The Huaraz airport is actually at Anta, 23km north of town. A taxi will cost about S40.

Bus Buses from Lima and most other destinations arrive in central Huaraz.

Where to Stay

Hotel prices can double during holiday periods and rooms become very scarce. Better hotels, at the southeast fringe of central Huaraz, are often perched higher, making for better views of Huascarán.

Cordillera Blanca lake

JOHN MILES / GETTY IMAGES ©

Cordillera Blanca

One of the most breathtaking parts of the continent, the Cordillera Blanca is the world's highest tropical mountain range and encompasses some of South America's highest mountains.

Great For...

☑ **Don't Miss**

Lakes, ruins and hot springs en route – it's not just about seeing the (spectacular) mountains.

Pick Your Peak

With 18 glaciated summits over 6000m and more than 50 over 5700m, the Cordillera Blanca is one of the most important ranges in the world for high-altitude climbers. Add to that the sheer multitude of options, generally short approaches and almost no red tape or summit fees (although you have to pay your park fee) and the appeal is obvious. While Huascarán Sur (6768m) is the undisputed granddaddy and Alpamayo (5947m) voted 'most beautiful' by climbers and photographers the world over, Pisco (5752m) is certainly the most popular climb for its straightforward accessibility and moderate technical requirements.

Laguna 69

BRIANBALDRATI / GETTY IMAGES ©

❶ Need to Know

Even experienced mountaineers would do well to add a local guide to their trekking group.

✕ Take a Break

Ask in Huaraz what amount of food and water is required for your trek, or bring a cook.

★ Top Tip
The dry season, May to September, offers the best trekking conditions.

Treks

Huaraz–Wilkahuaín–Laguna Ahuac

This is a relatively easy, well-marked day hike to Laguna Ahuac (4560m) starting from Huaraz or the Wilkahuaín ruins. From Huaraz, the walk will take six hours; from Wilkahuaín, four. It makes an excellent early acclimatization trip. Look for furry, rabbit-like vizcachas sniffing around and the big mountain views of the Cordillera Blanca.

Laguna Churup

If overnight trekking isn't your bag, but you'd like to experience the sight of some of the area's extravagant high-altitude lakes, this one-day hike is for you. It begins at the hamlet of Pitec (3850m), just above Huaraz, and takes you to the emerald green Laguna Churup (4450m), at the base of Nevado Churup. Note the altitudes and the

ascent (it's a steep 600m straight up). The walk takes roughly six hours and is a good acclimatization hike.

Laguna 69

A beautiful overnight trek offering backdrops dripping with marvelous views. The campsite is a true highlight: you'll wake up to morning views of Chopicalqui (6354m), Huascarán Sur (6768m) and Norte (6655m) all around you. From here, you'll then scramble up to Laguna 69, which sits right at the base of Chacraraju (6112m). From there, the journey takes you past the famous Llanganuco lakes – a lot of impressive scenery crammed into 48 hours.

Parque Nacional Huascarán

This 3400-sq-km park encompasses practically the entire area of the Cordillera Blanca above 4000m, including more than 600 glaciers and nearly 300 lakes, and protects such extraordinary and endangered species as the giant *Puya raimondii* plant, the spectacled bear and the Andean condor.

KEVIN WELLS NATURE PHOTOGRAPHY / GETTY IMAGES ©

Cordillera Huayhuash

South of the Cordillera Blanca is the smaller, more remote, but no less spectacular Cordillera Huayhuash. Containing Peru's second-highest mountain, it is a more rugged and less frequently visited range.

Often playing second fiddle to Cordillera Blanca, its limelight-stealing cousin, the Huayhuash hosts an equally impressive medley of glaciers, summits and lakes – all packed into a hardy area only 30km across. Increasing numbers of travelers are discovering this rugged and remote territory, where trails skirt around the outer edges of this stirring, peaked range.

Several strenuous high-altitude passes of over 4500m throw down a gauntlet to the hardiest of trekkers. The feeling of utter wilderness, particularly along the unspoiled eastern edge, is the big draw, and you are more likely to have majestic Andean condors for company than other trekking groups.

Great For...

☑ Don't Miss

The hardy *Stangea henrici*, a flat, grayish-green, rosette-shaped plant that only grows above 4600m.

KELLY CHENG TRAVEL PHOTOGRAPHY / GETTY IMAGES ©

ℹ Need to Know

Nine districts along the circuit charge user fees of S15 to S40, with costs for the basic circuit S195.

✕ Take a Break

Open fires are prohibited throughout the Huayhuash region; make sure you bring a gas cooker.

★ Top Tip

Look out for aggressively territorial dogs along the way; bending down to pick up a rock usually keeps them off.

The Huayhuash Circuit

Circling a tight cluster of high peaks, including Yerupajá (6634m), the world's second-highest tropical mountain, this stunning 10- to 12-day trek crosses multiple high-altitude passes with spine-tingling views. The dramatic lakes along the eastern flanks provide great campsites (and are good for trout fishing) and give hikers a wide choice of routes to make this trek as difficult as they want.

Daily ascents range from 500m to 1200m, but a couple of days in the middle and at the end of the trek involve major descents, which can be just as tough as going uphill. The average day involves about 12km on the trail, or anywhere from four to eight hours of hiking, although you may experience at least one 10- to 12-hour day.

Most trekkers take extra rest days along the way, partly because the length and altitude make the entire circuit very demanding, and partly to allow for the sensational sights to sink in. Others prefer a shorter version and can hike for as few as five days along the remote eastern side of the Huayhuash.

If you are trekking with an agency you may begin your trek at Matacancha.

Huayhuash Hogwash

Some travelers have complained that the community gatekeepers on the Cordillera Huayhuash Circuit sometimes try to resell used receipts or purposely write down the wrong date on your receipt in order to fine you later in a random check at the campsite, so keep a keen eye on your transactions and don't head out until all is squared away.

Courtyard, Chavín de Huántar

Chavín de Huántar

Chavín de Huántar is the most intriguing of the many relatively independent, competitive ceremonial centers constructed throughout the central Andes.

Great For...

ℹ Need to Know

Admission S10; ⊙9am-4pm Tue-Sun)

★ **Top Tip**

Stay overnight in underappreciated Chavín town and have the ruins to yourself in the morning.

The quintessential site of the Mid–Late Formative Period (c 1200–500 BC), Chavín de Huántar is a phenomenal achievement of ancient construction, with large temple-like structures above ground and labyrinthine (now electronically lit) underground passageways. Although looters and a major landslide have affected the site, it is still intact enough to provide a full-bodied glimpse into one of Peru's oldest complex societies.

Castillo

Chavín is a series of older and newer temple arrangements built between 1200 BC and 500 BC. From the central square, a broad staircase leads up to the portal in front of the largest and most important building, called the Castillo, which has withstood some mighty earthquakes over the years. Built on three different levels of stone-and-mortar masonry, the walls here were at one time embellished with tenon heads (blocks carved to resemble human heads, with animal or perhaps hallucinogen-induced characteristics, backed by stone spikes for insertion into a wall).

Lanzón de Chavín

A series of tunnels underneath the Castillo are an exceptional feat of engineering, comprising a maze of complex corridors, ducts and chambers. In the heart of this complex is an exquisitely carved, 4.5m monolith of white granite known as the Lanzón de Chavín. In typical terrifying Chavín fashion, the low-relief carvings on

Tenon head, Museo Nacional de Chavín

the Lanzón represent a person with snakes radiating from his head and a ferocious set of fangs, most likely feline. The Lanzón, almost certainly an object of worship given its prominent, central placement in this ceremonial center, is sometimes referred to as the Smiling God – although its appearance seems anything but friendly.

Shock & Awe

Several beguiling construction quirks, such as the strange positioning of water channels and the use of highly polished mineral mirrors to reflect light, led Stanford archaeologists to believe that the complex was used as an instrument of shock and awe. To instill fear in nonbelievers, priests manipulated sights and sounds. They blew on echoing Strombus-shell trumpets,

amplified the sounds of water running through specially designed channels and reflected sunlight through ventilation shafts. The disoriented cult novitiates were probably given hallucinogens such as San Pedro cactus shortly before entering the darkened maze. These tactics endowed the priests with the aura of awe-inspiring power.

Museo Nacional de Chavín

This outstanding **museum** (☑043-45-4011; 17 de Enero s/n; ☺9am-5pm Tue-Sun) FREE, funded jointly by the Peruvian and Japanese governments, houses most of the intricate and horrifyingly carved tenon heads from Chavín de Huántar (p242), as well as the magnificent Tello Obelisk, another stone object of worship with low relief carvings of a caiman and other fierce animals. The obelisk had been housed in a Lima museum since the 1945 earthquake that destroyed much of the original museum, and was only returned to Chavín in 2009.

The museum is located around 2km from the ruins on the other side of town.

INSIGHTS / CONTRIBUTOR / GETTY IMAGES ©

☑ Don't Miss

The carved tenon heads at the Museo Nacional de Chavín.

✕ Take a Break

There is plenty of Peruvian fare in the adjacent town of Chavín.

Huaraz

Huaraz is the restless capital of this Andean adventure kingdom and its rooftops command exhaustive panoramas of the city's dominion: one of the most impressive mountain ranges in the world. Nearly wiped out by the earthquake of 1970, Huaraz isn't going to win any Andean-village beauty contests anytime soon, but it does have personality – and personality goes a long way.

This is first and foremost a trekking metropolis. During high season the streets buzz with adventurers fresh from arduous hikes. And an endless lineup of quality restaurants and hopping bars keep the belly full and the place lively.

◉ SIGHTS

Monumento Nacional
Wilkahuaín   Ruin

(adult/student S5/2; ⊙9am-5pm Tue-Sun) This small Wari ruin about 8km north of Huaraz is remarkably well preserved, dating from about AD 600 to 900. It's an imitation of

the temple at Chavín done in the Tiwanaku style. Wilkahuaín means 'grandson's house' in Quechua. The three-story temple has seven rooms on each floor, each originally filled with bundles of mummies. The bodies were kept dry using a sophisticated system of ventilation ducts. Another smaller set of ruins, **Wilkahuaín Pequeno**, can be seen nearby.

Museo Regional
de Ancash   Museum

(Plaza de Armas; adult/child S5/1; ⊙8:30am-5:15pm Tue-Sat, 9am-2pm Sun) The Museo Regional de Ancash houses one of the most significant collections of ancient stone sculptures in South America. Small but interesting, it has a few mummies, some trepanned skulls and a garden of stone monoliths from the Recuay culture (400 BC–AD 600) and the Wari culture (AD 600–1100).

Jirón José Olaya   Architecture, Market

On the east side of town, Jirón José Olaya is the only street that remained intact through the earthquakes and provides a

Bouldering near Huaraz

CORY RICHARDS / GETTY IMAGES ©

glimpse of what old Huaraz looked like; go on Sunday when a street market sells regional foods.

Mirador de Retaqeñua   Viewpoint

Mirador de Retaqeñua is about a 45-minute walk southeast of the center and has great views of the city and its mountainous backdrop. It's best to take a S15 taxi here as robberies have been reported on the trail.

✪ ACTIVITIES

Huaraz is the epicenter for planning and organizing local Andean adventures. Dozens of companies help plan trips, rent equipment and organize adventure sports.

Rock climbing is one of the Cordillera Blanca's biggest pastimes. There are good climbs for beginners at Chancos, while the Los Olivos area offers something for all skill levels. Avid climbers will find some gnarly bolted sport climbs at Recuay and **Hatun Machay** (admission S5). For some big-wall action that will keep you chalked up for days, head to the famous **Torre de Parón**, known locally as the Sphinx. Most trekking tour agencies offer climbing trips, both for beginners and advanced, as part of their repertoire.

When it comes to trekking and mountaineering, it is well worth taking a guide, even for nontechnical activities, as conditions change rapidly in the mountains, plus a good guide will ensure you see things you otherwise may have missed.

Mountaineers and trekkers should check out Casa de Guías (p251), the headquarters of the Mountain Guide Association of Peru. It maintains a list of its internationally certified guides, all of whom are graduates of a rigorous training program. Bear in mind that international certification is not necessary to work in the park and there are also some excellent independent guides from other associations certified to work in the region.

Many agencies arrange full trekking and climbing expeditions that include guides, equipment, food, cooks, porters and transport. Depending on the number of

Martes Guerra

You might want to invest in a waterproof suit or brave the high-altitude chill in your bathing suit if you are in Huaraz on Carnaval's Fat Tuesday, a day of intense water fights throughout the city. Known as Martes Guerra (War Tuesday), thousands of kids run around the city with buckets searching for public sources of water and have huge water fights. Women, senior citizens and tourists are prime targets. Police are everywhere, even the military, but none of them can control these wild water bandits. Stay inside your hotel if you don't want to get drenched!

people, the length of your trip and what's included, expect to pay from under S100 for an easy day out to up to S750 for more technical mountains per person per day. Try not to base your selection solely on price, as you often get what you pay for. Do your research; things change, good places go bad and bad places get good.

One of the best resources regarding guides in Huaraz is other travelers who have just come back from a trek and can recommend (or not recommend) their guides based on recent experience. The South American Explorers club (www.saexplorers.org) in Lima is also an excellent source of information and maps.

Quechuandes   Trekking, Rock Climbing

(☑943-562-339; www.quechandes.com; Luzuriaga 522) A very well-organized agency that gets rave reviews for its quality guides and ethical approach to treks. In addition to offering treks and summit expeditions, its staff are experts in rock climbing and bouldering.

It also offers mountaineering courses and has an indoor climbing wall in the office. The detailed website offers a great overview of treks and climbs in the region.

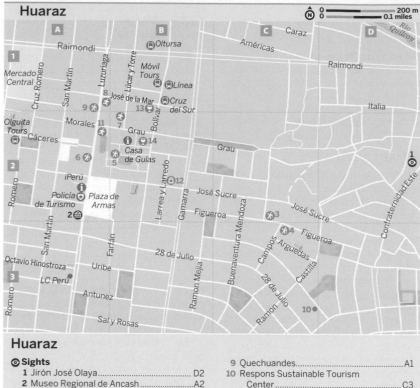

Huaraz

Eco Ice Peru — Trekking
(www.ecoice-peru.com; Figueroa 1185; ⊘8am-6pm) Run by a gregarious and passionate young guide, this new agency gets top reviews from travelers for its customer service. Treks often end with a dinner at the owner's pad in Huaraz.

Huascarán — Trekking
(☏043-42-2523; www.huascaran-peru.com; Campos 711) A well established operator offering the full gamut of excursions.

Montañero — Trekking, Mountaineering
(☏043-42-6386; www.trekkingperu.com; Parque Ginebra; ⊘9am-12pm & 4-8pm) This high-end agency arranges both treks and climbs. It also sells quality gear.

Monttrek — Trekking, Climbing
(☏043-1124; www.monttrek.com.pe; Luzuriaga 646, 2nd fl) A reputable agency that has lots of local information, including invaluable topo maps. Arranges rock climbing, mountain biking and paragliding trips. Top-end gear rental too.

Skyline
Adventures Trekking, Mountaineering
(📞043-42-7097; www.skyline-adventures.com;
Pasaje Industrial 137) Based just outside
Huaraz, this high-end operator comes highly recommended and provides guides for
treks and mountain climbs. Leads six- and
12-day mountaineering courses.

Mountain Bike
Adventures Mountain Biking
(📞043-42-4259; www.chakinaniperu.com;
Lúcar y Torre 530, 2nd fl; ⏰9am-1pm & 3-8pm)
Mountain Bike Adventures has been in
business for more than a decade and
receives repeated visits by mountain bikers
for its decent selection of bikes, knowledgeable and friendly service, and good safety
record. It offers guided tours, ranging from
an easy five-hour cruise to 12-day circuits
around the Cordillera Blanca. Rates start at
around S160 for a day circuit.

TOURS

Dozens of agencies along Luzuriaga can
organize outings to local sites, including
several day excursions.

One popular tour visits the ruins at
Chavín de Huántar; another passes
through Yungay to the beautiful Lagunas
Llanganuco, where there are superb vistas
of Huascarán and other mountains; a third
takes you through Caraz to Laguna Parón,
which is surrounded by ravishing glaciated
peaks; and a fourth travels to the glacier at
Nevado Pastoruri, the most accessible in
the cordillera.

All of these trips run between S35 and
S60 each; prices may vary depending on
the number of people going, but typically
include transport (usually in minibuses)
and a guide (who often doesn't speak English). Admission fees and lunch are extra.
Trips take a full day; bring a packed lunch,
warm clothes, drinking water and sunblock.

Two of the most popular agencies are
Pablo Tours (📞043-1145; www.pablotours.
com; Luzuriaga 501) and **Sechín Tours** (📞42-
1419; Morales 602).

Respons Sustainable
Tourism Center Cultural
(📞043-42-7949; www.responsibletravelperu.com;
Eulogio del Río 1364, La Soledad; ⏰9am-1pm &
3-7pm) 🌱 This company works as a clearing-
house for information about local community tourism and arranges homestays
in Humachucco, which is a good base for
exploring Lagunas Llanganuco and 69, and
Vicos, a very traditional mountain community. You will stay in bungalows next to family
homes and eat meals with your hosts. It also
arranges trips to Huaripampa, where visitors
learn about traditional weaving.

Activities in the villages range from
preparing traditional food to participating
in farming and craft production. There is
also a small shop in the office selling fair-
trade products from local artisans. Almost
anything you do with the agency will benefit
local families and contribute to growing
community tourism in the region.

🛍 SHOPPING

Inexpensive thick woolen sweaters,
scarves, hats, socks, gloves, ponchos and
blankets are available if you need to rug
up for the mountains; many of these are
sold at stalls on the pedestrian alleys off
Luzuriaga or at the *feria artesanal* (artisans'
market) off the Plaza de Armas. A few
shops on Parque Ginebra, plus several
agencies that rent equipment and gear,
also sell quality climbing gear and clothes.

Tejidos Turmanyé Clothing
(www.arcoiristurmanye.com; Larrea y Loredo,
cuadra 6; ⏰11am-1pm & 4-8pm Mon-Sat) 🌱 Sells
handsome locally made weavings and knit
garments to support a foundation that
provides occupational training to young
mothers.

EATING

Restaurants come in a surprising range of
flavors for such a small town. Hours are
flexible in Huaraz, with shorter opening
times during low-season slow spells and
longer hours at busy times.

⚠️ Tremors & Landslides

Records of *aluviónes,* a deadly mix of avalanche, waterfall and landslide, date back almost 300 years, but three recent ones have caused particular devastation.

The first occurred in 1941, when an avalanche in the Cojup Valley, west of Huaraz, caused the Laguna Palcacocha to break its banks and flow down onto Huaraz, killing about 5000 inhabitants and flattening the city. Then, in 1962, a huge avalanche from Huascarán destroyed the town of Ranrahirca, killing about 4000 people.

The worst disaster occurred on May 31, 1970, when a massive earthquake, measuring 7.7 on the Richter scale, devastated much of central Peru, killing an estimated 70,000 people. About half of the 30,000 inhabitants of Huaraz died, and only 10% of the city was left standing. The town of Yungay was completely buried by the *aluvión* caused by the quake and almost its entire population of 25,000 was buried with the city.

Since these disasters, a government agency (Hidrandina) has been formed to control the lake levels by building dams and tunnels, thus minimizing the chance of similar catastrophes. Today, warning systems are in place, although false alarms do occur.

Café Andino   Cafe $
(www.cafeandino.com; Lúcar y Torre 530, 3rd fl; breakfast S8-24, mains S18-25; 🛜🕹️) This modern top-floor cafe has space and light in spades, comfy lounges, art, photos, crackling fireplace, books and groovy tunes – it's the ultimate South American traveler hangout and meeting spot. You can get breakfast anytime (Belgian waffles, huevos rancheros), and snacks you miss (nachos). It's the best place in town for information about trekking in the area.

American owner Chris is the go-to java junkie in the Cordilleras and roasts his own organic beans here. He was responsible for first bringing excellent brew to town in 1997 – he showed up a year earlier and had to resort to using a rock to smash organic beans he'd brought from Alaska, straining it through a bandanna for his morning jolt.

California Café   Breakfast $
(www.huaylas.com; Jiron 28 de Julio 562; breakfast S13-25; 🕖7:30am-6:30pm, to 2pm Sun; 🛜) Managed by an American from California, this hip traveler magnet does breakfasts at any time, plus light lunches and salads – it's a funky, chilled space to while away many hours. You can spend the day listening to the sublime world-music collection or reading one of the hundreds of books available for exchange.

Novaplaza   Self-Catering $
(cnr Bolivar & Morales; 🕖7am-11:30pm) A good supermarket to pick up supplies for trekking or self-catering.

Mi Comedia   Italian $$
(Centenario 351; mains S25-32; 🕔5-11pm Mon-Sat) Pizzerias are ubiquitous in Huaraz but once you've eaten in this friendly place you won't go anywhere else. The pizzas are prepared right in the dining room and all feature a delicious crust and farm-fresh tomato sauce. There is also a small selection of excellent pasta dishes. Reservations are advisable.

Chili Heaven   Indian, Thai $$
(Parque Ginebra; mains S17-35; 🕛noon-11pm) Whether you send your appetite to India or Thailand, the fiery curries at this hot spot will seize your taste buds upon arrival, mercilessly shake them up and then spit them back out the other side as if you've died and gone to chili heaven (hence the name). It also bottles its own hot sauces. A critical Peruvian-food antidote.

Monte Rosa/Inca Pub   Fusion $$$
(📞043 42-1447; José de la Mar 661; mains S18-30; 🕚11am-11pm) This warm, snug Swiss-run restaurant has an Alpine vibe; it does an

international menu that includes fondue and raclette (melted cheese over potatoes or bread) as well as pizzas and Peruvian plates. If it's full, service can be slow. The owner also sells Victorinox Swiss army knives.

DRINKING & NIGHTLIFE

Los 13 Buhos   Bar

(Parque Ginebra; ⊙11am-late) A supremely cool cafe-bar in newly upgraded Parque Ginebra digs. The owner, Lucho, was the first craft-beer brewer in Huaraz and offers five tasty choices, including red and black ales. The bar also prepares top Thai curries and fantastic set-menu meals. It's the best bar in town for kicking back over cold home brews and liquid-courage-inspired conversation.

El Tambo   Bar, Club

(José de la Mar 776; ⊙9pm to 4am) If you're hankering to shake your groove-thang, this is the most popular disco in town, complete with dance-floor trees and loads of nooks and crannies so you can hide yourself away. Fashionable with both *extranjeros* (foreigners) and Peruvians, the music swings from techno-*cumbia* to Top 20, salsa and reggae, and most things in between.

❶ INFORMATION

Casa de Guías (☑043-42-1811; Parque Ginebra 28G; ⊙9am-1pm & 4-8pm Mon-Fri, 8am-noon Sat) Runs mountain safety and rescue courses and maintains a list of internationally certified guides. Also mounts rescue operations to assist climbers in emergencies. If you are heading out on a risky ascent, it's worth consulting with these guys first.

Clínica San Pablo (☑043-42-8811; www. sanpablo.com.pe; Huaylas 172; ⊙24hr) North of town, this is the best medical care in Huaraz. Some doctors speak English.

iPerú (☑043-42-8812; iperuhuaraz@promperu. gob.pe; Pasaje Atusparia, Oficina 1, Plaza de Armas; ⊙9am-6pm Mon-Sat, to 1pm Sun) Has general tourist information but little in the way of trekking info.

Policía de Turismo (☑043-42-1341; Luzuriaga 724; ⊙24hr) On the west side of the Plaza de Armas.

❶ GETTING THERE & AWAY

AIR

LC Perú (☑043-42-4734; www.lcperu.pe; Luzuriaga 904) operates flights from Lima to Huaraz every day at 5:30am; the return journey leaves at 7:05am. The Huaraz airport is actually at Anta, 23km north of town. A taxi will cost about S40.

BUS

Combis (minibuses) for Caraz, Carhuaz and Yungay leave every few minutes during the day from a lot on Cajamarca near Raimondi. These will drop you in any of the towns along the way.

Cruz del Sur (☑043-42-8726; Bolívar 491) Has 11am and 10pm luxury nonstop services to Lima.

Línea (☑043-42-6666; Bolívar 450) Excellent buses at 9:15pm and 9:30pm to Chimbote and Trujillo.

Móvil Tours (www.moviltours.com.pe; **Ticket Office** (Bolívar 452); **Terminal** (☑043-42-2555; Confraternidad Internacional Oeste 451) Buses to Lima at 9:30am, 1pm and 2:30pm and four night buses. Also has night buses to Chimbote via Casma, some of which continue on to Trujillo.

Olguita Tours (☑043-39-6309, 943-644-051; Mariscal Caceres 338) Departures to Chavín and Huari at 4am, 7:30am, 11am, 12:20pm and 8:30pm.

Oltursa (☑043-42-3717; www.oltursa.pe; Raimondi 825) The most comfortable Lima buses; departures at 12:15pm and 10:30pm.

THE AMAZON BASIN

The Amazon Basin at a Glance...

The best-protected tract of the world's most biodiverse forest is a strange, sweltering, seductive country-within-a-country. Tribes still exist here that have never had contact with outside civilization. More plant types flourish in one rainforest hectare than in any European country, and fauna is so fantastic it defies the most imaginative sci-fi comic.

As the 21st century encroaches on this enticing expanse of arboreal wilderness, exploitation of the rainforest's abundant natural resources threatens to irreversibly damage it. For now, though, the Peruvian Amazon offers phenomenal wildlife-spotting, forays into untamed forest from the jungle's best selection of lodges, and raucous city life.

The Amazon Basin in Four Days

Visits to **Parque Nacional Manu** (p256) are usually one week, but three-night stays are possible, letting you still spot a wide range of tropical wildlife. Trips to Manu often go overtime, so allow an extra day, which can be used to visit a 1906 Amazon riverboat housing the **Historical Ships Museum** (p263), if you have time.

The Amazon Basin in Six Days

With an extra two days, see more of Manu or get deep into the largest of Peru's parks, **Reserva Nacional Pacaya-Samiria** (p258). Camp and spot manatees, pink dolphins, giant turtles and hundreds of bird species. Hire a guide from Lagunas and go by dugout canoe, or take a comfortable ship from Iquitos.

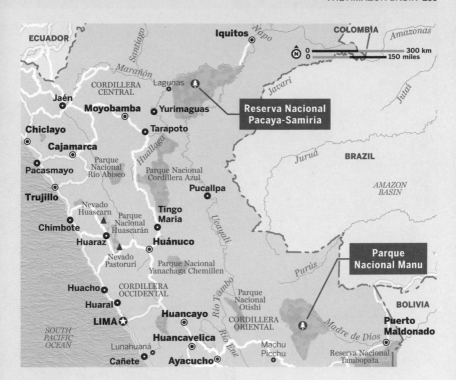

Arriving in the Amazon Basin

Coronel FAP Francisco Secada Vignetta International Airport Iquitos' airport is 7km from the center. A taxi into town costs about S15.

Ferry Three ports are situated between 2km and 3km north of the city center.

Where to Stay

If you are after the total jungle-immersion experience, there is no shortage of lodges. Find your base, then explore the jungle to your heart's content. (Features to look out for include pools, and jungle or plaza views.)

The best hotels tend to be booked up on Friday and Saturday nights, and on major festivals such as **San Juan** (p23). The busiest season is from May to September, when prices may rise slightly.

Rafting, Parque National Manu

PHILIP LEE HARVEY / LONELY PLANET ©

Parque Nacional Manu

Covering almost 20,000 sq km (about the size of Wales), this park is one of the best places in South America to scout out a whole shebang of tropical wildlife.

Great For...

☑ Don't Miss

Cocha Otorongo, an oxbow lake with a wildlife-viewing observation tower, half an hour's boat ride from Cocha Salvador.

This national park starts in the eastern slopes of the Andes and plunges down into the lowlands, hosting great diversity over a wide range of cloud forest and rainforest habitats. The most progressive aspect of the park is the fact that so much of it is very carefully protected – a rarity anywhere in the world. Unesco declared Manu a Biosphere Reserve in 1977 and a World Natural Heritage site in 1987.

Virgin jungle lies up the Río Manu northwest of Boca Manu (the entrance point for the park). Two hours upstream is the oxbow lake of **Cocha Juárez**, where giant river otters are often encountered. About four hours further, **Cocha Salvador**, one of the park's largest, most beautiful lakes, has guided camping and hiking possibilities.

Gould's jewelfront, Parque Nacional Manu

GLENN BARTLEY / GETTY IMAGES ©

Smaller mammals you might see include kinkajous, pacas, agoutis, squirrels, brocket deer, ocelots and armadillos. Other animals include river turtles and caiman (which are frequently seen), snakes (which are less often spotted) and a variety of other reptiles and amphibians. Colorful butterflies and less pleasing insects also abound.

Visiting & Staying

There are two lodges within the park, plus a tented camp: you can't stay at any of these accommodations independently, but all are included on tours. Note that it is illegal to enter the park without a guide. Going with an organized group can be arranged in Cuzco or with international tour operators.

Permits, which are necessary to enter the park, are arranged by tour agencies. Most visits are for a week, although three-night stays at a lodge can be arranged.

Travelers often report returning from Manu several days late. Don't plan an international airline connection the day after a Manu trip!

Wildlife-Spotting

These are not wide-open habitats like the African plains. Thick vegetation will obscure many animals, and a skilled guide is very useful in helping you to see them.

During a one-week trip, you can reasonably expect to see scores of different bird species, several monkey species and possibly a few other mammals.

Jaguars (sightings are on the increase in the *zona reservada*), tapirs, giant anteaters, tamanduas, capybaras, peccaries and giant river otters are among the common large Manu mammals. But they are elusive, and you can consider a trip very successful if you see two or three of these creatures during a week's visit.

Hiking in the rainforest

Reserva Nacional Pacaya-Samiria

This huge national reserve is home to Amazon manatees, pink and gray river dolphins, two species of caiman and giant South American river turtles, alongside around 450 bird species.

Iquitos

Reserva Nacional Pacaya-Samiria

Lagunas

Moyobamba   Yurimaguas

Tarapoto

Ucayali

Javari

Great For...

ⓘ Need to Know

3-day pass S60

★ **Top Tip**

Bring plenty of insect repellent and plastic bags (to cover luggage), and be prepared to camp out.

At 20,800 sq km, Pacaya-Samiria provides local people with food and a home, and protects ecologically important habitats. More than 40,000 people live on and around the reserve; juggling the needs of human inhabitants while protecting wildlife is the responsibility of 20 to 30 rangers. Staff also teach inhabitants how to best harvest the natural renewable resources to benefit the local people and to maintain thriving populations of plants and animals.

The area close to Lagunas has suffered from depletion: allow several days to get deep into the least disturbed areas. Noteworthy points in the reserve include **Lago Pantean**, where you can check out caimans and go medicinal-plant collecting; and **Tipischa de Huana**, where you can see the giant *Victoria regia* waterlilies, big enough for a small child to sleep upon without sinking.

When to Go

The best time to go is during the dry season, when you are more likely to see animals along the riverbanks. Rains ease off in late May; it then takes a month for water levels to drop, making July and August the best months to visit (with excellent fishing). February to June tend to be the hottest months, with animal-viewing best in the early morning and late afternoon.

Dugout canoe on the river near Iquitos

Visiting

Official information is available at the reserve office in Iquitos or (more limited and perhaps more biased) at tour-agency offices in Yurimaguas, Lagunas and Iquitos.

The best way to visit the reserve is to go by dugout canoe with a guide from Lagunas and spend several days camping and exploring. Alternatively, comfortable ships visit from Iquitos.

If coming from Lagunas, Santa Rosa is the main entry point, where you pay the park entrance fee (S20 per person per day; often included in tour prices).

☑ Don't Miss

Quebrada Yanayacu, where the river water is black from dissolved plants.

PAUL KENNEDY / GETTY IMAGES ©

Guided Tours from Lagunas

Spanish-speaking guides are available in Lagunas. It is illegal to hunt within the reserve (though fishing for the pot is OK). The going rate is a rather steep S120 to S150 per person per day for a guide, a boat and accommodations in huts, tents and ranger stations. Food and park fees are extra, although the guides can cook for you

Several years ago, there was a plethora of guides in Lagunas that harassment and price-cutting, an guides association was formed. This then split into two separate organizations, with the highly regarded **Estypel** (☑065-40-1080; www.estypel.com.pe; Jr Padre Lucero 1345, Lagunas), headed by the reputable guide Juan Manuel Rojas Arévalo, the only survivor of these two.

There's also **Huayruro Tours** (☑965-662-555, 065-40-1186; www.peruselva.com; Alfonso Aiscorbe 2), an increasingly prominent association that is great for helping plan tours (agency staff speak English; their guides are Spanish-speaking but know the reserve extremely well). They offer tours of up to 22 days and are involved in programs like turtle reintroduction within the reserve.

River Cruises from Iquitos

Cruising the Amazon is an expensive business: the shortest trips can cost over US$1000. Cruises naturally focus on the Río Amazonas, both downriver (northeast) toward the Brazil–Colombia border and upriver to Nauta, where the Ríos Marañón and Ucayali converge. Beyond Nauta, trips continue up these two rivers to the Pacaya-Samiria reserve.

★ Top Tip

Ask your guide what food is provided.

Iquitos

Linked to the outside world by air and by river, Iquitos is the world's largest city that cannot be reached by road. It's a prosperous, vibrant jungle metropolis teeming with the usual, inexplicably addictive Amazonian anomalies. Unadulterated jungle encroaches beyond town in full view of the air-conditioned, elegant bars and restaurants that flank the riverside.

◉ SIGHTS

Iquitos' cultural attractions, while limited, dwarf those of other Amazon cities, it's especially boosted by the arrival of two new museums. The cheery Malecón (riverside walk) runs between Nauta and Ricardo Palma.

Remnants of the rubber-boom glory days include *azulejos*, handmade tiles imported from Portugal to decorate the mansions of the rubber barons. Many buildings along Raimondi and Malecón Tarapaca are lavishly decorated with these tiles. Some of the best are various government buildings along or near the Malecón.

Belén   Area

At the southeast end of town is the floating shantytown of Belén, consisting of scores of huts, built on rafts, which rise and fall with the river. During the low-water months, these rafts sit on the river mud and are dirty and unhealthy, but for most of the year they float on the river – a colorful and exotic sight. Seven thousand people live here, and canoes float from hut to hut selling and trading jungle produce.

The best time to visit the shantytown is at 7am, when people from the jungle villages arrive to sell their produce. To get here, take a cab to 'Los Chinos,' walk to the port and rent a canoe to take you around.

The market here, located within the city blocks in front of Belén, is the raucous, crowded affair common to most Peruvian towns. All kinds of strange and exotic products are sold among the more mundane bags of rice, sugar, flour and cheap household goods. Look for the bark of the

Floating hut, Iquitos

chuchuhuasi tree, which is soaked in rum for weeks and used as a tonic (it's served in many of the local bars). *Chuchuhuasi* and other Amazon plants are common ingredients in herbal pain-reducing and arthritis formulas manufactured in Europe and the USA. The market makes for exciting shopping and sightseeing, but do remember to watch your wallet.

Historical Ships Museum — Museum

(Plaza Castilla; S10; ⊗8am-8pm) Moored below Plaza Castilla is the diverting new Historical Ships Museum, on a 1906 Amazon riverboat, the gorgeously restored three-deck *Ayapua*. The exhibitions reflect the Amazon River's hodgepodge past: explorers, tribes, rubber barons and the filming of the 1982 Herzog movie *Fitzcarraldo*. Included in the entrance price is a half-hour historic boat ride on the river (Río Itaya out to the Río Amazonas proper).

Casa de Fierro — Historic Building

(Iron House; cnr Putumayo & Raymondi) Every guidebook mentions the 'majestic' Casa de Fierro (Iron House), designed by Gustave Eiffel (of Eiffel Tower fame). It was made in Paris in 1860 and imported piece by piece into Iquitos around 1890, during the opulent rubber-boom days, to beautify the city. It's the only survivor of three different iron houses originally imported here. It resembles a bunch of scrap-metal sheets bolted together, was once the location of the Iquitos Club and is now, in humbler times, a general store.

Museum of Indigenous Amazon Cultures — Museum

(Malecón Tarapaca 332; S15; ⊗8am-7:30pm) This intuitively presented museum takes you on a romp through the traits, traditions and beliefs of the tribes of the Amazon Basin, with a focus on the Peruvian Amazon. Some 40 Amazonian cultures are represented.

ⓘ Jungle Checklist

First jungle voyage? You'll find things far more relaxing than the movies make out. The jungle, you'll see, has largely been packaged to protect delicate tourists. With lodge facilities and the below kit list, you should be ready for most eventualities.

○ Two pairs of shoes, one for jungle traipsing, one for camp.

○ Spare clothes – in this humidity clothes get wet quickly; take a spare towel too.

○ Binoculars and a zoom-lens camera, for wildlife in close-up.

○ Flashlight for night walks.

○ Mosquito repellent with DEET – bugs are everywhere.

○ Sunblock and sunglasses – despite that foliage, you'll often be in direct sun.

○ First-aid kit for basics such as bites, stings or diarrhea.

○ Plastic bags to waterproof gear and pack nonbiodegradable litter to take back with you.

○ Lightweight rainproof jacket.

○ Sleeping bag, mat or hammock if sleeping outside.

○ Books – cell phones rarely work and neither do TVs; electricity is often limited to several hours daily.

Owl monkey, Iquitos
GREGORY G DIMIJIAN / GETTY IMAGES ©

Herzog's Amazon

Eccentric German director Werner Herzog, often seen as obsessive and bent on filming 'reality itself,' shot two movies in Peru's jungle: *Aguirre, the Wrath of God* (1972) and *Fitzcarraldo* (1982). Herzog's accomplishments in getting these movies made at all – during havoc-fraught filming conditions – are in some ways more remarkable than the finished products.

Klaus Kinski, the lead actor in *Aguirre*, was a volatile man prone to extreme fits of rage. Herzog's documentary *My Best Fiend* details such incidents, as when Kinski, after altercations with a cameraman on the Río Nanay, prepared to desert the film crew on a speedboat. Herzog had to threaten to shoot him with a rifle to make him stay.

Filming *Fitzcarraldo*, the first choice for the lead fell ill and the second, Mick Jagger, abandoned the set to do a Rolling Stones tour. Herzog called upon Kinski once more, who soon antagonized the Matsiguenka tribespeople being used as extras: one even offered to murder him for Herzog. Then there was the weather: droughts so dire that the rivers dried and stranded the film's steamship for weeks, followed by flash floods that wrecked the boat entirely. The director once said he saw filming ...zon as 'challenging nature ...

⊕ ACTIVITIES

Cruising the Amazon is a popular pastime, and trips can be arranged on the three rivers surrounding Iquitos: the Itaya, the Amazonas and the Nanay.

Operators quote prices in US dollars. A useful booking website for cruises is www. amazoncruise.net. Advance reservations are often necessary (and often mean discounts).

Dawn on the Amazon Tours & Cruises   Cruise
(☑065-22-3730; www.dawnontheamazon. com; Malecón Maldonado 185; per person day trips incl lunch US$79, multiday cruises per day from US$150) This small outfit offers the best deal for independent travelers. The *Amazon I* is a beautiful 11m wooden craft with modern furnishings, available for either day trips or longer river cruises up to two weeks. Included are a bilingual guide, all meals and transfers. You can travel with host Bill Grimes and his experienced crew along the Amazon, or along its quieter tributaries (larger cruise ships will necessarily stick to the main waterways).

While many cruise operators have fixed departures and itineraries, Bill's can be adapted to accommodate individual needs. The tri-river cruise is a favorite local trip: while on board, fishing and bird-watching are the most popular activities.

Aqua Expeditions   Cruise
(☑965-83-2517, 065-60-1053, in US 1-866-603-3687; www.aquaexpeditions.com; Av La Marina s/n; 3-night Marañón & Ucayali cruise per person in suite from US$3135) Aqua operates two luxury riverboats, which depart twice weekly for the Pacaya-Samiria reserve. The 40m *MV Aqua* has 12 vast, luxury suite cabins (each over 22 sq meters) while the *MV Aria* has equally splendid accommodations, but in 16 similarly sized suites and with an onboard Jacuzzi. Both boats have beautiful observation lounges. Cruises last three, five or seven days.

The office is 1km along Av La Marina from the center.

Cruise boats come with a full crew and bilingual guides. Meals are included and small launches are carried for side trips. Activities can involve visiting indigenous communities (for dancing and craft sales), hikes, and bird- and pink-dolphin-watching (on big ships, don't expect to see too much rare wildlife).

SHOPPING

There are a few stands along the Malecón selling jungle crafts, some of high quality, some (not always the same ones) pricey. A good place for crafts is the **Mercado de Artesanía San Juan**, on the airport road – bus and taxi drivers know it. Don't buy items made from animal bones and skins, as they are made from jungle wildlife. It's illegal to import many such items into the US and Europe.

Mad Mick's
Trading Post   Outdoor Equipment
(📞50-7525; Putumayo 163; ⏱9am-8pm) You can buy, rent or trade almost anything needed for a jungle expedition at Mad Mick's Trading Post. Don't need it afterwards? Mick will buy anything back (if it's in good nick) for half price.

EATING

The city has excellent restaurants, but be aware that many regional specialties feature endangered animals, such as *chich-arrón de lagarto* (fried alligator) and *sopa de tortuga* (turtle soup). *Paiche,* a local river fish, is making a comeback thanks to breeding programs. More environmentally friendly esoteric dishes include ceviche made with river fish, *chupín de pollo (*a tasty soup of chicken, egg and rice) and *juanes* (banana leaves stuffed with chicken or pork and rice).

Belén Mercado   Market $
(cnr Prospero & Jirón 9 de Diciembre; menús from S5) There are great eats at Iquitos' markets, particularly the Belén *mercado* where a *menú*, including *jugo especial* (jungle juice) costs S5. Look out for specialties including meaty Amazon worms, *ishpa* (simmered sabalo fish intestines and fat) and *sikisapa* (fried leafcutter ants; abdomens are supposedly tastiest) and watch your valuables. Another good market for cheap eats is **Mercado Central** (Lores cuadra 5).

Ivalú   Peruvian $
(Lores 215; snacks from S3; ⏱8am-early afternoon) One of the most popular local spots for juice and cake and tamales

Belén Mercado

Al Frio y al Fuego restaurant

(corn cakes filled with chicken or fish and wrapped in jungle leaves). As for the opening hours: go earlier, before they sell out!

Al Frio y al Fuego   Fusion $$

(☎965-607-474; www.alfrioyalfuego.com; Embarcadero Av La Marina 138; mains S20-40; ☺noon-4pm & 7-11pm Tue-Sat, noon-5pm Sun) Take a boat out to this floating foodie paradise in the middle of the mouth of the Río Itaya to sample some of the city's best food. The emphasis is on river fish (such as the delectable *doncella*), but the *parrillas* (grills) are inviting too. The address given is the boat embarkation point.

Amazon Bistro   International $$

(Malecón Tarapaca 268; breakfasts S12, mains S20-40; ☺6am-midnight; 🛜) Laid out with TLC by the Belgian owner, this place has a New York–style breakfast bar (OK, Amazon version thereof) and upper-level mezzanine seating looking down on the main eating area. The cuisine refuses to be pigeonholed: there are Argentine steaks not to mention the Belgian influence,

which creeps across in the crepes, and with the escargot and the range of Belgian beers.

Fitzcarraldo Restaurant-Bar   International $$

(☎065-50-7545; www.restaurantefitzcarraldo. com; Napo 100; mains S15-40; ☺noon-late; ❄) The Fitzcarraldo is an upscale option on the riverside strip, with very good food and service. It does good pizzas (delivery available) and various local and international dishes. Try the S80 Amazon tasting platter – all the jungle specialties on one massive plate. And beware of that icy air-con!

🍷 DRINKING & NIGHTLIFE

Iquitos is a party city. The Malecón is the cornerstone of the lively nightlife scene.

Arandú Bar   Bar

(Malecón Maldonado 113; ☺till late) The liveliest of several thumping Malecón bars, great for people-watching and always churning out loud rock-and-roll classics.

Musmuqui Bar

(Raimondi 382; ☺to midnight Sun-Thu, to 3am Fri & Sat) Locally popular lively bar with two floors and an extensive range of aphrodisiac cocktails concocted from wondrous Amazon plants.

 INFORMATION

BCP (Próspero & Putamayo) Has a secure ATM.

iPerú (☏065-23-6144; Napo 161; ☺9am-6pm Mon-Sat, to 1pm Sun) There's also a branch at the **airport** (☏065-26-0251; Main Hall, Francisco Secada Vignetta Airport; ☺whenever flights are arriving/departing).

 GETTING THERE & AWAY

AIR

Iquitos' small but busy airport, 7km from the center, currently receives flights from Lima, Pucallpa, Tarapoto and Panama City with **LAN** (☏065-23-2421; Próspero 232), **Star Perú** (☏065-23-6208; Napo 260) and **Copa Airlines** (☏1-800-359-2672 in Panama; www.copaair.com).

Charter companies at the airport have five-passenger planes to almost anywhere in the Amazon, if you have a few hundred US dollars to spare.

BOAT

Iquitos is Peru's largest, best-organized river port. If you choose to arrive by river, you'll end up at one of three ports, which are situated between 2km and 3km north of the city center.

The city's numerous riverboats dock at **Puerto Masusa,** about 3km north of the town center.

 GETTING AROUND

Squadrons of *mototaxis* (three-wheeled motorcycle rickshaw taxis) are the bona fide transport round town. They are fun to ride, though they don't provide much protection in an accident. Always enter *mototaxis* from the sidewalk side – and keep your limbs inside at all times. Scrapes and fender benders are common. Most rides around Iquitos cost a standard S1.50 to S3; to the airport it's about S8 for a *mototaxi* and S15 for the harder-to-spot cabs.

 Need to Know

Allow plenty of time for your Amazon adventure: erratic weather causes delays, in forms such as landslides, broken boats and cancelled flights. Even on a good day, road and river transport is prone to overcrowding and severe hold-ups.

Lagunas

Travelers come to muddy, mosquito-rich Lagunas because it is the best embarkation point for a trip to the Reserva Nacional Pacaya-Samiria. It's a spread-out, remote place; there are stores, but stock (slightly pricier than elsewhere in Peru) is limited, so it's wise to bring your own supplies as backup. There are no money-changing facilities and hardly any public phones.

The most popular route to Lagunas is from Tarapoto via Yurimaguas. Tarapoto has a reasonable bus network as well as a mainline airport with connections to Lima and Iquitos.

From Tarapoto, taxis and buses (S15, three hours) run to Yurimaguas. Multiple companies with *colectivos* (shared transportation; S20, two hours) also offer services to Yurimaguas.

Regular boats downriver from Yurimaguas to Lagunas take about 10 to 12 hours and leave Yurimaguas' La Boca port between 7am and 8am most days. Times are posted on boards at the port in both Yurimaguas and Lagunas for a day in advance. Fast boats from Yurimaguas head off either at 2:30am (from La Boca) or between 7am and 8am from the port near the Plaza: they take 4½ to 5½ hours.

Action time is, indeed, between 7am and 8am in Lagunas' ramshackle port. This is when many fast boats rock up for the journey upriver to Yurimaguas (S40, 5½ to 6½ hours) and downriver to Iquitos (S100, 10 hours).

Traditional Peruvian wedding, Inca site near Cuzco

In Focus

Miraflores cliffs, Lima

FOTOS593 / SHUTTERSTOCK ©

Peru Today

From the happening capital of Lima to cobblestoned Andean villages, Peru leaves an indelible impression as a place of incredible diversity, bustling commerce and innovation. In 2011 it became one of the world's fastest growing economies.

Unparalleled Boom

Between the violence of the Spanish conquest, the chaos of the early republic and the succession of dictatorships that swallowed up much of the 20th century, stability has been a rare commodity in Peru. But the new millennium has treated the country with uncharacteristic grace. Peru's economy has grown every year since 2003. Foreign investment is up and the country's exports – in the areas of agriculture, mining and manufacturing – have been strong. Tourism is also big: the number of foreign travelers going to Peru almost tripled between 2003 and 2014 from 1.3 to 3.2 million, according to World Bank data.

In addition, since 2000, a succession of peaceful elections has provided political stability. In 2011 former army officer Ollanta Humala was elected to the presidency. The son of a Quechua labor lawyer from Ayacucho, he has made social inclusion a theme of his pres-

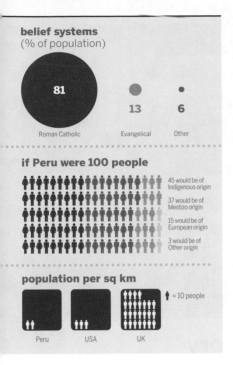

belief systems
(% of population)

81 — Roman Catholic

13 — Evangelical

6 — Other

if Peru were 100 people

45 would be of Indigenous origin

37 would be of Mestizo origin

15 would be of European origin

3 would be of Other origin

population per sq km

Peru   USA   UK

♦ ≈ 10 people

idency. One of his early acts was to make it a legal requirement for native peoples to be consulted on mining or other extractive activities in their territories.

Upon Humala ending his term, Peru passed from left wing to the middle ground. Pedro Pablo Kuczynski, a Princeton- and Oxford-educated former Wall Street banker, became President in 2016, winning the election by a narrow margin. Kuczynski's strategy is economic, seeing growth as the key to funding social wellbeing.

Keiko Fujimori may have barely lost the presidency election to Kuczynski but her presence remains, with her party holding the majority of seats in Congress, and with it great power.

Cultural Renaissance

The good times have resulted in a surge of cultural productivity – much of it revolving around food. Once considered a place to avoid, Lima is now a foodie bastion, where gastronomic festivals attract visitors from all over the world. La Mistura, a culinary gathering organized by celebrity chef Gastón Acurio, has drawn around 400,000 people annually in recent years.

The relentless focus on food has had a ripple effect on other aspects of the culture. Young fashion designers produce avant-garde clothing lines with alpaca knits. Innovative musical groups fuse folk and electronica. And the contemporary arts scene has been re-freshed with the opening of the Museo Mario Testino, a top-to-bottom renovation of Museo de Arte de Lima (MALI), and galleries blossoming in the capital's bohemian quarters.

Work in Progress

None of this means there aren't serious challenges. Though the country's poverty rate has been roughly cut in half since 2002, the economic boom has not trickled down to every-one: rural poverty, for one, is nearly double the national average.

In addition, Sendero Luminoso (Shining Path), the Maoist guerrilla group that took the country to the brink of civil war in the 1980s, has seen a comeback with a small political following and offshoots reportedly in the drug trade. Peru now rivals Colombia in terms of cocaine production, which represented 17% of the Gross Domestic Product in 2009. Coca and cocaine production also affects Peru's environment through deforestation in remote growing areas and the chemical contamination that is a byproduct of production.

Above all, there are environmental pressures. Antimining strikes in Cajamarca and Arequipa continue the regional civil unrest, enmeshed with regional corruption and envi-ronmental concerns. The Amazon is now bisected by the Interoceanic Hwy, an important overland trade route connecting Peru and Brazil both physically and economically. The engineering marvel has generated deep apprehension among scientists about its future impact on one of the world's last great wilderness areas.

Embroidered fabric, Chimú culture

History

In 1532, when Francisco Pizarro landed to conquer Peru
in the name of God and the Spanish Crown, the region
had already seen the epic rise and fall of civilizations.
Yet the conquest changed everything: from that seismic
clash between Inca and Spaniard came new cultures,
new races, new voices, new cuisines – ultimately, a new
civilization.

8000 BC
Hunting scenes are painted
in caves by hunter-gatherers
in the central highlands and
in Toquepala in the south.

c 3000 BC
Settlement of Peru's coastal
oases begins; some of the
first structures are built
north of present-day Lima.

200 BC
The Nazca culture on the
coast starts construction of
a series of giant glyphs that
adorn the desert to this day.

Huaca del Sol (p227)

Earliest Settlers

There is some debate about how long, exactly, there has been a human presence in Peru. Some scholars have suggested that humans occupied the Andes as far back as 14,000 BC (with at least one academic reporting that it could precede even that early date). The most definitive archaeological evidence, however, puts humans in the region at around 8000 BC. Caves in Lauricocha (near Huánuco) and Toquepala (outside Tacna) bear paintings that record hunting scenes from that era. The latter shows a group of hunters cornering and killing what appears to be a group of camelid animals.

In 4000 BC taming of llamas and guinea pigs began in the highlands, followed by the domestication of potatoes, gourds, cotton, *lúcuma* (an earthy Andean fruit), quinoa, corn and beans. By 2500 BC, once-nomadic hunters and gatherers clustered into settlements along the Pacific, surviving on fishing and agriculture.

In recent years studies at some of these archaeological sites have revealed that these early societies were far more developed than previously imagined. Along with Egypt, India

200	**500**	**c 800**
The Tiwanaku begin their 400-year domination of the area around Lake Titicaca, into what is today Bolivia and northern Chile.	In the north, the Moche culture begins construction on the Huaca del Sol y de la Luna, outside present-day Trujillo.	The fiercely independent Chachapoyas build Kuélap, a citadel in the northern highlands composed of upwards of 400 constructions.

Kitchen, Monasterio de Santa Catalina

★ **Best Historic Churches**

Iglesia de Santo Domingo (p51), Lima

Iglesia de La Compañía de Jesús (p161), Cuzco

Monasterio de Santa Catalina (p94), Arequipa

Basílica Menor Catedral (p226), Trujillo

and China, Peru is considered one of the six cradles of civilization (a site where urbanization accompanied agricultural innovation) – the only one located in the southern hemisphere. Ongoing excavations at Caral, on the coast about 200km north of Lima, continue to uncover evidence of what is the oldest civilization in the Americas.

Chavín Horizon

Lasting roughly from 1000 BC to 300 BC, and named after the site of Chavín de Huántar, this was a rich period of development for Andean culture – when artistic and religious phenomena appeared, perhaps independently, over a broad swath of the central and northern highlands, as well as the coast. The salient feature of this era is the repeated representation of a stylized feline deity, perhaps symbolizing spiritual transformations experienced under the influence of hallucinogenic plants.

Birth of Local Cultures

After 300 BC, numerous local settlements achieved importance at a regional level. South of Lima, in the area surrounding the Península de Paracas, lived a coastal community whose most significant phase is referred to as Paracas Necropolis (AD 1–400), after a large burial site. It is here that some of the finest pre-Columbian textiles in the Americas have been unearthed: colorful, intricate fabrics that depict oceanic creatures, feline warriors and stylized anthropomorphic figures.

To the south, the people of the Nazca culture (200 BC–AD 600) carved giant, enigmatic designs into the desert landscape that can only be seen from the air. Known as the Nazca Lines, these were mapped early in the 20th century – though their exact purpose remains up for debate.

During this time, the Moche culture settled the area around Trujillo between AD 100 and 800. This was an especially artistic group (they produced some of the most remarkable portrait art in history), leaving behind important temple mounds, such as the Huacas del Sol y de la Luna (Temples of the Sun and Moon), near Trujillo, and the burial site of Sipán, outside Chiclayo.

c 850	1100–1200	1438–71
The Chimú begin development of Chan Chan, a sprawling adobe urban center, outside present-day Trujillo.	The Incas emerge as a presence in Cuzco.	The reign of Inca Yupanqui – also known as Pachacutec – represents a period of aggressive empire-building for the Incas.

Wari Expansion

As the influence of regional states waned, the Wari, an ethnic group from the Ayacucho basin, emerged as a force to be reckoned with for 500 years beginning in AD 600. They were vigorous military conquerors who built and maintained important outposts throughout a vast territory that covered an area from Chiclayo to Cuzco. Though their ancient capital lay outside present-day Ayacucho, they also operated the major lowland ceremonial center of Pachacamac, just outside Lima, where people from all over the region came to pay tribute.

As with many conquering cultures, the Wari attempted to subdue other groups by emphasizing their own traditions over local belief. Thus from about AD 700 to 1100, Wari influence is noted in the art, technology and architecture of most areas in Peru. These include elaborate, tie-dyed tunics, and finely woven textiles, some of which contained a record-breaking 398 threads per linear inch. They are most significant, however, for developing an extensive network of roadways and for greatly expanding the terrace agriculture system – an infrastructure that served the Incas well just a few centuries later.

Regional Kingdoms

The Wari were eventually replaced by a gaggle of small nation-states that thrived from about 1000 until the Inca conquest of the early 15th century. One of the biggest and best studied of these are the Chimú of the Trujillo area, whose capital was the famed Chan Chan, the largest adobe city in the world. Their economy was based on agriculture and they had a heavily stratified society with a healthy craftsman class, which produced painted textiles and beautifully fashioned pottery that is distinctive for its black stain.

Closely connected to the Chimú are the Sicán from the Lambayeque area, renowned metallurgists who produced the *tumi* (a ceremonial knife with a rounded blade used in sacrifices). The knife has since become a national symbol in Peru and replicas can be found in craft markets everywhere.

To the south, in the environs of Lima, the Chancay people (1000–1500) produced fine, geometrically patterned lace and crudely humorous pottery, in which just about every figure seems to be drinking.

The formation of chiefdoms in the Amazon began during this period too.

Enter the Incas

According to Inca lore, their civilization was born when Manco Cápac and his sister Mama Ocllo, children of the sun, emerged from Lake Titicaca to establish a civilization in the Cuzco Valley. Whether Manco Cápac was a historical figure is up for debate, but what is certain is that the Inca civilization was established in the area of Cuzco at some point in the 12th century. The reign of the first several *incas* (kings) is largely unremarkable, and for a couple of centuries they remained a small, regional state.

1532	1717	1781
Atahualpa wins control over Inca territories; and the Spanish land in Peru – in less than a year, Atahualpa is dead.	The Spanish Crown establishes the Viceroyalty of New Granada, covering modern-day Ecuador, Colombia and Panama.	Inca noble Túpac Amaru II is brutally executed by the Spanish in Cuzco after leading an unsuccessful indigenous rebellion.

Expansion took off in the early 15th century, when the ninth king, Inca Yupanqui, defended Cuzco – against incredible odds – from the invading Chanka people to the north. After the victory, he took on the boastful new name of Pachacutec (Transformer of the Earth) and spent the next 25 years bagging much of the Andes. Under his reign, the Incas grew from a regional fiefdom in the Cuzco Valley into a broad empire of about 10 million people known as Tawantinsuyo (Land of Four Quarters). The kingdom covered most of modern Peru, in addition to sections of Ecuador, Bolivia and Chile. This was made more remarkable by the fact that the Incas, as an ethnicity, never numbered more than about 100,000.

Pachacutec allegedly gave Cuzco its layout in the form of a puma and built fabulous stone monuments in honor of Inca victories, including Sacsaywamán; the temple-fortress at Ollantaytambo; and possibly Machu Picchu. He also improved the network of roads that connected the empire, further developed terrace agricultural systems and made Quechua the lingua franca.

Atahualpa's Brief Reign

Inca kings continued the expansions of the empire first started by Pachacutec. Pachacutec's grandson, Huayna Cápac, who began his rule in 1493, took over much of modern-day Ecuador all the way into Colombia. Consequently, he spent much of his life living in, governing and commanding his armies from the north, rather than Cuzco.

By this time, the Spanish presence was already being felt in the Andes. Smallpox and other epidemics transmitted by European soldiers were sweeping through the entire American continent. These were so swift, in fact, that they arrived in Peru before the Spanish themselves, claiming thousands of indigenous lives – including, in all likelihood, that of Huayna Cápac, who succumbed to some sort of plague in 1525.

Without a clear plan of succession, the emperor's untimely death left a power vacuum. The contest turned into a face-off between two of his many children: the Quito-born Atahualpa, who commanded his father's army in the north, and Huáscar, who was based in Cuzco. The ensuing struggle plunged the empire into a bloody civil war, reducing entire cities to rubble. Atahualpa emerged as the victor in April 1532. But the vicious nature of the conflict left the Incas with a lot of enemies throughout the Andes – which is why some tribes were so willing to cooperate with the Spanish when they arrived just five months later.

The Spanish Invade

In September 1528 explorer Francisco Pizarro and his right-hand-man Diego de Almagro landed in Tumbes with a shipload of arms, horses and slaves, as well as a battalion of 168 men. Atahualpa, in the meantime, was in the process of making his way down from Quito to Cuzco to claim his hard-won throne. When the Spanish arrived, he was in the highland settlement of Cajamarca, enjoying the area's mineral baths.

Pizarro quickly deduced that the empire was in a fractious state. He and his men charted a course to Cajamarca and approached Atahualpa with royal greetings and promises of

1821	1826	1879–83
José de San Martín declares Peru independent, but true sovereignty doesn't come until Simón Bolívar's forces vanquish the Spanish three years later.	The last of the Spanish military forces depart from Callao, after which the country descends into a period of anarchy.	Chile wages war against Peru and Bolivia over nitrate-rich lands in the Atacama Desert; Peru loses the war and the Tarapacá region.

brotherhood. But the well-mannered overtures quickly devolved into a surprise attack that left thousands of Incas dead and Atahualpa a prisoner of war. (Between their horses, their armor and the steel of their blades, the Spanish were practically invincible against fighters armed only with clubs, slings and wicker helmets.)

In an attempt to regain his freedom, Atahualpa offered the Spanish a bounty of gold and silver. Thus began one of the most famous ransoms in history – with the Incas attempting to fill an entire room with the precious stuff in order to placate the unrelenting appetites of the Spanish. But it was never enough. The Spanish held Atahualpa for eight months before executing him with a garrote at the age of 31.

The Inca empire never recovered from this fateful encounter. The arrival of the Spanish brought on a cataclysmic collapse of indigenous society. One scholar estimates that the native population – around 10 million when Pizarro arrived – was reduced to 600,000 within a century.

Tumultuous Colony

Following Atahualpa's death, the Spanish got to work consolidating their power. On January 6, 1535, Pizarro sketched out his new administrative center in the sands that bordered the Río Rímac on the central coast. This would be Lima, the so-called 'City of Kings' (named in honor of Three Kings' Day), the new capital of the viceroyalty of Peru, an empire that for more than 200 years would cover much of South America.

It was a period of great turmoil. As elsewhere in the Americas, the Spanish ruled by terror. Rebellions erupted regularly. Atahualpa's half-brother Manco Inca (who had originally sided with the Spanish and served as a puppet emperor under Pizarro) tried to regain control of the highlands in 1536 – laying siege to the city of Cuzco for almost a year – but was ultimately forced to retreat. He was stabbed to death by a contingent of Spanish soldiers in 1544.

Throughout this, the Spanish were doing plenty of fighting among themselves, splitting into a complicated series of rival factions, each wanting control of the new empire. In 1538 De Almagro was sentenced to death by strangulation for attempting to take over Cuzco. Three years later, Pizarro was assassinated in Lima by a band of disgruntled De Almagro supporters. Other conquistadors met equally violent fates. Things grew relatively more stable after the arrival of Francisco de Toledo as viceroy, an efficient administrator who brought some order to the emergent colony.

Until independence, Peru was ruled by a series of these Spanish-born viceroys, all of whom were appointed by the crown. Immigrants from Spain held the most prestigious positions, while *criollos* (Spaniards born in the colony) were confined to middle management. *Mestizos* – people of mixed blood – were placed even further down the social scale. Full-blooded *indígenas* (people of indigenous descent) resided at the bottom, exploited as *peones* (expendable laborers) in *encomiendas,* a feudal system that granted Spanish colonists land titles that included the property of all the indigenous people living in that area.

Tensions between *indígenas* and Spaniards reached a boiling point in the late 18th century, when the Spanish Crown levied a series of new taxes that hit indigenous people

1911	1924	1932
US historian Hiram Bingham arrives at the ruins of Machu Picchu; his 'discovery' of the ancient city is chronicled in *National Geographic*.	Víctor Raúl Haya de la Torre founds APRA, a populist, anti-imperialist political party that is immediately declared illegal.	More than a thousand APRA party followers are executed by the military at Chan Chan, following an uprising in Trujillo.

the hardest. In 1780 José Gabriel Condorcanqui – a descendant of the Inca monarch Túpac Amaru – arrested and executed a Spanish administrator on charges of cruelty. His act unleashed an indigenous rebellion that spread into Bolivia and Argentina. Condorcanqui adopted the name Túpac Amaru II and traveled the region fomenting revolution.

The Spanish reprisal was swift – and brutal. In 1781 the captured indigenous leader was dragged to the main plaza in Cuzco, where he watched his followers, his wife and his sons killed in a day-long orgy of violence, before being drawn and quartered himself. Pieces of his remains were displayed in towns around the Andes as a way of discouraging further insurrection.

Independence

By the early 19th century, *criollos* in many Spanish colonies had grown increasingly dis- satisfied with their lack of administrative power and the crown's heavy taxes – leading to revolutions all over the continent. In Peru, the winds of change arrived from two directions. Argentine revolutionary José de San Martín led independence campaigns in Argentina and Chile, before entering Peru by sea at the port of Pisco in 1820. With San Martín's arrival, royalist forces retreated into the highlands, allowing him to ride into Lima unobstructed. On July 28, 1821, independence was declared. But real independence wouldn't materialize for another three years. With Spanish forces still at large in the interior, San Martín needed more men to fully defeat the Spanish.

Enter Simón Bolívar, the Venezuelan revolutionary who had been leading independence fights in Venezuela, Colombia and Ecuador. In 1823, the Peruvians gave Bolívar dictatorial powers (an honor that had been bestowed on him in other countries). By the latter half of 1824, he and his lieutenant, Antonio José de Sucre, had routed the Spanish in decisive battles at Junín and Ayacucho. The revolutionaries had faced staggering odds, but none- theless managed to capture the viceroy and negotiate a surrender. As part of the deal, the Spanish retired all of their forces from Peru and Bolivia.

New Republic

The lofty idealism of the revolution was soon followed by the harsh reality of having to govern. The young nation of Peru proved to be just as anarchic as the viceroyalty of Peru. Between 1825 and 1841, there was a revolving door of regime changes (two dozen) as re- gional *caudillos* (chieftains) scrambled for power. The situation improved in the 1840s with the mining of vast deposits of guano off the Peruvian coast; the nitrate-rich bird droppings reaped unheard-of profits as fertilizer on the international market. (Nineteenth-century Peruvian history is – literally – rife with poop jokes.)

The country found some measure of stability under the governance of Ramón Castilla (a *mestizo*), who was elected to his first term in 1845. The income from the guano boom – which he had been key in exploiting – helped Castilla make much-needed economic improvements. He abolished slavery, paid off some of Peru's debt and established a public

1948	1968	1970
General Manuel Odría assumes power for eight years, encouraging foreign investment and cracking down on APRA.	General Juan Velasco Alva- rado takes power in a coup d'état.	A 7.7-magnitude earthquake in northern Peru kills almost 80,000 people, leaves 140,000 injured and another 500,000 homeless.

school system. Castilla served as president three more times over the course of two decades – at times, by force; at others, in an interim capacity; at one point, for less than a week. Following his final term, he was exiled by competitors who wanted to neutralize him politically.

He died in 1867, in northern Chile, attempting to make his way back to Peru. (Visitors can see his impressive crypt at the Panteón de los Proceres in Central Lima.)

War of the Pacific

With Castilla's passing, the country once again descended into chaos. A succession of *caudillos* squandered the enormous profits of the guano boom and, in general, managed the economy in a deplorable fashion. Moreover, military skirmishes ensued with Ecuador (over border issues) and Spain (which was trying to dominate its former South American colonies). The conflicts left the nation's coffers empty. By 1874, Peru was bankrupt.

This left the country in a weak position to deal with the expanding clash between Chile and Bolivia over nitrate-rich lands in the Atacama Desert. Borders in this area had never been clearly defined, and escalating tensions eventually led to military engagement. To make matters worse for the Peruvians, President Mariano Prado abandoned the country for Europe on the eve of the conflict. The war was a disaster for Peru at every level (not to mention Bolivia, which lost its entire coastline).

Despite the very brave actions of military figures such as Navy Admiral Miguel Grau, the Chileans were simply better organized and had more resources, including the support of the British. In 1881 they led a land campaign deep into Peru, occupying the capital of Lima, during which time they ransacked the city, making off with the priceless contents of the National Library. By the time the conflict came to a close in 1883, Peru had permanently lost its southernmost region of Tarapacá – and it wouldn't regain the area around Tacna until 1929.

A New Intellectual Era

As one century gave way to the next, intellectual circles saw the rise of *indigenismo*, a continent-wide movement that advocated for a dominant social and political role for indigenous people. In Peru, this translated into a wide-ranging (if fragmented) cultural movement. Historian Luis Valcárcel attacked his society's degradation of the indigenous class. Poet César Vallejo wrote critically acclaimed works that took on indigenous oppression as themes. And José Sabogal led a generation of visual artists who explored indigenous themes in their paintings. In 1928 journalist and thinker José Carlos Mariátegui penned a seminal Marxist work – *Seven Interpretive Essays on Peruvian Reality* – in which he criticized the feudal nature of Peruvian society and celebrated the communal aspects of the Inca social order. (It remains vital reading for the Latin American left to this day.)

In this climate, in 1924, Trujillo-born political leader Victor Raúl Haya de la Torre founded the Alianza Popular Revolucionaria Americana (American Popular Revolutionary

1980

Guerrilla group Sendero Luminoso (Shining Path) takes its first violent action – burning ballot boxes – in the Ayacucho region.

1985

Alan García becomes president, but his term is marked by hyperinflation and increased attacks by terrorist groups.

1990

Alberto Fujimori is elected president; his rule leads to improvements in the economy, but charges of corruption plague his administration.

Alliance) – otherwise known as APRA. The party espoused populist values, celebrated 'Indo-America' and rallied against US imperialism. It was quickly declared illegal by the autocratic regime of Augusto Leguía – and remained illegal for long stretches of the 20th century. Haya de la Torre, at various points in his life, lived in hiding and in exile and, at one point, endured a 15-month stint as a political prisoner.

Dictatorships & Revolutionaries

After the start of the Great Depression in 1929, the country's history becomes a blur of dictatorships punctuated by periods of democracy. Leguía, a sugar baron from the north coast, ruled on a couple of occasions: for his first period in office (1908–12) he was elected; for the second (1919–30) he made it in via coup d'état. He spent his first term dealing with a morass of border conflicts, and the second stifling press freedom and political dissidents.

Legúia was followed by Colonel Luis Sánchez Cerro, who served a couple of short terms in the 1930s. (Though his time in office was turbulent, Sánchez would be celebrated in some sectors for abolishing a conscription law that required able-bodied men to labor on road-building projects. The law affected poor indigenous men disproportionately, since they couldn't afford to pay the exemption fee.) By 1948 another dictator had taken power: former army colonel Manuel Odría, who spent his time in office cracking down on APRA and encouraging US foreign investment.

The most fascinating of Peru's 20th-century dictators, however, is Juan Velasco Alvarado, the former commander-in-chief of the army who took control in 1968. Though he was expected to lead a conservative regime, Velasco turned out to be an inveterate populist – so much so that some APRA members complained that he had stolen their party platform away from them. He established a nationalist agenda that included 'Peruvianizing' (securing Peruvian majority ownership) various industries. In his rhetoric he celebrated the indigenous peasantry, championed a radical program of agrarian reform and made Quechua an official language. He also severely restricted press freedom, which drew the wrath of the power structure in Lima. Ultimately, his economic policies were failures – and in 1975, in declining health, he was replaced by another, more conservative military regime.

Internal Conflict

Peru returned to civilian rule in 1980, when President Fernando Belaúnde Terry was elected to office; it was the first election in which leftist parties were allowed to participate, including APRA, which was now legal. Belaúnde's term was anything but smooth. Agrarian and other social reforms took a back seat as the president tried desperately to jump-start the moribund economy.

It was at this time that a radical Maoist group from the poor region of Ayacucho began its unprecedented rise. Founded by philosophy professor Abimael Guzmán, Sendero Luminoso (Shining Path) wanted nothing less than an overthrow of the social order via violent armed struggle. Over the next two decades, the situation escalated into a phantasmagoria

1992	1996	2001
Alan García flees the country in 1992, clouded by allegations of embezzlement.	Guerrillas from the Movimiento Revolucionario Túpac Amaru storm the Japanese ambassador's residence and hold 72 hostages for four months.	Alejandro Toledo becomes the first indigenous person to govern an Andean country.

of violence, with the group assassinating political leaders and community activists, carrying out attacks on police stations and universities and, at one point, stringing up dead dogs all over downtown Lima.

To quell the violence, the government sent in the military, a heavy-handed outfit that knew little about handling a guerrilla insurgency. There was torture and rape, plus disappearances and massacres, none of which did anything to put a stop to Sendero Luminoso. Caught in the middle were tens of thousands of poor *campesinos,* who bore the brunt of the casualties.

In the midst of this, Alan García was elected to the presidency in 1985. Initially, his ascent generated a great deal of hope. He was young, he was a gifted public speaker, he was popular – and he was the first member of the storied APRA party to win a presidential election. But his economic program was catastrophic, and, by the late 1980s, Peru faced a staggering hyperinflation rate of 7500%. Thousands of people were plunged into poverty. There were food shortages and riots, and the government was forced to declare a state of emergency.

Two years after completing his term, García fled the country after being accused of embezzling millions of dollars. He returned to Peru in 2001, when the statute of limitations on his case finally ran out.

Fujishock

With the country in a state of chaos, the 1990 presidential elections took on more importance than ever. The contest was between famed novelist Mario Vargas Llosa and Alberto Fujimori, a little-known agronomist of Japanese descent. During the campaign, Vargas Llosa promoted an economic 'shock treatment' program that many feared would send more Peruvians into poverty, while Fujimori positioned himself as an alternative to the status quo. Fujimori won handily. But as soon as he got into office, he implemented an even more austere economic plan that, among other things, drove up the price of gasoline by 3000%. The measures, known as 'Fujishock,' ultimately succeeded in reducing inflation and stabilizing the economy – but not without costing the average Peruvian dearly.

Fujimori followed this, in April 1992, with an *autogolpe* (coup from within). He dissolved the legislature and generated an entirely new congress, one stocked with his allies. Peruvians, not unused to *caudillos,* tolerated the power grab, hoping that Fujimori might help stabilize the economic and political situation – which he did. The economy grew. And by the end of the year, leaders of both Sendero Luminoso and the Marxist-Leninist Movimiento Revolucionario Túpac Amaru (MRTA) had been apprehended (though not before Sendero Luminoso had brutally assassinated community activist María Elena Moyano and detonated lethal truck bombs in Lima's tony Miraflores district).

By the end of his second term, Fujimori's administration was plagued by allegations of corruption. He ran for a third term in 2000 (which was technically unconstitutional) and remained in power despite the fact that he didn't have the simple majority necessary to claim the election. Within the year, however, he was forced to flee the country after it was

2003	**2005**	**2006**
The country's Truth and Reconciliation Commission releases its final report on Peru's internal conflict: estimates of the dead reach 70,000.	Construction of the Interoceanic Hwy, which opens an overland trade route between Peru and Brazil, begins in the southern Amazon Basin.	Alan García is elected to a second, nonconsecutive term as president after a runoff contest.

revealed that his security chief Vladimiro Montesinos had been embezzling government funds and bribing elected officials and the media. Fujimori formally resigned the presidency from abroad, but the legislature rejected the gesture, voting him out of office and declaring him 'morally unfit' to govern.

Peru, however, hadn't heard the last of Fujimori. In 2005 he returned to South America, only to be arrested in Chile on long-standing charges of corruption, kidnapping and human-rights violations. He was extradited to Peru in 2007 and, that same year, was convicted of ordering an illegal search. Two years later, he was convicted of ordering extrajudicial killings, and three months after that, was convicted of channeling millions of dollars in state funds to Montesinos. In 2009 he also pleaded guilty to wiretapping and bribery. He is currently serving 25 years in prison. Montesinos, in the meantime, is doing 20 – for bribery and selling arms to Colombian rebels.

The 21st Century

The new millennium has, thus far, been pretty good to Peru. In 2001, shoeshine-boy-turned-Stanford-economist Alejandro Toledo became the first person of Quechua ethnicity to be elected to the presidency. (Until then, Peru had had *mestizo* presidents, but never a full-blooded *indígena*.) Unfortunately, Toledo inherited a political and economic mess. This was amplified by the fact that he lacked a majority in congress, hampering his effectiveness in the midst of an economic recession.

Toledo was followed in office by – of all people – the APRA's Alan García, who was reelected in 2006. His second term was infinitely more stable than the first. The economy performed well and the government invested money in upgrading infrastructure such as ports, highways and the electricity grid. But it wasn't without problems. For one, there was the issue of corruption (García's entire cabinet was forced to resign in 2008 after widespread allegations of bribery) and the touchy issue of how to manage the country's mineral wealth. In 2008, García signed a law that allowed foreign companies to exploit natural resources in the Amazon. The legislation generated a backlash among various Amazon tribes and led to a fatal standoff in the northern city of Bagua in 2009.

The Peruvian congress quickly revoked the law, but this issue remain a challenge for president Ollanta Humala, elected in 2011. Having campaigned on a broader inclusion of all social classes, he passed the Prior Consultation Law, a historic new law to guarantee indigenous rights to consent to projects affecting them and their lands. The former army officer was initially thought to be a populist in the Hugo Chávez vein (the Lima stock exchange dropped precipitously when he was first elected). But his administration has been quite friendly to business. Though the economy functioned well under his governance, civil unrest over a proposed gold mine in the north, as well as a botched raid on a Sendero Luminoso encampment in the highlands, sent his approval rating into a tailspin in the middle of 2012.

2009	2011	2014
Fujimori is convicted of embezzling; this is in addition to prior convictions for ordering military death squads to carry out extrajudicial killings.	Populist former army officer Ollanta Humala assumes the Presidency after winning a tight run-off election against Fujimori's daughter Keiko.	A Greenpeace protest that puts a message in the Nazca Lines irreparably damages the World Heritage site and causes international outrage.

Horseback riding, Sacred Valley

Outdoor Activities

Scale icy Andean peaks. Raft one of the world's deepest canyons. Surf heavenly Pacific curlers. Walk the flanks of a smoldering volcano known locally as a living deity. With its breathtaking, diverse landscapes, Peru is a natural adventure hub. So gear up – you're in for a wild ride.

Hiking & Trekking

Pack the hiking boots because the variety of trails in Peru is downright staggering. The main trekking centers are Cuzco and Arequipa in the southern Andes, and Huaraz in the north. Hikers will find many easily accessible trails around Peru's archaeological ruins, which are also the final destinations for more-challenging trekking routes.

Peru's most famous trek is the Inca Trail to Machu Picchu. Limited permits mean this guided-only trek sells out months in advance. For those who haven't planned so far ahead, there are worthwhile alternative routes. Other possibilities around Cuzco include the spectacular six-day trek around the venerated Ausangate (6384m), which will take you over 5000m passes, through huge herds of alpacas and past tiny hamlets unchanged in centuries. Likewise, the isolated Inca site of Choquequirau is another intriguing destination for a trek.

Masked crimson tanager, Parque Nacional Manu (p256)

★ **Best Wildlife-Watching Spots**

Parque Nacional Manu (p256)

Cañón del Colca (p107)

Islas Ballestas (p69)

Parque Nacional Huascarán (p239)

In nearby Arequipa, you can get down in some of the world's deepest canyons – the world-famous Cañón del Colca and the Cañón del Cotahuasi. The scenery is guaranteed to knock you off your feet, and it's easier going than some higher-altitude destinations. During the wet season, when some Andean trekking routes are impassable, Colca is the best place in Peru for DIY trekking between rural villages. The more remote and rugged Cañón del Cotahuasi is best visited with an experienced local guide and only during the dry season.

Cuzco and Huaraz (and, to a lesser degree, Arequipa) have outfitters that can provide equipment, guides and even *arrieros* (mule drivers). If you prefer to trek ultralight, you might want to purchase your own gear, especially a sleeping bag, as old-generation rental items tend to be heavy. Whether you'll need a guide depends on where you trek. Certain areas of Peru, such as along the Inca Trail, require guides; in other places, such as in the Cordillera Huayhuash, there have been muggings, so it's best to be with a local. Thankfully, scores of other trekking routes are wonderfully DIY. Equip yourself with topographic maps for major routes in the nearest major gateway towns or, better yet, at the Instituto Geográfico Nacional (IGN) or at the South American Explorers Club (www.saexplorers.org) in Lima.

Whatever adventure you choose, be prepared to spend a few days acclimating to the dizzying altitudes – or face a heavy-duty bout of altitude sickness.

Trekking is most rewarding during the dry season (May to September) in the Andes. Avoid the wet season (December to March), when rain makes some areas impassable.

Mountain, Rock & Ice Climbing

Peru has the highest tropical mountains in the world, offering some absolutely inspired climbs, though acclimatization to altitude is essential. The Cordillera Blanca, with its dozens of snowy peaks exceeding 5000m, is one of South America's top destinations. The Andean town of Huaraz has tour agencies, outfitters, guides, information and climbing equipment for hire. Still, it's best to bring your own gear for serious ascents. Near Huaraz, Ishinca (5530m) and Pisco (5752m) provide two ascents easy enough for relatively inexperienced climbers. For experts, these mountains are also good warm-up climbs for bigger adventures such as Huascarán (6768m), Peru's highest peak.

In southern Peru, the snowy volcanic peaks around Arequipa can be scaled by determined novice mountaineers. The most popular climb is El Misti (5822m), a site of Inca human sacrifice. Despite its serious altitude, it is basically a very long, tough walk. Chachani (6075m) is one of the easier 6000m peaks in the world – though it still requires crampons, an ice ax and a good guide.

For beginners looking to bag their first serious mountains, Peru may not be the best place to start. Not all guides know the basics of first aid or wilderness search and rescue. Check out a prospective guide's credentials carefully and seek out those who are personally recommended. Carefully check any rental equipment before setting out.

As with trekking, high-elevation climbing is best done during the dry season (mid-June to mid-July).

Rafting & Kayaking

River running is growing in popularity around Peru, with trips that range from a few hours to more than two weeks.

Cuzco is the launch point for the greatest variety of river-running options. Choices range from a few hours of mild rafting on the Urubamba to adrenaline-pumping rides on the Santa Teresa to several days on the Apurímac, technically the source of the Amazon (with world-class rafting between May and November). A river-running trip on the Tambopata, available from June through October, tumbles down the eastern slopes of the Andes, culminating in a couple of days of floating in unspoiled rainforest.

Arequipa is another rafting center. Here, the Río Chili is the most frequently run, with a half-day novice trip leaving daily between March and November. Further afield, the more challenging Río Majes features class II and III rapids. On the south coast, Lunahuaná, not far from Lima, is a prime spot for beginners and experts alike. Between December and April, rapids here can reach class IV.

Note that rafting is not regulated in Peru. There are deaths every year and some rivers are so remote that rescues can take days. In addition, some companies are not environmentally responsible and leave camping beaches dirty. Book excursions only with reputable, well-recommended agencies and avoid cut-rate trips. A good operator will have insurance, provide you with a document indicating that they are registered, and have highly experienced guides with certified first-aid training who carry a properly stocked medical kit. Choose one that provides top-notch equipment, including self-bailing rafts, US Coast Guard–approved life jackets, first-class helmets and spare paddles. Many good companies raft rivers accompanied by a kayaker experienced in river rescue.

For more on river running in Peru, visit www.peruwhitewater.com.

Surfing

With consistent, uncrowded waves and plenty of remote breaks to explore, Peru has a mixed surfing scene that attracts dedicated locals and international die-hards alike. Kite-surfing and paddleboarding are also emerging as popular sports, particularly in Máncora and Paracas.

Waves can be found from the moment you land. All along the southern part of Lima, surfers ride out popular point and beach breaks at Miraflores (known as Waikiki), Barranquito and La Herradura. Herradura's outstanding left point break gets crowded when there is a strong swell. In-the-know surfers prefer the smaller crowds further south at Punta Hermosa. International and national championships are held at nearby Punta Rocas as well as Pico Alto, an experts-only 'kamikaze' reef break with some of the largest waves in Peru. Isla San Gallán, off the Península de Paracas, also provides experts with a world-class right-hand point break only accessible by boat; ask local fishers or at hotels.

The water is cold from April to mid-December (as low as 15°C/60°F), when wet suits are generally needed. Indeed, many surfers wear wet suits year-round (2/3mm will suffice), even though the water is a little warmer (around 20°C, or 68°F, in the Lima area) from January to March. The far north coast (north of Talara) stays above 21°C (70°F) most of the year.

Though waves are generally not crowded, surfing can be a challenge – facilities are limited and equipment rental is expensive. The scene on the north coast is the most organized, with surf shops and hostels that offer advice, rent boards and arrange surfing day trips. Huanchaco is a great base for these services. Serious surfers should bring their own board.

The best surfing websites include www.peruazul.com, www.vivamancora.com and www.wannasurf.com, with a comprehensive, highly detailed list of just about every break in Peru. Good wave and weather forecasts can be found at www.magicseaweed.com and www.windguru.com.

Sandboarding

Sandboarding down the giant desert dunes is growing in popularity at Huacachina and around Nazca, on Peru's south coast. Nazca's Cerro Blanco (2078m) is the highest known sand dune in the world. Some hotels and travel agencies offer tours in *areneros* (dune buggies), where you are hauled to the top of the dunes, then get picked up at the bottom. (Choose your driver carefully; some are notoriously reckless.)

Mountain Biking & Cycling

In recent years mountain biking has exploded in popularity. It is still a fledgling sport in Peru, but there is no shortage of incredible terrain. Single-track trails ranging from easy to expert await mountain bikers outside Huaraz, Arequipa and even Lima. If you're experienced, there are incredible mountain-biking possibilities around the Sacred Valley and downhill trips to the Amazon jungle, all accessible from Cuzco. Easier cycling routes include the wine country around Lunahuaná and in the Cañón del Colca, starting from Chivay.

Mountain-bike rental in Peru tends to be basic; if you are planning on serious biking it's best to bring your own. (Airline bicycle-carrying policies vary, so shop around.) You'll also need a repair kit and extra parts.

Swimming

Swimming is popular along Peru's desert coast from January to March, when the Pacific Ocean waters are warmest and skies are blue. Some of the best spots are just south of Lima. Far more attractive is the stretch of shore on the north coast, especially at laid-back Huanchaco, around Chiclayo and the perennially busy jet-set resorts of Máncora.

Only north of Talara does the water stay warm year-round. Watch for dangerous currents and note that beaches near major coastal cities are often polluted.

Horseback Riding

Horse rentals can be arranged in many tourist destinations, but the rental stock is not always treated well, so check your horse carefully before you saddle up. For a real splurge, take a ride on a graceful Peruvian *paso* horse. These descendants of horses with royal Spanish and Moorish lineage, like those ridden by the conquistadors, are reputed to have the world's smoothest gait. Stables around Peru advertise rides for half a day or longer, especially in the Sacred Valley at Urubamba.

Paragliding

Popular paragliding sites include the coastal cliff tops of suburban Miraflores in Lima and various points along the south coast, including Pisco and Paracas (even, possibly, over the Nazca Lines). There are few paragliding operators in Peru. Book ahead through the agencies in Lima.

Llamas in the Cordilleras (p235)

CHARTON FRANCK / HEMIS.FR / GETTY IMAGES ©

The Natural World

Few countries have topographies as rugged, forbidding and wildly diverse as Peru. Between snaking rivers, plunging canyons and zigzagging mountain roads, navigating Peru's landscape is about circumventing natural obstacles, a path of excitement and jaw-dropping beauty.

The Land

The third-largest country in South America (at 1.285 million sq km), Peru is five times larger than the UK, almost twice the size of Texas and one-sixth the size of Australia. On the coast, a narrow strip of land that lies below 1000m in elevation hugs the country's 3000km-long shoreline. Consisting primarily of scrubland and desert, it eventually merges, in the south, with Chile's Atacama Desert, one of the driest places on earth. The coast includes Lima, the capital, and several major agricultural centers – oases watered by dozens of rivers that cascade down from the Andes. These settlements make for a strange sight: barren desert can give way to bursts of green fields within the course of a few meters. The coast contains some of Peru's flattest terrain, so it's no surprise that the country's best road, the Carretera Panamericana (Pan-American Hwy), borders much of the Pacific from Ecuador to Chile.

Wildflowers, Parque Nacional Huascarán (p239)

The Andes, the world's second-greatest mountain chain, form the spine of the country. Rising steeply from the coast, and growing sharply in height and gradient from north to south, they reach spectacular heights of more than 6000m just 100km inland. Peru's highest peak, Huascarán (6768m), located northeast of Huaraz, is the world's highest tropical summit and the sixth-tallest mountain in the Americas. Though the Peruvian Andes reside in the tropics, the mountains are laced with a web of glaciers above elevations of 5000m. Between 3000m and 4000m lie the agricultural highlands, which support more than a third of Peru's population.

The eastern Andean slopes receive much more rainfall than the dry western slopes and are draped in lush cloud forests as they descend into the lowland rainforest of the Amazon. Here, the undulating landscape rarely rises more than 500m above sea level as various tributary systems feed into the mighty Río Amazonas (Amazon River), the largest river in the world. Weather conditions are hot and humid year-round, with most precipitation falling between December and May.

Wildlife

With its folds, bends and plunging river valleys, Peru is home to countless ecosystems, each with its own unique climate, elevation, vegetation and soil type. As a result, it boasts a spectacular variety of plant and animal life. Colonies of sea lions occupy rocky outcroppings on the coast, while raucous flocks of brightly colored macaws descend on clay licks in the Amazon. In the Andes, rare vicuñas (endangered relatives of the alpaca) trot about in packs as condors take to the wind currents. Peru is one of only a dozen or so countries in the world considered to be 'megadiverse.'

Birds

Peru has more than 1800 bird species – that's more than the number of species found in North America and Europe together. From the tiniest hummingbirds to the majestic Andean condor, the variety is colorful and seemingly endless; new species are discovered regularly.

Along the Pacific, marine birds of all kinds are most visible, especially in the south, where they can be found clustered along the shore. Here you'll see exuberant Chilean flamingos, oversized Peruvian pelicans, plump Inca terns sporting white-feather mustaches and bright-orange beaks, colonies of brown boobies engaged in elaborate mating dances, cormorants, and endangered Humboldt penguins, which can be spotted waddling around the Islas Ballestas.

In the highlands, the most famous bird of all is the Andean condor. Weighing up to 10kg, with a 3m-plus wingspan, this monarch of the air (a member of the vulture family) once ranged over the entire Andean mountain chain from Venezuela to Tierra del Fuego. Considered the largest flying bird in the world, the condor was put on the endangered-species list in the 1970s, due mostly to loss of habitat and pollution. But it was also hunted to the brink of extinction because its body parts were believed to increase male virility and ward off nightmares. Condors usually nest in impossibly high mountain cliffs that prevent predators from snatching their young. Their main food source is carrion and they're most easily spotted riding thermal air currents in the canyons around Arequipa.

Other prominent high-altitude birds include the Andean gull (don't call it a seagull!), which is commonly sighted along lakes and rivers as high as 4500m. The mountains are also home to several species of ibis, such as the puna ibis, which inhabits lakeside marshes, as well as roughly a dozen types of cinclodes, a type of ovenbird (their clay nests resemble ovens) endemic to the Andes. Other species include torrent ducks, which nest in small waterside caves, Andean geese, spotted Andean flickers, black-and-yellow Andean siskins and, of course, a panoply of hummingbirds.

Swoop down toward the Amazon and you'll catch sight of the world's most iconic tropical birds, including boisterous flocks of parrots and macaws festooned in brightly plumed regalia. You'll also see clusters of aracaris, toucans, parakeets, toucanets, ibises, regal gray-winged trumpeters, umbrella birds with gravity-defying feathered hairdos, crimson colored cocks-of-the-rock, soaring hawks and harpy eagles. The list goes on.

Mammals

The Amazon is home to a bounty of mammals. More than two dozen species of monkey are found here, including howlers, acrobatic spider monkeys and wide-eyed marmosets. With the help of a guide, you may also see sloths, bats, piglike peccaries, anteaters, armadillos and coatis (ring-tailed members of the raccoon family). And if you're really lucky, you'll find giant river otters, capybaras (a rodent of unusual size), river dolphins, tapirs and maybe one of half a dozen elusive felines, including the fabled jaguar.

Toward the west, the cloud forests straddling the Amazon and the eastern slopes of the Andean highlands are home to the endangered spectacled bear. South America's only bear is a black, shaggy mammal that grows up to 1.8m in length, and is known for its white, masklike face markings.

The highlands are home to roving packs of camelids: llamas and alpacas are the most easily spotted since they are domesticated, and used as pack animals or for their wool; vicuñas and guanacos live exclusively in the wild. On highland talus slopes, watch out for the viscacha, which looks like the world's most cuddly rabbit. Foxes, deer and domesticated *cuy* (guinea pigs) are also highland dwellers, as is the puma (cougar or mountain lion).

On the coast, huge numbers of sea lions and seals are easily seen on the Islas Ballestas. While whales are very rarely seen offshore, dolphins are commonly seen. In the coastal desert strip, there are few unique species of land animals. One is the near-threatened Sechuran fox, the smallest of the South American foxes (found in northern Peru), which has a black-tipped tail, pale, sand-colored fur and an omnivorous appetite for small rodents and seed pods.

Reptiles, Amphibians, Insects & Marine Life

The greatest variety of reptiles, amphibians, insects and marine life can be found in the Amazon Basin. Here, you'll find hundreds of species, including toads, tree frogs and thumbnail-sized poison dart frogs (indigenous peoples once used the frogs' deadly poison on the points of their blow-pipe darts). Rivers teem with schools of piranhas, *paiche* and *doncella* (both are types of freshwater fish), while the air buzzes with the activity of thousands of insects: armies of ants, squadrons of beetles, as well as katydids, stick insects, caterpillars, spiders, praying mantis, transparent moths, and butterflies of all shapes and sizes. A blue morpho butterfly in flight is a remarkable sight: with wingspans of up to 10cm, their iridescent-blue coloring can seem downright hallucinogenic.

Naturally, there are all kinds of reptiles too, including tortoises, river turtles, lizards, caimans and, of course, that jungle-movie favorite: the anaconda. An aquatic boa snake that can measure more than 10m in length, it will often ambush its prey by the water's edge, constrict its body around it and then drown it in the river. Caimans, tapirs, deer, turtles and peccaries are all tasty meals for this killer snake; human victims are almost unheard of (unless you're Jennifer Lopez and Ice Cube in a low-rent Hollywood production). Far more worrisome to the average human is the bushmaster, a deadly, reddish-brown viper that likes to hang out inside rotting logs and among the buttress roots of trees. Thankfully, it's a retiring creature, and is rarely found on popular trails.

Plants

At high elevations in the Andes, especially in the Cordilleras Blanca and Huayhuash, outside Huaraz, there is a cornucopia of distinctive alpine flora. Plants encountered in this region include native lupins, spiky tussocks of *ichu* grass, striking *queñua* (Polylepis) trees with their distinctive curly, red paper-like bark, in addition to unusual bromeliads. Many alpine wildflowers bloom during the trekking season, between May and September.

In the south, you'll find the distinctive puna ecosystem. These areas have a fairly limited flora of hard grasses, cushion plants, small herbaceous plants, shrubs and dwarf trees. Many plants in this environment have developed small, thick leaves that are less susceptible to frost and radiation. In the north, you can find some *páramo* (high-altitude Andean grasslands), which have a harsher climate, are less grassy and have an odd mixture of landscapes, including peat bogs, glacier-formed valleys, alpine lakes, wet grasslands and patches of scrubland and forest.

National Parks

Peru's vast wealth of wildlife is protected by a system of national parks and reserves with 60 areas covering almost 15% of the country. The newest is the Sierra del Divisor Reserve Zone, created in 2006 to protect 1.5 million hectares of rainforest on the Brazilian border. All of these protected areas are administered by the Instituto Nacional de Recursos Nacionales (Inrena; www.inrena.gob.pe), a division of the Ministry of Agriculture.

Unfortunately, resources are lacking to conserve protected areas, which are subject to illegal hunting, fishing, logging and mining. The government simply doesn't have the funds to hire enough rangers and provide them with the equipment necessary to patrol the parks. That said, a number of international agencies and not-for-profit organizations contribute money, staff and resources to help with conservation and education projects.

Environmental Issues

Peru faces major challenges in the stewardship of its natural resources, with problems compounded by a lack of law enforcement and its impenetrable geography. Deforestation and erosion are major issues, as is industrial pollution, urban sprawl and the continuing attempted eradication of coca plantations on some Andean slopes. In addition, the Interoceánica Hwy through the heart of the Amazon may imperil thousands of square kilometers of rainforest.

Reduced growth in mining earnings in recent years has led the government to install protectionist measures, much to the detriment of the environment. A new law enacted in July 2014 weakened environmental protections by removing Peru's environmental ministry's jurisdiction over air-, soil-, and water-quality standards.

Chupe de pollo (chicken chowder)

RUIDOBLANCO / GETTY IMAGES ©

Food & Drink

In Peru, fusion was always a natural part of everyday cooking. Over the last 400 years, Andean stews mingled with Asian stir-fries, and Spanish rice dishes absorbed Amazonian flavors, producing the country's famed criollo *(creole) cooking. More recently, a generation of experimental young innovators has pushed local fare to gastronomic heights.*

Staples & Specialties

Given the country's craggy topography, there are an infinite number of regional cuisines. But at a national level much of the country's cooking begins and ends with the humble potato – which originally hails from the Andes. (All potatoes can be traced back to a single progenitor from Peru.)

Standout dishes include *ocopa* (potatoes with a spicy peanut sauce), *papa a la huancaína* (potato topped with a creamy cheese sauce) and *causa* (mashed-potato terrines stuffed with seafood, vegetables or chicken). Also popular is *papa rellena*, a mashed potato filled with ground beef and then deep-fried. Potatoes are also found in the chowder-like soups known as *chupe* and in *lomo saltado*, the simple beef stir-fries that headline every Peruvian menu.

Ceviche

★ **Most Influential Chefs**

Gastón Acurio, at Astrid y Gastón Casa Moreyra (p43) and others

Virgilio Martínez, at Central (p42)

Pedro Miguel Schiaffino, at Malabar (p59) and ámaZ (p42)

Rafael Osterling, at Rafael (p61) and El Mercado (Map p56)

Other popular items include tamales (corn cakes), which are made in numerous regional variations, such as *humitas* (created with fresh corn) and *juanes* (made from cassava).

Amazon

Though not as popular throughout the entire country, Amazon ingredients have begun to make headway in recent years. Several high-end restaurants in Lima have started giving gourmet treatment to jungle mainstays, with wide acclaim. This includes the increased use of river snails and fish (including *paiche* and *doncella*), as well as produce such as *aguaje* (the fruit of the *moriche* palm), *yucca* (cassava) and *chonta* (hearts of palm). *Juanes* (a bijao leaf stuffed with rice, *yucca*, chicken and/or pork) is a savory area staple.

Coast

The coast is all about seafood – and ceviche, naturally, plays a starring role. A chilled concoction of fish, shrimp or other seafood marinated in lime juice, onions, cilantro and chili peppers, it is typically served with a wedge of boiled corn and sweet potato. The fish is cooked in the citrus juices through a process of oxidation. (Some chefs, however, have begun to cut back on their marinating time, which means that some ceviches are served with a sushi-like consistency.) Another popular seafood cocktail is *tiradito,* a Japanese-inflected ceviche consisting of thin slices of fish served without onions, sometimes bathed in a creamy hot-pepper sauce.

Cooked fish can be prepared dozens of ways: *al ajo* (in garlic), *frito* (fried) or *a la chorrillana* (cooked in white wine, tomatoes and onions), the latter of which hails from the city of Chorrillos, south of Lima. Soups and stews are also a popular staple, including *aguadito*

Top Eats

For a meal so good it will (almost certainly) bring unbridled joy, try the following places:

Arequipa At **Zig Zag** (p103), the succulent combination meat plate of alpaca, beef and lamb – cooked over hot volcanic rocks – is a carnivore's delight.

Cuzco Elegant **Uchu Peruvian Steakhouse** (p172) serves stone-grilled alpaca with piquant sauces. You can also order from the menu of Marcelo Batata upstairs – twice-baked Andean potatoes are a must.

Iquitos Set at the mouth of the Río Itaya, **Al Frío y al Fuego** (p266) has excellent nighttime views of Iquitos and scrumptious dishes crafted from Amazon river fish.

Lima Ceviche at **Al Toke Pez** (p59)and **Pescados Capitales** (p61)

Trujillo The bamboo-lined **Mar Picante** (p229) is known for serving up behemoth orders of divine *ceviche mixto,* piled high with shrimp, fish, crab and scallops.

(a soupy risotto), *picante* (a spicy stew) and *chupe* (bisque), all of which can feature fish, seafood and other ingredients.

Other items that make a regular appearance on seafood menus are *conchitas a la parmesana* (scallops baked with cheese), *pulpo al olivo* (octopus in a smashed-olive sauce) and *choros a la chalaca* (chilled mussels with fresh corn salsa). On the north coast, around Chiclayo, omelets made with manta ray *(tortilla de manta raya)* are a typical dish.

None of this means that pork, chicken or beef aren't popular. *Aji de gallina* (shredded chicken-walnut stew) is a Peruvian classic. In the north, a couple of local dishes bear repeat sampling: *arroz con pato a la chiclayana* (duck and rice simmered with cilantro, typical of Chiclayo) and *seco de cabrito* (goat stewed with cilantro, chilis and beer).

Highlands

In the chilly highlands, it's all about soups, which tend to be a generous, gut-warming experience, filled with vegetables, squash, potatoes, locally grown herbs and a variety of meats. *Sopa a la criolla* (a mild, creamy noodle soup with beef and vegetables) is a regular item on menus, as is *caldo de gallina* (a nourishing chicken soup with potatoes and herbs). In the area around Arequipa, *chupe de camarones* (chowder made from river shrimp) is also a mainstay.

The highlands are also known as the source of all things *cuy* – guinea pig. It is often served roasted or *chactado* (pressed under hot rocks). It tastes very similar to rabbit and is often served whole. River trout – prepared myriad ways – is also popular.

Arequipa has a particularly dynamic regional cuisine. The area is renowned for its *picantes* (spicy stews served with chunks of white cheese), *rocoto relleno* (red chilis stuffed with meat) and *solterito* (bean salad).

For special occasions and weddings, families will gather to make *pachamanca:* a mix of marinated meats, vegetables, cheese, chilis and fragrant herbs baked on hot rocks in the ground.

Desserts

Desserts tend to be hypersweet concoctions. *Suspiro limeña* is the most famous, consisting of *manjar blanco* (caramel) topped with sweet meringue. Also popular are *alfajores* (cookie sandwiches with caramel) and *crema volteada* (flan). Lighter and fruitier is *mazamorra morada,* a purple-corn pudding of Afro-Peruvian origin that comes with chunks of fruit.

During October, bakeries sell *turrón de Doña Pepa,* a sticky, molasses-drenched cake eaten in honor of the Lord of Miracles.

Drinks

The main soft-drink brands are available, but locals have a passion for Inca Kola – which tastes like bubble gum and comes in a spectacular shade of nuclear yellow. Fresh fruit juices are also popular, as are traditional drinks such as *chicha morada,* a refreshing, non-alcoholic beverage made from purple corn and spices.

Though the country exports coffee to the world, many Peruvians drink it instant: some restaurants dish up packets of Nescafé or an inky coffee reduction that is blended with hot water. In cosmopolitan and touristy areas, cafes serving espresso and cappuccino have proliferated. Tea and *mates* (herbal teas), such as *manzanilla* (chamomile), *menta* (mint) and *mate de coca* (coca-leaf tea), are also available. Coca-leaf tea will not get you high, but it can soothe stomach ailments and it's believed to help in adjusting to high altitude.

Pisco

It is the national beverage: pisco, the omnipresent grape brandy served at events from the insignificant to the momentous. Production dates back to the early days of the Spanish colony in Ica, where it was distilled on private haciendas and then sold to sailors making their way through the port of Pisco. In its early years, pisco was the local firewater: a great way to get ripped – and wake up the following morning feeling as if you had been hammered over the head.

By the early 20th century, the pisco sour (pisco with lime juice and sugar) arrived on the scene, quickly becoming the national drink. In recent decades, as production has become more sophisticated, piscos have become more nuanced and flavorful (without the morning-after effects).

The three principal types of Peruvian pisco are Quebranta, Italia and acholado. Quebranta (a pure-smelling pisco) and Italia (slightly aromatic) are each named for the varieties of grape from which they are crafted, while acholado is a blend of varietals that has more of an alcohol top-note (best for mixed drinks). There are many small-batch specialty piscos made from grape must (pressed juice with skins), known as mosto verde. These have a fragrant smell and are best sipped straight.

The most common brands include Tres Generaciones, Ocucaje, Ferreyros and La Botija, while Viñas de Oro, Viejo Tonel, Estirpe Peruano, LaBlanco and Gran Cruz are among the finest. Any pisco purchased in a bottle that resembles the head of an Inca will make for an unusual piece of home decor – and not much else.

Where to Eat & Drink

For the most part, restaurants in Peru are a community affair, and local places will cater to a combination of families, tourists, teenagers and packs of chatty businesspeople. At lunch time, many eateries offer a *menú* (a set meal consisting of two or three courses). This is generally good value. (Note: if you request the *menú*, you'll get the special. If you want the menu, ask for *la carta*.)

Cevicherías – places where ceviche is sold – are popular along the coast, and most commonly open for lunchtime service, as most places proudly serve fish that is at its freshest. In the countryside, informal local restaurants known as *picanterías* are a staple. In some cases these operate right out of someone's home.

Embracing Local Cuisine

Peru, once a country where important guests were treated to French meals and Scotch whisky, is now a place where high-end restaurants spotlight deft interpretations of Andean favorites, including quinoa and *cuy*. The dining scene has blossomed. And tourism outfits have swept in to incorporate a culinary something as part of every tour. In 2000 the country became the site of the first Cordon Bleu academy in Latin America, and in 2009 *Bon Appétit* magazine named Lima the 'next great food city.' In Lima, La Casa de La Gastronomia Peruana is a new museum fully dedicated to celebrating the country's complex culinary heritage. In 2015 Peru won 'best culinary destination' from the World Travel Awards for the third time. Of Peru's 3.1 million annual visitors, 40% take part in gastronomic tourism. And maybe you should too.

Foodie fever has infected Peruvians at every level, with even the most humble *chicharrón* (fried-pork) vendor hyperattentive to the vagaries of preparation and presentation. No small part of this is due to celebrity chef Gastón Acurio, whose culinary skill and business acumen (he owns dozens of restaurants around the globe) have given him rock-star status.

GAVIN HELLIER / ROBERTHARDING / GETTY IMAGES ©

Music & the Arts

The country that has been home to both indigenous and European empires has a wealth of cultural and artistic tradition. Perhaps the most outstanding achievements are in the areas of music (both indigenous and otherwise), painting and literature — the latter of which received plenty of attention in 2010, when Peruvian novelist Mario Vargas Llosa won the Nobel Prize.

Music

Like its people, Peru's music is an intercontinental fusion of elements. Pre-Columbian cultures contributed bamboo flutes, the Spaniards brought stringed instruments and the Africans gave it a backbone of fluid, percussive rhythm. By and large, music tends to be a regional affair: *criollo* waltzes, and African-influenced *landó,* with its thumping bass beats, are predominant on the coast, while high-pitched indigenous *huayno,* heavy on bamboo wind instruments, is heard in the Andes.

Over the last several decades, the *huayno* has blended with surf guitars and Colombian *cumbia* (a type of Afro-Caribbean dance music) to produce *chicha*, a danceable sound closely identified with the Amazon region, growing in popularity even with cool urban youth. Well-known *chicha* bands include Los Shapis and Los Mirlos. *Cumbia* (Colombian

Peruvian flute

RUSLANA LURCHENKO / SHUTTERSTOCK ©

★ **Must-Read Fiction**

The War of the End of the World (Mario Vargas Llosa, 1981)

War by Candlelight (Daniel Alarcón, 2006)

Chronicle of San Gabriel (Julio Ramón Ribeyro, 2004)

salsa-like dance and musical style) is also popular. Grupo 5, which hails from Chiclayo, is currently a favorite in the genre.

On the coast, guitar-inflected *música criolla* (*criollo* music) has its roots in both Spain and Africa. The most famous *criollo* style is the *vals peruano* (Peruvian waltz), a three-quarter-time waltz that is fast moving and full of complex guitar melodies. The most legendary singers in this genre include singer and composer Chabuca Granda (1920–83), Lucha Reyes (1936–73) and Arturo 'Zambo' Cavero (1940–2009). Cavero, in particular, was revered for his gravelly vocals and soulful interpretations. *Landó* is closely connected to this style of music, but features the added elements of call-and-response. Standout performers in this vein include singers Susana Baca (b 1944) and Eva Ayllón (b 1956).

Peru is making significant contributions to today's alt-rock scene, with fusion bands such as Uchpa, NovaLima, Bareto, the award-winning Lucho Quequezana, and La Sarita, integrating Quechua, Afro-Peruvian and other influences. Band La Mente sets a party tone and Bareto remakes Peruvian *cumbia* classics with great appeal.

Visual Arts

The country's most famous art movement dates to the 17th and 18th centuries, when the artists of the *escuela cuzqueña* (Cuzco school) produced thousands of religious paintings, the vast majority of which remain unattributed. Created by native and *mestizo* (person of mixed indigenous and Spanish descent) artists, the pieces frequently feature holy figures laced in gold paint and rendered in a style inspired by mannerist and late Gothic

Traditional Crafts

Peru has a long tradition of producing extraordinarily rendered crafts and folk art. Here's what to look for:

Textiles You'll see intricate weavings with elaborate anthropomorphic and geometric designs all over Peru. Some of the finest can be found around Cuzco.

Pottery The most stunning pieces of pottery are those made in the tradition of the pre-Columbian Moche people of the north coast. But also worthwhile is Chancay-style pottery: rotund figures made from sand-colored clay. Find these at craft markets in Lima.

Religious crafts These abound in all regions, but the *retablos* (three-dimensional ornamental dioramas) from Ayacucho are the most spectacular.

art – but bearing traces of an indigenous color palette and iconography. Today, these hang in museums and churches throughout Peru and reproductions are sold in many craft markets.

One of the most well-known artistic figures of the 19th century is Pancho Fierro (1807–79), the illegitimate son of a priest and a slave, who painted highly evocative watercolors of the everyday figures that occupied Lima's streets: fishmongers, teachers and Catholic religious figures clothed in lush robes.

In the early 20th century, an indigenist movement led by painter José Sabogal (1888–1956) achieved national prominence. Sabogal often painted indigenous figures and incorporated pre-Columbian design in his work. As director of the National School of Arts in Lima, he influenced a whole generation of painters, who looked to Andean tradition for inspiration, including Julia Codesido (1892–1979), Mario Urteaga (1875–1957) and Enrique Camino Brent (1909–60).

Literature

Mario Vargas Llosa (b 1936) is Peru's most famous writer, hailed alongside 20th-century Latin American luminaries such as Gabriel García Márquez, Julio Cortázar and Carlos Fuentes. His novels evoke James Joyce in their complexity, meandering through time and shifting perspectives. Vargas Llosa is also a keen social observer, casting a spotlight on the naked corruption of the ruling class and the peculiarities of Peruvian society. More than two dozen of his novels are available in translation. The best place to start is *La ciudad y los perros* (The Time of the Hero; 1962), based on his experience at a Peruvian military academy. (The soldiers at his old academy responded to the novel by burning it.)

Another keen observer includes Alfredo Bryce Echenique (b 1939), who chronicles the ways of the upper class in novels such as *El huerto de mi amada* (My Beloved's Garden; 2004), which recounts an affair between a 33-year-old woman and a teenage boy in 1950s Lima. Demonstrating a distinctly Peruvian penchant for dark humor is Julio Ramón Ribeyro (1929–94). Though never a bestselling author, he is critically acclaimed for his insightful works, which focus on the vagaries of lower-middle-class life. His work is available in English in *Marginal Voices: Selected Stories* (1993). If you are just learning to read Spanish, his clearly and concisely written pieces are an ideal place to start exploring Peruvian literature.

Also significant is Daniel Alarcón (b 1977), a rising Peruvian-American writer whose award-winning short stories have appeared in the *New Yorker* magazine. His debut novel, *Lost City Radio* (2007), about a country recovering from civil war, won a PEN award in 2008.

If Vargas Llosa is the country's greatest novelist, then César Vallejo (1892–1938) is its greatest poet. In his lifetime he published only three slim books – *Los heraldos negros* (The Black Heralds; 1919), *Trilce* (1922) and *Poemas humanos* (Human Poems; 1939) – but he has long been regarded as one of the most innovative Latin American poets of the 20th century. Vallejo frequently touched on existential themes and was known for pushing the language to its limits, inventing words when real ones no longer suited him.

Llama trek near Cuzco

Survival Guide

Directory A–Z

Accommodations

Peru has accommodations to suit every budget, especially in tourist hubs and cities. Lodgings are considerably more expensive in tourist areas, such as Lima, Cuzco and the Sacred Valley.

Rates

Note that prices may fluctuate with exchange rates.

Extra charges Foreigners do not have to pay the 19% hotel tax (sometimes included in rates quoted in soles), but may have to present their passport and tourist card to photocopy. A credit card transaction surcharge of 7% or more does not include the home bank's foreign-currency exchange fee. US dollars may be accepted, but the exchange rate may be poor.

Packages In the remote jungle lodges of the Amazon and in popular beach destinations such as Máncora, all-inclusive resort-style pricing is more the norm.

High season In Cuzco, demand is very high during the peak season (June to August). During Inti Raymi (p23), Semana Santa (p22) and Fiestas Patrias (p24), advance reservations are a must. In Lima, prices remain steady throughout the year; look for last-minute specials online. Paying cash always helps; ask for discounts for long-term stays.

Reservations

Street noise can be an issue in any lodging, so select your room accordingly. It's always OK to ask to see a room before committing. Other things to consider:

Airport arrival Since many flights into Lima arrive late at night, it's inadvisable to begin searching for a place to sleep upon arrival. Reserve your first night ahead; most hotels also can arrange airport pickup.

Late arrival Cheap budget places may not honor a reservation if you arrive late, so it is best to confirm your arrival time. Late check-in is not a problem at many midrange and top-end hotels, but a deposit may be required.

Book Online

For more accommodations reviews by Lonely Planet writers, check out hotels.lonelyplanet.com. You'll find independent reviews, as well as recommendations on the best places to stay. Best of all, you can book online.

When to Book Around the country, reservations are a necessity for stays during a major festival (such as Inti Raymi in Cuzco) or a holiday such as Semana Santa (Easter Week), when all of Peru is on vacation. In the Amazon, reservations

Climate

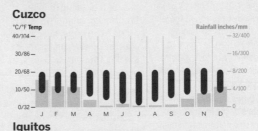

Cuzco

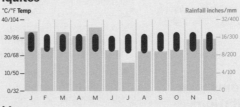

Iquitos

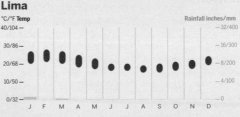

Lima

A Note About Prices

Prices are generally listed in Peruvian nuevos soles. Many package lodgings and higher-end hotels, however, will only quote prices in US dollars, as will many travel agencies and tour operators. In these cases, we list prices in US dollars.

Both currencies have experienced fluctuations in recent years, so expect many figures to be different from what you have read.

Electricity

Electrical current is 220V, 60Hz AC. Standard outlets accept round prongs, some have dual-voltage outlets that take flat prongs. Even so, your adapter may need a built-in surge protector.

220V/60Hz

are needed at remote lodges. In smaller villages and areas off the beaten path, service tends to be on a first-come, first-served basis.

Advance payment Some lodges, especially in the Amazon, may require all or part of the payment up front. Make sure your travel plans are firm if you are paying in advance, as securing refunds can be a challenge.

Discounts Reserving online is convenient, but off-season walk-in rates may be lower. At top-end hotels, however, last-minute online deals are the norm, so always check a hotel's website for discounts and special promotional packages.

Room types *Habitación simple* refers to a single room. A *habitación doble* features twin beds while a *habitación matrimonial* has a double or queen-sized bed.

Customs Regulations

Peru allows duty-free importation of 3L of alcohol and 20 packs of cigarettes, 50 cigars or 250g of tobacco. You can import US$300 of gifts. Legally, you are allowed to bring

in such items as a laptop, camera, portable music player, kayak, climbing gear, mountain bike or similar items for personal use.

○ It is illegal to take pre-Columbian or colonial artifacts out of Peru, and it is illegal to bring them into most countries. If purchasing reproductions, buy only from a reputable dealer and ask for a detailed receipt. Purchasing animal products made from endangered species or even just transporting them around Peru is also illegal.

○ Coca leaves are legal in Peru, but not in most other countries, even in the form of tea bags. People subject to random drug testing should be aware that coca, even in the form of tea, may leave trace amounts in urine.

○ Check with your own home government about customs restrictions and duties on any expensive or rare items you intend to bring back. Most countries allow their citizens to import a limited number of items duty-free, though these regulations are subject to change.

220V/60Hz

Food

See Food & Drink, p291.

Mid- to high-end restaurants charge a 10% service fee and a 19% tax. The following price ranges refer to a main dish:

$ less than S25
$$ S20–S60
$$$ more than S60

LGBT Travelers

Peru is a strongly conservative, Catholic country. In 2015, the Peruvian Congress rejected a bill for gay and lesbian civil unions, despite the adoption of similar measures in neighboring countries in the Southern Cone. While many Peruvians will tolerate homosexuality on a 'don't ask, don't tell' level when dealing with foreign travelers, gay rights remain a struggle. As a result, many gays and lesbians in Peru don't publicly identify as homosexual.

Public displays of affection among homosexual couples are rarely seen. Outside gay clubs, it is advisable to keep a low profile. Lima is the most accepting of gay people, but this is on a relative scale. Beyond that, the tourist towns of Cuzco, Arequipa and Trujillo tend to be more tolerant than the norm. Social apps Tinder and Grindr are good places to find out more about the gay scene.

FYI: the rainbow flag seen around Cuzco and in the Andes is *not* a gay pride flag – it's the flag of the Inca empire.

Health

It's not unusual to suffer from altitude sickness in the Andes or tummy problems, despite Peru's wonderful culinary reputation. Peru's many climates mean that travelers will face different risks in different areas. While food-borne as well as mosquito-borne infections happen, many of these illnesses are not life-threatening. However, they can certainly ruin your trip. Besides getting the proper vaccinations, it's important that you take insect repellent and exercise care in what you eat and drink.

Before You Go

Since most vaccines don't produce immunity until at least two weeks after they're given, visit a physician four to eight weeks before departure. Ask your doctor for an International Certificate of Vaccination (otherwise known as the 'yellow booklet'), which will list all the vaccinations you've received. This is mandatory for countries that require proof of yellow-fever vaccination upon entry, but it's a good idea to carry it wherever you travel.

Bring medications in their original containers, clearly labeled. A signed, dated letter from your physician describing all medical conditions and medications, including generic names, is also a good idea. If carrying syringes or needles, be sure to have a physician's letter documenting their medical necessity.

Most doctors and hospitals expect payment in cash, regardless of whether you have travel health insurance.

Availability of Health Care

Lima has high-quality 24-hour medical clinics, and English-speaking doctors and dentists. See the guide at the website for the US embassy (http://lima.usembassy.gov). Rural areas may have only the most basic medical services. You may have to pay in cash, regardless of whether you have travel insurance.

Life-threatening medical problems may require evacuation. For a list of medical-evacuation and travel-insurance companies, see the website of the US State Department (http://travel.state.gov).

Pharmacies are known as *farmacias* or *boticas,* identified by a green or red cross. They offer most of the medications available in other countries, though tampons, birth-control pills and other contraceptives (even condoms) are scarce outside metropolitan areas and not always reliable, so stock up in cities or from home.

Altitude Sickness

Altitude sickness may result from rapid ascents to altitudes greater than 2500m (8100ft). In Peru, this includes Cuzco, Machu Picchu and Lake Titicaca. Being physically fit offers no protection. Symptoms may include headaches, nausea, vomiting, dizziness, malaise, insomnia and loss of appetite. Severe cases may be complicated by fluid in the lungs (high-altitude pulmonary edema) or swelling of the brain (high-altitude cerebral edema). If symptoms persist for more than 24 hours, descend immediately by at least 500m and see a doctor.

The best prevention is to spend two nights or more at each rise of 1000m. Diamox may be taken starting 24 hours before ascent. A natural alternative is ginkgo.

It's also important to avoid overexertion, eat light meals and abstain from alcohol. Altitude sickness should be taken seriously; it can be life threatening when severe.

Insurance

Having a travel-insurance policy to cover theft, loss, accidents and illness is highly recommended. Always carry your insurance card with you. Not all policies compensate travelers for misrouted or lost luggage. Check the fine print to see if it excludes 'dangerous activities,' which can include scuba diving, motorcycling and even trekking. Also check if the policy coverage includes worst-case scenarios, such as evacuations and flights home.

You must usually report any loss or theft to local police (or airport authorities) within 24 hours. Make sure you keep all documentation to make any claim.

Worldwide travel insurance is available at www.lonelyplanet.com/travel-insurance. You can buy, extend and claim online anytime – even if you're already on the road.

Internet Access

Most regions have excellent internet connections and reasonable prices; it is typical for hotels and hostels to have wi-fi or computer terminals. Family guesthouses, however, particularly outside urban areas, lag behind in this area.

Internet cafes are widespread. Rates start at S1 per hour, with high rates only in remote areas.

Legal Matters

Legal assistance Your own embassy is of limited help if you get into trouble with the law in Peru, where you are presumed guilty until proven innocent. If you are the victim, the *policía de turismo* (Poltur; tourist police) can help, with limited English. Poltur stations are found in major cities.

Bribery Though some police officers (even tourist police) have a reputation for corruption, bribery is illegal. Beyond traffic police, the most likely place officials might request a little extra is at land borders. Since this too is illegal, those with time and fortitude can and should stick to their guns.

Drugs Avoid having any conversation with someone who offers you drugs. Peru has draconian penalties for possessing even a small amount of drugs; minimum sentences are several years in jail.

Police Should you be stopped by a plainclothes officer, don't hand over any documents or money. Never get into a vehicle with someone claiming to be a police officer, but insist on going to a real police station on foot.

Protests It's not recommended to attend political protests or to get too close to blockades – these are places to avoid.

Detention If you are imprisoned for any reason, make sure that someone else knows about it as soon as possible. Extended pretrial detentions are not uncommon. Peruvians bring food and clothing to family members who are in prison, where conditions are extremely harsh.

Complaints For issues with a hotel or tour operator, register your complaint with the **National Institute for the Defense of Competition and the Protection of Intellectual Property** (Indecopi; ☑01-224-7800; www.indecopi.gob.pe) in Lima.

Maps

The best road map of Peru is the 1:2,000,000 *Mapa Vial* published by Lima 2000 and available in better bookstores. The 1:1,500,000 *Peru South and Lima* country map, published by International Travel Maps, covers the country in good detail south of a line drawn east to west through Tingo María, and has a good street map of Lima, San Isidro, Miraflores and Barranco on the reverse side.

For topographical maps, go to the **Instituto Geográfico Nacional** (IGN; ☎01-475-3030, ext 119; www.ign.gob.pe; Aramburu 1190-98, Surquillo, Lima; ☺8am-6pm Mon-Fri, to 1pm Sat), which has reference maps and others for sale. In January the IGN closes early, so call ahead. High-scale topographic maps for trekking are available, though sheets of border areas might be hard to get. Geological and demographic maps and CD-ROMs are also sold.

Topographic, city and road maps are also at the South American Explorers' clubhouses (www.saexplorers.org) in Lima and Cuzco.

Up-to-date topo maps are often available from outdoor outfitters in major trekking centers such as Cuzco, Huaraz and Arequipa. If you are bringing along a GPS unit, ensure that your power source adheres to Peru's 220V, 60Hz AC standard and always carry a compass.

Money

○ Peru uses the nuevo sol (S).

○ Carrying cash, an ATM card, and a credit card that can be used for cash advances in case of emergency, is advisable.

○ Credit-card fraud is rampant. Tell your bank you will be in Peru and use your cards with care.

○ Ask for *billetes pequeños* (small bills), as S100 bills are hard to change in small towns or for small purchases.

○ *Casas de cambio* (foreign-exchange bureaus) are fast, have longer hours and often give slightly better rates than banks.

○ Many places accept US dollars.

○ Do not accept torn money as it will likely not be accepted by Peruvians.

○ Don't change money on the street as counterfeits are a problem.

ATMs

○ *Cajeros automáticos* (ATMs) proliferate in nearly every city and town in Peru, as well as at major airports, bus terminals and shopping areas.

○ ATMs are linked to the international Plus (Visa) and Cirrus (Maestro/MasterCard) systems, as well as American Express and other networks.

○ Users should have a four-digit PIN. To avoid problems, notify your bank that you'll be using your ATM card abroad.

○ If your card works with Banco de la Nacion it may be the best option, as it doesn't charge fees (at least at the time of writing).

○ Both US dollars and nuevos soles are readily available from Peruvian ATMs.

○ Your home bank may charge an additional fee for each foreign ATM transaction.

○ ATMs are normally open 24 hours.

○ For safety reasons, use ATMs inside banks with security guards, preferably during daylight hours. Cover the keyboard for pin entry.

Cash

The nuevo sol (new sun) comes in bills of S10, S20, S50, S100 and (rarely) S200. It is divided into 100 céntimos, with copper-colored coins of S0.05, S0.10 and S0.20, and silver-colored S0.50 and S1 coins. In addition, there are bimetallic S2 and S5 coins with a copper-colored center inside a silver-colored ring.

US dollars are accepted by many tourist-oriented businesses, though you'll need nuevos soles to pay for local transportation, meals and other incidentals.

Counterfeit bills (in both US dollars and nuevo soles) often circulate in Peru. Merchants question both beat-up and large-denomination bills. Consumers should refuse them too.

To detect fakes, check for a sheer watermark and examine a metal strip crossing the note that repeats Peru in neat, not misshapen, letters. Colored thread, holographs and writing along the top of the bill should be embossed, not glued on.

Changing Money

The best currency for exchange is the US dollar, although the euro is accepted in major tourist centers. Other hard currencies can be exchanged, but usually with difficulty and only in major cities. All foreign currencies must be in flawless condition.

Cambistas (money changers) hang out on street corners near banks and *casas de cambio* and give competitive rates (there's only a little flexibility for bargaining), but are not always honest. Officially, they should wear a vest and badge identifying themselves as legal. They're useful after regular business hours or at borders where there aren't any other options.

Credit Cards

Midrange and top-end hotels and shops accept *tarjetas de crédito* (credit cards) with a 7% (or greater) fee. Your bank may also tack on a surcharge and additional fees for each foreign-currency transaction. The most widely accepted cards in Peru are Visa and MasterCard.

Taxes, Tipping & Refunds

- Expensive hotels add a 19% sales tax and 10% service charge; the latter is generally not included in quoted rates. Non-Peruvians may be eligible for a refund of the sales tax only.

- A few restaurants charge combined taxes of more than 19%, plus a service charge (*servicio* or *propina*) of 10%.

- Otherwise, tip waitstaff 10% for good service. Taxi drivers do not generally expect tips (unless they've assisted with heavy luggage), but porters and tour guides do.

- There is no system of sales-tax refunds for shoppers, except for the possibility of accommodations sales tax refunds.

Opening Hours

Hours are variable and liable to change, especially in small towns, where regular hours are, in fact, irregular. Posted hours are a guideline. Lima has the most continuity of services. In other major cities, taxi drivers often know where the late-night stores and pharmacies are.

Banks 9am to 6pm Monday to Friday, 9am to 1pm Saturday

Government offices and businesses 9am to 5pm Monday to Friday

---

Practicalities

Internet resources Helpful online resources in English include www.expatperu.com and www.theperuguide.com.

Magazines The most well-known political and cultural weekly is *Caretas* (www.caretas.com.pe), while *Etiqueta Negra* (etiquetanegra.com.pe) focuses on culture. A good bilingual travel publication is the monthly *Rumbos* (www.rumbosdelperu.com).

Newspapers Peru's government-leaning *El Comercio* (www.elcomercioperu.com.pe) is the leading daily. There's also the slightly left-of-center *La República* (www.elcomercioperu.com.pe), and the *Peruvian Times* (www.peruviantimes.com) and *Peru this Week* (www.peruthisweek.com) in English.

TV Cable and satellite TV are widely available for a fix of CNN or even Japanese news.

Weights & measures Peru uses the metric system, but gas (petrol) is measured in US gallons.

Museums Often close on Monday

Restaurants 10am to 10pm, many close between 3pm and 6pm

Shops 9am to 6pm Monday to Friday, some 9am to 6pm Saturday

Public Holidays

Major holidays may be celebrated for days around the official date.

Fiestas Patrias (National Independence Days) are the biggest national holidays, when the entire nation seems to be on the move.

New Year's Day January 1

Good Friday March/April

Labor Day May 1

Inti Raymi June 24

Feast of Sts Peter & Paul June 29

National Independence Days July 28–29

Feast of Santa Rosa de Lima August 30

Battle of Angamos Day October 8

All Saints Day November 1

Feast of the Immaculate Conception December 8

Christmas December 25

Safe Travel

The safety situation in Peru has improved significantly in recent years, especially in Lima. Yet street crimes

---

Government Travel Advice

The following government websites offer travel advisories and information on current hot spots.

Australian Department of Foreign Affairs (☎1300-139-281; www.smarttraveller.gov.au)

British Foreign Office (☎0845-850-2829; www.fco.gov.uk/en/travelling-and-living-overseas)

Canadian Department of Foreign Affairs (☎800-267-6788; www.dfait-maeci.gc.ca)

US State Department (☎888-407-4747; travel.state.gov)

---

such as pickpocketing, bag-snatching and muggings are still common. Sneak theft is by far the most widespread type of crime, while muggings happen with less regularity. Even so, they do happen.

Use basic precautions and a reasonable amount of awareness, however, and you probably won't be robbed. Following are some tips:

○ Crowded places such as bus terminals, train stations, markets and fiestas are the haunts of pickpockets; wear your day pack in front of you or carry a bag that fits snugly under your arm.

○ Thieves look for easy targets, such as a bulging wallet in a back pocket or a camera held out in the open; keep your spending money in your front pocket and your camera stowed when it's not in use.

○ Passports and larger sums of cash are best carried in a money belt or an inside pocket that can be zipped or closed – or better yet, stowed in a safe at your hotel.

○ Snatch theft can occur if you place a bag on the ground (even for a few seconds), or while you're asleep on an overnight bus; never leave a bag with your wallet and passport in the overhead rack of a bus.

○ Don't keep valuables in bags that will be unattended.

○ Blending in helps: walking around town in brand-new hiking gear or a shiny leather jacket will draw attention; stick to simple clothing.

○ Leave jewelry and fancy watches at home.

○ Hotels – especially cheap ones – aren't always trustworthy; lock valuables inside your luggage, or use safety-deposit services.

○ Walk purposefully wherever you are going, even if you are lost; if you need to examine your map, duck into a shop or restaurant.

○ Always take an official taxi at night and from the airport or bus terminals.

○ If threatened, it's better just to give up your goods than face harm.

Telephone

A few public pay phones operated by Movistar and Claro are still around, especially in small towns. They work with coins or phone cards, which can be purchased at supermarkets and groceries. Often internet cafes have 'net-to-phone' and 'net-to-net' capabilities (such as Skype), to talk for pennies or even for free.

Cell Phones

In stands in supermarkets in Lima and other larger cities, you can buy cell phones that use SIM cards for about S40, then pop in a SIM card that costs from S15. Credit can be purchased in pharmacies and supermarkets. Claro is a popular pay-as-you-go plan. Cell-phone rentals may be available in major cities and tourist centers. Cell-phone reception may be poor in the mountains or jungle.

Emergency & Important Numbers

Directory assistance	☎103
National tourist information (24hr)	☎511-574-800
Police	☎105

Phone Codes

When calling Peru from abroad, dial the international access code for the country you're in, then Peru's country code (☎51), then the area code without the 0 and finally, the local number. When making international calls from Peru, dial the international access code (☎00), then the country code of where you're calling to, then the area code and finally, the local phone number.

In Peru, any telephone number beginning with a 9 is a cell-phone number. Numbers beginning with 0800 are often toll-free only when dialed from private phones. To make a credit-card or collect call using AT&T, dial ☎0800-50288. For an online telephone directory, see www.paginas amarillas.com.pe.

Phone Cards

Called *tarjetas telefónicas*, these cards are widely available and are made by many companies in many price ranges, with some designed specifically for international calls.

Time

Peru is five hours behind Greenwich Mean Time (GMT). It's the same as Eastern Standard Time (EST) in North America. At noon in Lima, it's 9am in Los Angeles, 11am in Mexico City, noon in New York, 5pm in London and 4am (the following day) in Sydney. Note that daylight saving time (DST) isn't used in Peru, so these times may vary by an hour during other countries' DST.

○ Punctuality is not one of the things that Latin America is famous for, so be prepared to wait around. Buses rarely depart or arrive on time. Savvy travelers should allow some flexibility in their itineraries.

○ Bring your own travel alarm clock – tours and long-distance buses often depart before 6am.

Toilets

Peruvian plumbing leaves something to be desired. There's always a chance that flushing a toilet will cause it to overflow, so you should avoid putting anything other than human waste into the toilet. Even a small amount of toilet paper can muck up the entire system – that's why a small plastic bin is routinely provided for disposal of the paper. This may not seem sanitary, but it is definitely better than the alternative of clogged toilets and flooded floors. A well-run hotel or restaurant, even a cheap one, will empty the bin and clean the toilet daily. In rural areas, there may be just a rickety wooden outhouse built around a hole in the ground.

Public toilets are rare outside of transportation terminals, restaurants and museums, but restaurants will generally let travelers use a restroom (sometimes for a charge). Those in terminals usually have an attendant who will charge you about S0.50 to enter and then give you a few sheets of toilet paper. Public restrooms frequently run out of toilet paper, so always carry extra.

Travelers with Disabilities

Peru offers few conveniences for travelers with disabilities. Features such as signs in Braille or phones for the hearing-impaired are virtually nonexistent, while wheelchair ramps and lifts are few and far between, and the pavement is often badly potholed and cracked. Most hotels do not have wheelchair-accessible rooms, at least not rooms specially designated as such. Bathrooms are often barely large enough for an able-bodied person to walk into, so few are accessible to wheelchairs.

Nevertheless, there are Peruvians with disabilities who get around, mainly through the help of others.

Access-Able Travel Source (www.access-able.com) Partial listings of accessible transportation and tours, accommodations, attractions and restaurants.

Apumayo Expediciones (☑/fax 084-24-6018; www.apumayo. com; Jr Ricardo Palma Ñ-11, Urb Santa Monica Wanchaq, Cuzco) An adventure-tour company that takes disabled travelers to

Machu Picchu and other historic sites in the Sacred Valley.

Conadis (☑01-332-0808; www.conadisperu.gob.pe; Av Arequipa 375, Santa Beatriz, Lima) Governmental agency for Spanish-language information and advocacy for people with disabilities.

Emerging Horizons (www. emerginghorizons.com) Travel magazine for the mobility-impaired, with handy advice columns and news articles.

Mobility International (☑541-343 1284; www.miusa.org; 132 E Broadway, Suite 343, Eugene, USA) Advises disabled travelers on mobility issues and runs an educational exchange program.

Visas

With a few exceptions, visas are not required for travelers entering Peru. Tourists are permitted a 183-day, non-extendable stay, stamped into passports and onto a tourist card called a Tarjeta Andina de Migración (Andean Immigration Card). Keep it – it must be returned upon exiting the country. If you will need it, request the full amount of time to the immigration officer at the point of entry, since they have a tendency to issue 30- or 90-day stays.

○ If you lose your tourist card, visit an *oficina de migraciónes* (immigration office; www.digemin.gob.pe) for a replacement. Information in English can be found

online. Extensions are no longer officially available.

○ Anyone who plans to work, attend school or reside in Peru for any length of time must obtain a visa in advance. Do this through the Peruvian embassy or consulate in your home country.

○ Carry your passport and tourist card on your person at all times, especially in remote areas (it's required by law on the Inca Trail). For security, make a photocopy of both documents and keep them in a separate place from the originals.

Women Travelers

Machismo is alive and well in Latin America. Most female travelers to Peru will experience little more than shouts of *mi amor* (my love) or an appreciative hiss. If you are fair-skinned with blond hair, however, be prepared to be the center of attention. Peruvian men consider foreign women to have looser morals and be easier sexual conquests than Peruvian women and will often make flirtatious comments to single women.

Unwanted attention Staring, whistling, hissing and catcalls in the streets are run-of-the-mill – and should be treated as such. Many men make a pastime of dropping *piropos* (cheeky, flirtatious or even vulgar 'compliments'). However, these are generally not meant to be insulting. Most men rarely, if ever, follow up on the idle chatter (unless they feel you've insulted their manhood). Ignoring all provocation and staring ahead is generally the best response. If someone is particularly persistent, try a potentially ardor-smothering phrase such as *soy casada* (I'm married). If you appeal directly to locals, you'll find most Peruvians to be protective of lone women, expressing surprise and concern if you tell them you're traveling without your family or husband.

Bricheros It's not uncommon for fast-talking charmers, especially in tourist towns such as Cuzco, to attach themselves to gringas. Known in Peru as *bricheros,* many of these young Casanovas are looking for a meal ticket, so approach any professions of undying love with extreme skepticism. This happens to men too.

First impressions Use common sense when meeting men in public places. In Peru, outside of a few big cities, it is rare for a woman to belly up to a bar for a beer, and the ones that do tend to be prostitutes. If you feel the need for an evening cocktail, opt for a restaurant. Likewise, heavy drinking by women might be misinterpreted by some men as a sign of promiscuity. When meeting someone, make it very clear if only friendship is intended. This goes double for tour and activity guides. When meeting someone for the first time, it is also wise not to divulge where you are staying until you feel sure that you are with someone you can trust.

Transport

Getting There & Away

Air

Peru (mainly Lima) has direct flights to and from cities all over the Americas, as well as to continental Europe. Other locations require a connection. The international departure tax is included in ticket costs.

Land & River

Because no roads bridge the Darien Gap, it is not possible to travel to South America by land from the north (unless you spend a week making your way through swampy, drug-dealer-infested jungle). Driving overland from neighboring Bolivia, Brazil, Chile, Colombia and Ecuador requires careful logistical planning.

With any form of transportation, it may be a bit cheaper to buy tickets to the border, cross over and then buy onward tickets on the other side, but it's usually much easier, faster and safer to buy a cross-border through-ticket. When traveling by bus, check carefully with the company about what is included in the price of the ticket, and whether the service is direct or involves a transfer, and possibly a long wait, at the border.

Bus & Train

The main international bus company that travels to Chile, Ecuador, Colombia, Bolivia and Argentina is **Ormeño** (☎01-472-1710; www.grupo-ormeno.com.pe). Smaller regional companies do cross-border travel, but on a more limited basis. The only rail service that crosses the Peru border is the train between Arica, Chile, and Tacna on Peru's south coast.

Boat

Getting to Peru by boat is possible from points on the Amazon River in Brazil and from Leticia, Colombia, as well as to the port cities on Peru's Pacific coast.

Getting Around

Peru has a constant procession of flights and buses connecting the country. In particular, driving routes to the jungle have improved drastically. Keep in mind, poor weather conditions can cancel flights and buses. Strikes can be another obstacle in regional travel – consult travel experts on the routes you will be taking.

Air

Most domestic airlines have offices in Lima. Smaller carriers and charters are also an option. The most remote towns may require connecting flights, and smaller towns are not served every day. Many airports for these places are no more than a dirt strip.

Be at the airport at least two hours before your flight departs. Flights may be overbooked, baggage handling and check-in procedures tend to be chaotic, and flights may even leave *before* their official departure time because of predicted bad weather.

Most airlines fly from Lima to regional capitals, but service between provincial cities is limited.

LAN (LPE; ☎01-213-8200; www.lan.com) Peru's major domestic carrier flies to Arequipa, Chiclayo, Cuzco, Iquitos, Juliaca, Piura, Puerto Maldonado, Tacna, Tarapoto, Trujillo and Tumbes. Additionally it offers link services between Arequipa and Cuzco, Arequipa and Juliaca, Arequipa and Tacna, Cuzco and Juliaca, and Cuzco and Puerto Maldonado.

LC Peru (☎01-204-1313; www.lcperu.pe; Av Pablo Carriquirry 857, San Isidro) Flies from Lima to Andahuaylas, Ayacucho, Cajamarca, Huánuco, Huaraz, Iquitos and Huancayo (Jauja) on smaller turbo-prop aircraft.

Peruvian Airlines (www.peruvianairlines.pe) Flies to Lima, Arequipa, Cuzco, Piura, Iquitos and Tacna.

Star Perú (SRU; ☎01-705-9000; www.starperu.com) Domestic carrier, flying to Ayacucho, Cajamarca, Cuzco, Huancayo (Jauja), Iquitos, Pucallpa, Puerto Maldonado, Talara and Tarapoto; with link service between Tarapoto and Iquitos.

Tickets

Most travelers travel in one direction overland and save time returning by air. You can sometimes buy tickets at the airport on a space-available basis, but don't count on it.

Peak season The peak season for air travel within Peru is late May to early September, as well as around major holidays. Buy tickets for less popular destinations as far in advance as possible, as these infrequent flights book up quickly. It's almost impossible to buy tickets just before major holidays, notably Semana Santa (the week leading up to Easter) and Fiestas Patrias (the last week in July). Overbooking is the norm.

Discounts Domestic flights are usually cheaper when advertised on the Peruvian website (versus its international version), so if you can wait until you arrive in Peru to buy regional tickets, you may save money.

Reconfirming flights Buying tickets and reconfirming flights are best done at airline offices in remote areas; otherwise, you can do so online or via a recommended travel agent. Ensure all flight reservations are *confirmed and reconfirmed* 72 and 24 hours in advance; airlines are notorious for overbooking and flights are changed or canceled with surprising frequency, so it's even worth calling the airport or the airline just before leaving for the airport. Confirmation is especially essential during the peak travel season.

Bicycle

Safety The major drawback to cycling in Peru is the country's bounty of kamikaze motorists. On narrow, two-lane highways, drivers can be a serious hazard to cyclists. Cycling is more enjoyable and safer, though very challenging, off paved roads. Mountain bikes are recommended, as road bikes won't stand up to the rough conditions.

Rentals Reasonably priced rentals (mostly mountain bikes) are available in popular tourist destinations, including Cuzco, Arequipa, Huaraz and Huancayo.

Climate Change & Travel

Every form of transport that relies on carbon-based fuel generates CO_2, the main cause of human-induced climate change. Modern travel is dependent on airplanes, which might use less fuel per kilometer per person than most cars but travel much greater distances. The altitude at which aircraft emit gases (including CO_2) and particles also contributes to their climate-change impact. Many websites offer 'carbon calculators' that allow people to estimate the carbon emissions generated by their journey and, for those who wish to do so, to offset the impact of the greenhouse gases emitted with contributions to portfolios of climate-friendly initiatives throughout the world. Lonely Planet offsets the carbon footprint of all staff and author travel.

These bikes are rented to travelers for local excursions, not to make trips all over the country. For long-distance touring, bring your own bike from home.

Transporting bicycles Airline policies on carrying bicycles vary, so shop around.

Boat

There are no passenger services along the Peruvian coast. In the Andean highlands, there are boat services on Lake Titicaca. Small motorized vessels take passengers from the port in Puno to visit various islands on the lake, while catamarans zip over to Bolivia.

In Peru's Amazon Basin, boat travel is of major importance. Larger vessels ply the wider rivers. Dugout canoes powered by outboard motors act as water taxis on smaller rivers. Those called *peki-pekis* are slow and rather noisy. In some places, modern aluminum launches are used.

Bus

Buses are the usual form of transportation for most Peruvians and many travelers. Fares are cheap and services are frequent on the major long-distance routes, but buses are of varying quality. Remote rural routes are often served by older, worn-out vehicles. Seats at the back of the bus yield a bumpier ride.

Many cities do not have a main bus terminal. Buses rarely arrive or depart on time, so consider most average trip times as best-case

scenarios. Buses can be significantly delayed during the rainy season, particularly in the highlands and the jungle. From January to April, journey times may double or face indefinite delays from landslides and bad road conditions.

Fatal accidents are not unusual in Peru. Avoid overnight buses, on which muggings and assaults are more likely to occur.

Classes

Luxury buses Invariably called Imperial, Royal, Business or Executive, these higher-priced express services feature toilets, videos and air-conditioning. Luxury buses serve paltry snacks and don't stop.

Bus-camas Feature seats which recline halfway or almost fully. Better long-distance buses stop for bathroom breaks and meals in special rest areas with inexpensive but sometimes unappetizing fare. Almost every bus terminal has a few kiosks with basic provisions.

Económico For trips under six hours, you may have no choice but to take an *económico* bus, and these are usually pretty beaten up. While *económico* services don't stop for meals, vendors will board and sell snacks.

Costs & Reservations

Schedules and fares change frequently and vary from company to company; quoted prices, therefore, are only approximations.

Fares fluctuate during peak and off-peak travel times. For long-distance or overnight journeys, or for

travel to remote areas with only limited services, buy your ticket at least the day before. Most travel agencies offer reservations, but shockingly overcharge for the ticket. Except in Lima, it's cheaper to take a taxi to the bus terminal and buy the tickets yourself.

You can check schedules online (but not make reservations, at least not yet) for the major players, including:

Cruz del Sur (www.cruzdelsur.com.pe)

Oltursa (www.oltursa.com.pe)

Ormeño (022-779-3443; www.grupo-ormeno.com.pe)

Transportes Línea (www.transporteslinea.com.pe)

Car & Motorcycle

○ Distances in Peru are long so it's best to bus or fly to a region and rent a car from there. Hiring a taxi is often cheaper and easier.

○ At roadside checkpoints police or military conduct meticulous document checks. Drivers who offer an officer some money to smooth things along consider it a 'gift' or an 'on-the-spot fine' to get on their way. Readers should know that these transactions are an unsavory reality in Peru and Lonely Planet does not condone them.

○ When filling up, make sure the meter starts at zero.

Car & Motorcycle Rental

A driver's license from your home country is sufficient

for renting a car. An International Driving Permit (IDP) is only required if you'll be driving in Peru for more than 30 days.

Major rental companies have offices in Lima and a few other large cities. Renting a motorcycle is an option mainly in jungle towns, where you can go for short runs around town on dirt bikes, but not much further.

Economy car rental starts at US$25 a day without the 19% sales tax, 'super' collision-damage waiver, personal accident insurance and so on, which together can climb to more than US$100 per day, not including excess mileage. Vehicles with 4WD are more expensive.

Make sure you completely understand the rental agreement before you sign. A credit card is required, and renters normally need to be over 25 years of age.

Road Rules & Hazards

Bear in mind that the condition of rental cars is often poor, roads are potholed (even the paved Pan-American Hwy), gas is expensive, and drivers are aggressive, regarding speed limits, road signs and traffic signals as mere guides, not the law. Moreover, road signs are often small and unclear.

o Driving is on the right-hand side of the road.

o Driving at night is not recommended because of poor conditions, speeding buses and slow-moving, poorly lit trucks.

o Theft is all too common, so you should not leave your vehicle parked on the street. When stopping overnight, park the car in a guarded lot (common in better hotels).

o Gasoline or petrol stations (called *grifos*) are few and far between.

Local Transport

In most towns and cities, it's easy to walk everywhere or take a taxi. Using local buses, *colectivos* (shared transportation) and *combis* (minibuses) can be tricky, but they are very inexpensive.

Tours

Travelers who prefer not to travel on their own, or have a limited amount of time have ample tours to choose from. Travel with knowledgeable guides comes at a premium. It's worth it for highly specialized outdoor activities such as rafting, mountaineering, bird-watching or mountain biking.

If you want to book a tour locally, Lima, Cuzco, Arequipa, Puno, Trujillo, Huaraz, Puerto Maldonado and Iquitos have the most travel agencies offering organized tours. For more specialized, individual or small-group tours, you can generally hire a bilingual guide starting at US$20 an hour or US$80 a day plus expenses (keep in mind that exchange rates may affect this); tours in other languages may be more expensive. Some students

or unregistered guides are cheaper, but the usual caveat applies – some are good, others aren't.

For more guide listings, check out www.leaplocal. org, a resource promoting socially responsible tourism.

Train

The privatized rail system, PeruRail (www.perurail. com), has daily services between Cuzco and Aguas Calientes, aka Machu Picchu Pueblo, and services between Cuzco and Puno on the shores of Lake Titicaca three times a week. Passenger services between Puno and Arequipa have been suspended indefinitely, but will run as a charter for groups. **Inca Rail** (☑084-25-2974; www.incarail.com; Portal de Panes 105, Plaza de Armas, Cuzco; ⏱8am-9pm Mon-Fri, 9am-7pm Sat, to 2pm Sun) also offers service between Ollantaytambo and Aguas Calientes.

Train buffs won't want to miss the lovely **Ferrocarril Central Andino** (☑01-226-6363; www.ferrocarrilcentral. com.pe), which reaches a head-spinning altitude of 4829m. It usually runs between Lima and Huancayo weekly from mid-April through October. In Huancayo, cheaper trains to Huancavelica leave daily from a different station. Another charmingly historic railway makes inexpensive daily runs between Tacna on Peru's south coast and Arica, Chile.

Language

Spanish pronunciation is not difficult as most of its sounds are also found in English. You can read our pronunciation guides below as if they were English and you'll be understood just fine.

Peruvian Spanish is considered one of the easiest varieties of Spanish, with less slang in use than in many other Latin American countries, and relatively clear enunciation.

To enhance your trip with a phrasebook, visit **lonelyplanet.com**. Lonely Planet iPhone phrasebooks are available through the Apple App store.

Basics

Hello.
Hola. — o·la

How are you?
¿Qué tal? — ke tal

I'm fine, thanks.
Bien, gracias. — byen *gra*·syas

Excuse me. (to get attention)
Disculpe. — dees·*kool*·pe

Yes./No.
Sí./No. — see/no

Thank you.
Gracias. — *gra*·syas

You're welcome./That's fine.
De nada. — de *na*·da

Goodbye./See you later.
Adiós./Hasta luego. — a·*dyos*/*as*·ta *lwe*·go

Do you speak English?
¿Habla inglés? — a·bla een·*gles*

I don't understand.
No entiendo. — no en·*tyen*·do

How much is this?
¿Cuánto cuesta? — *kwan*·to *kwes*·ta

Can you reduce the price a little?
¿Podría bajar un poco el precio? — po·*dree*·a ba·*khar* oon *po*·ko el *pre*·syo

Accommodations

I'd like to make a booking.
Quisiera reservar una habitación. — kee·*sye*·ra re·ser·*var oo*·na a·bee·ta·*syon*

How much is it per night?
¿Cuánto cuesta por noche? — *kwan*·to *kwes*·ta por *no*·che

Eating & Drinking

I'd like ..., please.
Quisiera ..., por favor. — kee·*sye*·ra ... por fa·*vor*

That was delicious!
¡Estaba buenísimo! — es·*ta*·ba bwe·*nee*·see·mo

Bring the bill/check, please.
La cuenta, por favor. — la *kwen*·ta por fa·*vor*

I'm allergic to ...
Soy alérgico/a al ... (m/f) — soy a·*ler*·khee·ko/a al ...

I don't eat ...
No como ... — no *ko*·mo ...

chicken	*pollo*	*po*·yo
fish	*pescado*	pes·*ka*·do
meat	*carne*	*kar*·ne

Emergencies

I'm ill.
Estoy enfermo/a. (m/f) — es·*toy* en·*fer*·mo/a

Help!
¡Socorro! — so·*ko*·ro

Call a doctor!
¡Llame a un médico! — *ya*·me a oon *me*·dee·ko

Call the police!
¡Llame a la policía! — *ya*·me a la po·lee·*see*·a

Directions

I'm looking for (a/an/the) ...
Estoy buscando ... — es·*toy* boos·*kan*·do ...

ATM
un cajero automático — oon ka·*khe*·ro ow·to·*ma*·tee·ko

bank
el banco — el *ban*·ko

... embassy
la embajada de ... — la em·ba·*kha*·da de ...

market
el mercado — el mer·*ka*·do

museum
el museo — el moo·*se*·o

toilet
los servicios — los ser·*vee*·syos

tourist office
la oficina de turismo — la o·fee·*see*·na de too·*rees*·mo

Behind the Scenes

Acknowledgements

Climate map data adapted from Peel MC, Finlayson BL & McMahon TA (2007) 'Updated World Map of the Koppen-Geiger Climate Classification', *Hydrology and Earth System Sciences*, 11, pp1633–44.

This Book

This book was curated by Phillip Tang and researched and written by Phillip, Greg Benchwick, Alex Egerton, Carolyn McCarthy and Luke Waterson.

This guidebook was produced by the following:

Destination Editor MaSovaida Morgan

Product Editors Kate Chapman, Luna Soo

Senior Cartographer David Kemp

Book Designers Michael Buick, Katherine Marsh

Assisting Editors Victoria Harrison, Charlotte Orr, Saralinda Turner

Cover Researcher Naomi Parker

Thanks to Indra Kilfoyle, Kate Mathews, Kirsten Rawlings, Dianne Schallmeiner, Angela Tinson, John Taufa, Tony Wheeler, Tracy Whitmey, Juan Winata

Index

000 Map pages

E

F

G

Symbols & Map Key

Look for these symbols to quickly identify listings:

- ◉ Sights
- ✚ Activities
- ⊖ Courses
- ⊙ Tours
- ✦ Festivals & Events
- ✖ Eating
- ⊖ Drinking
- ✪ Entertainment
- ⊖ Shopping
- ⓘ Information & Transport

These symbols and abbreviations give vital information for each listing:

🌿 Sustainable or green recommendation

FREE No payment required

- ☎ Telephone number
- ◷ Opening hours
- P Parking
- ⊖ Nonsmoking
- ❄ Air-conditioning
- @ Internet access
- 🛜 Wi-fi access
- 🏊 Swimming pool
- 🚌 Bus
- ⛴ Ferry
- 🚊 Tram
- 🚆 Train
- 📋 English-language menu
- 🥗 Vegetarian selection
- 👪 Family-friendly

Find your best experiences with these Great For... icons.

 Budget

 Food & Drink

 Drinking

 Cycling

 Shopping

 Sport

 Art & Culture

 Events

 Photo Op

 Scenery

 Family Travel

 Short Trip

 Detour

Walking

Local Life

History

Entertainment

Beaches

Winter Travel

Cafe/Coffee

 Nature & Wildlife

Sights

- 🏖 Beach
- 🐦 Bird Sanctuary
- 🛕 Buddhist
- 🏰 Castle/Palace
- ✝ Christian
- ☯ Confucian
- 🕉 Hindu
- ☪ Islamic
- 卐 Jain
- ✡ Jewish
- 🗿 Monument
- 🏛 Museum/Gallery/ Historic Building
- 🏚 Ruin
- ⛩ Shinto
- ☬ Sikh
- ☯ Taoist
- 🍷 Winery/Vineyard
- 🦁 Zoo/Wildlife Sanctuary
- ◉ Other Sight

Points of Interest

- © Bodysurfing
- 🏕 Camping
- ☕ Cafe
- 🛶 Canoeing/Kayaking
- • Course/Tour
- 🤿 Diving
- 🍸 Drinking & Nightlife
- ✖ Eating
- ✪ Entertainment
- ♨ Sento Hot Baths/ Onsen
- 🛍 Shopping
- ⛷ Skiing
- 🛏 Sleeping
- 🤿 Snorkelling
- 🏄 Surfing
- 🏊 Swimming/Pool
- 🚶 Walking
- 🏄 Windsurfing
- ✚ Other Activity

Information

- ⓢ Bank
- 🏛 Embassy/Consulate
- ✚ Hospital/Medical
- @ Internet
- 👮 Police
- 📮 Post Office
- ☎ Telephone
- 🚻 Toilet
- ⓘ Tourist Information
- • Other Information

Geographic

- 🏖 Beach
- ⊶ Gate
- 🛖 Hut/Shelter
- 🗼 Lighthouse
- 🔭 Lookout
- ▲ Mountain/Volcano
- 🌴 Oasis
- 🌳 Park
-)(Pass
- 🧺 Picnic Area
- 💧 Waterfall

Transport

- ✈ Airport
- Ⓑ BART station
- ⊗ Border crossing
- Ⓣ Boston T station
- 🚍 Bus
- ➕🚠➕ Cable car/Funicular
- ─⊗─ Cycling
- ─⊖─ Ferry
- Ⓜ Metro/MRT station
- ⊶🚝⊷ Monorail
- P Parking
- ⛽ Petrol station
- Ⓢ Subway/S-Bahn/ Skytrain station
- 🚕 Taxi
- ➕🚉➕ Train station/Railway
- ⊠⊠⊠ Tram
- ⊖ Tube Station
- Ⓤ Underground/ U-Bahn station
- • Other Transport

Carolyn McCarthy

Carolyn McCarthy first discovered *cumbia* camping on the Inca Trail many years ago. On this trip she embarked on a quest for the perfect ceviche (with success). She has contributed to more than 30 titles for Lonely Planet, including *Panama*, *Trekking in the Patagonian Andes*, *Argentina*, *Chile*, *Colorado*, *Southwest USA* and national parks guides. She has also written for *Outside*, *BBC Magazine*, *National Geographic* and other publications. For more information, visit www.carolyn mccarthy.pressfolios.com or follow her on Instagram @masmerquen and Twitter @RoamingMcC.

Luke Waterson

A regular contributor to Lonely Planet's *Peru* guidebook, Luke has a love for getting off the beaten track. He specialises in writing about Andean and Amazonian South America as a travel writer and as a novelist: his debut novel, *Roebuck: Adventures of an Admirable Adventurer,* is set in the 16th-century South American jungle. He writes on Latin America for the *Independent*, the *Telegraph* and the BBC, and runs a travel-and-culture blog about his current home, Slovakia: Englishmaninslovakia.com.

Our Story

A beat-up old car, a few dollars in the pocket and a sense of adventure. In 1972 that's all Tony and Maureen Wheeler needed for the trip of a lifetime – across Europe and Asia overland to Australia. It took several months, and at the end – broke but inspired – they sat at their kitchen table writing and stapling together their first travel guide, *Across Asia on the Cheap*. Within a week they'd sold 1500 copies. Lonely Planet was born.

Today, Lonely Planet has offices in Melbourne, Franklin, London, Oakland, Dublin, Beijing and Delhi, with more than 600 staff and writers. We share Tony's belief that 'a great guidebook should do three things: inform, educate and amuse'.

Our Writers

Phillip Tang

A degree in Latin America studies brought Phillip Tang to these shores, and over a decade later he still finds himself breathless (slightly literally) pondering a canyon in Colca or the ocean in Miraflores. He writes about travel on his two loves, Asia and Latin America, and contributes to Lonely Planet's guides to *Peru*, *Mexico*, *China* and *Japan*. Find more of Phillip's Peru photos and social media through philliptang.co.uk.

Greg Benchwick

Greg Benchwick has been trucking around South America for the past 15 years. For this trip, the Lonely Planet veteran covered over 5000km of coastline, going that extra mile to explore offbeat surf destinations along the way. Greg has written speeches for the United Nations, interviewed Grammy-award winners and created dozens of videos and web features for LonelyPlanet.com, *National Geographic Traveler* and other international publications. He is an expert on sustainable travel, international development, food, wine and having a good time.

Alex Egerton

A journalist by trade, Alex writes about travel and culture in destinations all over Latin America but has a particular passion for the Andes and the seldom-visited jungle-covered parts of the map. Based in southern Colombia, he makes regular trips down to Peru in search of the best spicy eats and most spectacular/sketchy mountain bus rides. When not on the road for work, you'll find him hiking in the mountain plains or watching way too much football.

← ——————— More Writers ←

STAY IN TOUCH LONELYPLANET.COM/CONTACT

EUROPE Unit E, Digital Court, The Digital Hub, Rainsford St, Dublin 8, Ireland

AUSTRALIA Levels 2 & 3 551 Swanston St, Carlton, Victoria 3053 ☎ 03 8379 8000, fax 03 8379 8111

USA 150 Linden Street, Oakland, CA 94607 ☎ 510 250 6400, toll free 800 275 8555, fax 510 893 8572

UK 240 Blackfriars Road, London SE1 8NW ☎ 020 3771 5100, fax 020 3771 5101

 twitter.com/ lonelyplanet

 facebook.com/ lonelyplanet

 instagram.com/ lonelyplanet

 youtube.com/ lonelyplanet

 lonelyplanet.com/ newsletter